A BODY IN BERKELEY SQUARE

CAPTAIN LACEY REGENCY MYSTERIES BOOK 5

ASHLEY GARDNER

JA / AG PUBLISHING

CHAPTER 1

$\mathcal{A}$t two o'clock in the morning on the fifth of April, 1817, I stood in an elegant bedchamber in Berkeley Square and looked down at the dead body of Mr. Henry Turner.

Mr. Turner was in his twenties. He had brown hair arranged in fashionable, drooping curls and wore a black suit with an ivory and silver waistcoat, elegant pantaloons, and dancing slippers. An emerald stickpin glittered in his cravat, and his collar points were exceedingly high.

Only a slight red gash marred the waistcoat where a knife had gone in to stop his life. Except for the waxen paleness of his face, Mr. Turner might be asleep.

"And he died where?" I asked.

"In a little anteroom off the ballroom downstairs," Milton Pomeroy, my former sergeant, now a Bow Street Runner said. "Right in the middle of a fancy ball with the crème de la crème. Lord Gillis had him brought up here, so the guests would not be disturbed by a dead body, so he said."

Lord Gillis was an earl who lived in this opulent mansion on Berkeley Square. Tonight he had hosted a ball which the top of society had attended, including Lucius Grenville, Lady Breckenridge, Lady Jersey, and the Duke of Wellington.

Colonel Brandon and Louisa Brandon had been invited also because Lord Gillis had been an officer before he'd inherited his title, and he loved to gossip with military men — at least those ranked colonel and above.

After supper had finished and dancing had recommenced — about midnight — Mr. Turner had been found in a small anteroom, alone and dead.

"What about the weapon?" I asked.

For answer, Pomeroy held up a knife. It was slim and utilitarian, with a plain handle, unmarked. I'd had one much like it in the army and regretted its loss when I wagered it away in a game of cards.

Pomeroy laid it carefully on Mr. Turner's chest.

"Belongs to one Colonel Aloysius Brandon," he said.

I stared at it in sudden shock, then back at Pomeroy.

"I am afraid so, sir," he said. "He admitted the knife was his, but has no idea how it came to be a-sticking out of the chest of Mr. Turner."

I at last understood why Pomeroy had so urgently sent for me. Colonel Brandon had been my commanding officer during the recent Peninsular War. He'd also at one time been my mentor and my friend.

Currently, Brandon was my enemy. His actions had ended my career as a cavalry officer and brought me back to London tired and defeated.

"And where is Colonel Brandon now?" I asked tersely.

"Bow Street. I sent him off with my patroller. He'll face the magistrate tomorrow."

Like a common criminal, I thought. The magistrate would examine him and decide whether he had enough evidence to hold Brandon at Newgate for a trial.

I studied the knife. Nothing remarkable about it except that it had belonged to Colonel Brandon.

"Did Brandon offer any explanation as to how the knife got there?" I asked.

Pomeroy rocked on his heels. "None whatsoever. Our colonel looked blank, said he didn't do it, and I should take him at his word." He cocked his head. "Now what kind of Runner would I be if I believed every criminal what told me that?"

I could imagine Brandon, his back straight, his blue eyes chill, telling Pomeroy that his word should be enough to clear him of a charge of murder. He had likely marched off with the patroller, head high, indignation pouring from every inch of him.

"That the knife belongs to Brandon does not mean he stabbed Turner," I said. "Colonel Brandon could have used the knife at any time this evening—to pare an apple or some other thing. He might have laid down the knife, and anyone might have picked it up."

Pomeroy tapped the side of his nose. "Ah, but the good colonel told me that was nonsense. Said he never remembered taking the knife out of his pocket."

Typical of Brandon to make everything worse with heated protests. He would expect Pomeroy to obey him without question, as though we still stood on the battlefields of the Peninsular War.

But we'd left Spain three years ago, Napoleon had been defeated, and Brandon and Pomeroy and I were now civilians. Brandon, with a large private income, lived in a rather opulent house on Brook Street, and I, with no private income, lived in rooms over a bake shop near Covent Garden.

Even so, Pomeroy's instant acceptance that Brandon had stabbed this young man through his so elegant suit irritated me a bit. Pomeroy liked solutions to be simple.

"I never remember Brandon mentioning having acquaintance with Mr. Turner," I said. "He does not look like the sort of young man Brandon would even consider speaking to."

"True, the colonel did not know Mr. Turner, he says. I believe him, for the reasons you give. But he didn't have to know him, did he? Turner was annoying the colonel's paramour, and the colonel killed him in a fit of jealousy."

I stared at Pomeroy in abject astonishment. "Paramour?"

The Colonel Brandon I knew would never have anything so common as a paramour.

Pomeroy nodded. "A woman named Mrs. Harper, Christian name, Imogene. According to guests at the ball, Colonel Brandon became angry at Mr. Turner's pursuit of Mrs. Harper and threatened to kill him."

I stood still in incredulity. Brandon in a temper might call out a man who behaved badly to a lady, but what Pomeroy said was unbelievable.

"Sergeant, you are speaking of Colonel Aloysius Brandon. He does not have a paramour. He never did. He is the most moral and faithful husband a wife could have. He is tiresome about it. The idea that he murdered a rival lover in a fit of jealousy is beyond absurd."

Pomeroy held up his forefinger. "And yet, not a few witnesses put him walking off alone with her several times during the evening, never mind escorting her in to supper. These same witnesses say they overheard quarrels between himself and Mr. Turner about Mrs. Harper. Besides"—Pomeroy played his trump card—"Colonel Brandon admitted to me that Imogene Harper was his mistress."

My mind whirled. "Pomeroy, this is astonishment on top of astonishment. I cannot credit it."

"It has much credit, sir, and 'twill be the colonel's debit, so to speak." He chuckled at his joke.

I stood still a moment, trying to take it all in. "Mrs. Brandon was at the ball with him, you say?"

"Aye. That she was."

"Did he admit this in front of her?"

Pomeroy nodded, losing his smile. "Aye, that he did. Mrs. Brandon refused to leave his side while I questioned him."

She would have insisted on staying, thinking it must all be a mistake. I imagined the blow of Brandon's admission striking her, her face whitening, her gray eyes growing moist with pain. I would wring Brandon's neck when I saw him.

"Where is Mrs. Brandon?" I asked sharply.

"Gone home."

"Alone?"

"No, sir. Her maid toddled off with her, and the Viscountess Breckenridge and Lady Aline Carrington."

Aline Carrington was Louisa's closest woman friend, and I was happy the lady had chosen to take care of her. The addition of Lady Breckenridge surprised me. She was a young widow, friend to Lady Aline, but she'd not been acquainted with Louisa. Also, Lady Breckenridge was a woman about whose motives I was not always clear.

Pomeroy went on, "Mrs. Brandon told me to fetch you here."

"Mrs. Brandon is a wise woman."

"Aye, sir. I always obey when Mrs. Brandon gives orders."

"Good man."

I lifted the knife and held it between my palms, the point touching one hand and the handle touching the other. The knife told me little. The blade was slim and stained with blood. Neither blade nor hilt contained any markings or engravings. In itself, the knife indicated nothing.

I laid the knife on the table. "Please show me where he was found."

Pomeroy raised thick yellow brows. "Don't know what good that is. It's just a room."

"All the same."

Pomeroy gave me the look he'd always reserved for my more questionable orders, but he lumbered away.

Before I left I looked down at Turner once more. A young

man, his life abruptly ended. Did he have a father and mother, brothers, a wife, an affianced? His face told me nothing. He'd been a dandy and a well-to-do young man — his clothes and the emerald stickpin attested to that.

Lucius Grenville would know all about him. Grenville would know the young man's crowd, his intimates, his family. Grenville would also be able to tell me where Mr. Turner went to school, what wagers he liked to place at White's, and what kind of horses he drove. The Polite World knew everything about everyone, and this was definitely a crime of the Polite World.

I followed Pomeroy down the staircase. This house was opulent, with no expense spared to impress the invited guest. Lord Gillis had remodeled his abode with modern conveniences — large windows, airy rooms, and hidden halls and stairs through which servants could pass without being seen by the inhabitants or their guests. The main staircase lifted three stories from a wide hall paved with marble, and paintings of Gillis ancestors by Reynolds and Holbein marched up the walls to the domed ceiling at the top. The stair railing was wrought iron, shaped in fantastic curlicues.

Pomeroy's boots clumped swiftly as we descended. I followed more slowly, my footsteps punctuated by the sharp tap of my walking stick. At forty-one, I already walked like an old man, courtesy of a painful wound in my left leg — a wound for which Colonel Brandon was directly responsible.

We left the staircase and trudged through an equally grand corridor that led to the ballroom, and down a short sweep of stairs that took us to the ballroom floor. The ballroom's ceiling was punctuated with ponderous chandeliers, each holding about fifty candles.

All but a few candles had been extinguished, rendering the room gloomy. Hours ago, this chamber had blossomed with light and music, with gentlemen in evening dress and ladies in velvets and jewels gliding elegantly about.

Lucius Grenville waited for us with Lord Gillis. Lord Gillis drank brandy, and from his pink complexion, he'd consumed quite a few glasses.

Grenville, brandy glass in hand, cool sangfroid in place, greeted us with a nod. "Lord Gillis, may I present my friend, Captain Gabriel Lacey. Captain Lacey, Lord Gillis."

We might have been at a soiree. Lord Gillis was fifty and gray, but he had the physique of a man who enjoyed hearty walking and riding. He looked up at my six-foot height with strong eyes.

According to Pomeroy, Lord Gillis had been serving as a major on the Peninsula in 1811, when he'd received word that his cousin, the previous earl, had died. He'd quit the army and returned home, but he still retained his military bearing and his interest in military men and events.

"I wish the circumstances of the meeting were happier, Captain," Lord Gillis said, shaking my offered hand. "Our little ball will be a nine days' wonder."

"Will you show me where it happened?" I asked.

Lord Gillis pointed. "In the room at the foot of the stairs. Forgive me, but somehow I never want to see it again."

"I am sorry," I said. "Did you know Mr. Turner well?"

Lord Gillis looked surprised. "Not at all. Henry Turner was the friend of a friend of my wife's. So she tells me. But murder is a grim business, Captain. It was a gruesome sight."

Death in battle was far more gruesome. I recalled piles of bodies before the walls at Badajoz, young men torn in half by blasts, some ripped open but still alive, screaming in pain and fear. Henry Turner had looked peaceful, hardly touched.

Grenville volunteered to show me the room. His face, which was rather pointed, revealed no emotion, and his dark eyes did not glitter with as much curiosity as I'd thought they would.

Tonight, Grenville wore the finest clothes I'd ever seen on him. His coat was black superfine, cut in a style likely invented this morning and which would be all the rage by tomorrow. Next week, Grenville would return to his tailor and invent yet another fashion, and this week's coat would be discarded by one and all.

Black pantaloons hugged muscular legs ladies liked to admire. I'd seen caricatures and cartoons in newspapers about his legs and the way ladies ogled them. The diamond stickpin in his cravat was large and elegant, though not so large as to be vulgar.

"It was not pleasant, I must tell you," Grenville said as we crossed the inlaid floor toward the stairs. We walked alone; Lord Gillis stayed behind to speak to Pomeroy. "Mrs. Harper found him a little past midnight. She began screaming in a horrible way, half mad with it. She had blood on her hand and it seemed to make her crazed."

"Blood?" Turner's wound had been small and nearly clean.

"I saw it on her glove. The poor woman was horrified. The ladies near her seemed more inclined to recoil from her than to help her. I was able to take her aside to pour brandy into her."

"Where is Mrs. Harper now?"

"Home. Her servants rallied round and got her away."

I was becoming more and more intrigued by this Imogene Harper. Why had she gone into the room where she'd found Turner? How had she gotten the blood on her glove without putting her hand on the knife or the wound itself? And why the devil did Brandon agree to Pomeroy's accusation that Mrs. Harper was his mistress?

"I must meet this woman," I said.

Grenville gave me an odd look. "I'd never seen her before tonight. You did not know her?"

"No."

"Hmm."

He opened a door with panels picked out in gold. The room behind the door was small, a retiring room for the convenience of the guests.

Scarlet damask covered the upper walls which were framed by gold-painted panels. The wainscoting was pale gray, also framed in gold leaf. The ceiling, much lower than that of the ballroom, had been painted with a gaudy scene of Apollo and his chariot chasing nymphs across an arch of sky.

The only furniture in the room was a slim-legged Sheraton writing table and a small Sheraton chair with two carved slats on its back. The tastefully austere table and chair contrasted sharply with the ornamentation of the walls and ceiling.

"He was found here." Grenville pointed to the chair. "Slumped forward, as though he'd fallen asleep or was foxed. Lord Gillis himself lifted him, and then we saw the knife in his chest. His eyes were open, but he was quite dead."

I studied the chair and writing table. Both pieces of furniture were innocuous, betraying nothing of Turner's sudden and violent death. The desk presented a smooth, golden satinwood surface with an inlaid design on its edges. Nothing rested on its top.

The chair faced the desk, away from the door. I circled chair and desk once then stopped.

"Grenville, would you mind?"

"Show you how he looked, you mean?" Grenville gave his usual cool shrug, but his face was white. He strolled to the chair and sat down. "Slumped over the desk, as I said." He arranged himself in an untidy hunch, resting his head and one arm on the desk and letting the other arm hang to the floor. "Like this, I think." His voice was muffled.

I moved to the doorway and looked in. "Interesting."

Grenville sat up. "I found it rather appalling, myself. Are you finished?"

I started to tell him to stay a moment longer, then I realized he found sitting in the dead man's chair distasteful. "Of course. I beg your pardon."

Grenville stood, removed a handkerchief from his pocket, and dabbed his lips. "I know you must have seen worse sights than a man dead in a chair, but the entire business gave me a turn. It was so quick — "

He broke off and patted his lips again.

I thought I understood. The month before, Grenville had received a deep knife wound in his chest, one that had barely missed killing him. The sight of the knife and the fact that it had killed Turner instantly must have given him pause.

Grenville tucked his handkerchief back into his pocket and assumed his usual air of calm. If I hadn't come to know him well, I would think he'd found the whole thing a dead bore. But he betrayed himself with the twitching of his fingers and the tight lines about his mouth.

"If Imogene Harper entered and saw Turner sitting here, she might have thought him drunk or asleep," I said. "But as soon as she touched him . . ." I moved to the chair and laid my hand on an imaginary Turner's shoulder. "She would have noticed he was dead. How, then, did she get the blood on her glove?"

I saw Grenville's interest stir. "Yes, I see what you mean. He bled very little. If she'd merely shaken his shoulder, where would she have picked up the blood? She would have had to reach down to grasp the knife or press her fingers to the wound."

"And why should she?"

Grenville looked grim. "Unless she did the deed herself."

"Then why scream and draw attention to herself and the blood on her glove? Why not quietly walk away and dispose of the glove somewhere?"

"Perhaps she never meant to kill him. Perhaps there was a quarrel, she shoved the knife in, then realized what she'd done in her anger. Horrified, she began screaming."

I wandered around the desk again. "He was sitting down when he was killed, or the killer took the time to arrange his body so. He was a healthy young man. Would he not be able to deflect a blow from a woman? Even one crazed with anger?"

"Not if he were taken by surprise."

"As you were," I finished for him. "This is different. It was pitch dark when you were stabbed. You did not have a chance to defend yourself."

"No, I didn't."

I remembered fighting to save Grenville's life, remembered him lying in the dark on cold stone cobbles, his breath so very shallow. I had watched him, fearing every breath he drew would be his last. But Grenville's constitution was strong, and he'd recovered.

The incident had happened over a month ago, but the wound still pained him, I knew. It had made him a bit more nervous as well, though he strove to hide it.

"The circumstances here are entirely different," I said. "A brightly lit room, a hundred guests outside, a strong man facing his attacker. In addition, if Imogene Harper indeed killed him, how did she obtain Brandon's knife? I refuse to believe Brandon handed it to her and told her to kill Turner with it."

"She might have stolen it," Grenville suggested. "Or Brandon might have left it lying somewhere. Or it might be her knife, and Brandon lied to protect her."

"No, I do believe the knife belonged to Colonel Brandon. Such knives were common in the army—they are utilitarian and handy to have."

For a time we both looked at the desk and its herringbone inlay. I imagined Turner lying there, his curled brown hair, nearly the same color as the satinwood, splayed over the desk.

"Lacey," Grenville said in a quiet voice, "we can speculate all night, but the fact is, it looks pretty damning for your colonel. Brandon tried to place himself next to Imogene Harper from the moment he arrived. He was seen speaking sharply with Turner by more than one person—myself included. He even followed Turner into this room, although, admittedly, they emerged together not a few minutes later. An overheard quarrel, the knife, and Brandon seen chasing Turner from Mrs. Harper earlier, all point to one conclusion."

"I know." I closed my fists. "And yet, it is the wrong conclusion. It feels wrong."

"Your Sergeant Pomeroy does not much care about how a thing feels."

"He is a practical man, is Pomeroy. It makes him a good sergeant, but not a good investigator."

"No?" Pomeroy boomed behind me.

He filled the doorway, the tall bulk of him crowned with pomaded yellow hair. His face was red, his right cheekbone creased by a scar from a cut he'd recently received from a thief reluctant to be caught. Pomeroy grinned at me, his stalwart good humor in place.

"No," I said. "You see much and see nothing at the same time."

"Now that, Captain, is why you are the captain and I am the sergeant. You do the plotting and the planning and the inspiring, and I do the drilling and the fighting. We get it done in the end. You should have seen him on the Peninsula, Mr. Grenville. His men would have followed him to the mouth of hell itself. A fine sight."

"You flatter me," I said dryly.

My men had followed me because they'd known I'd make damn sure they'd come back. I'd seen no reason for us all to die in a heroic charge to satisfy a general's lust for glory. The generals had often disagreed with me, and I'd told them exactly what I'd thought. Shouting back at those above me, many of them aristocrats, had earned me the reputation as a hothead and made certain I never progressed to the rank of major. Colonel Brandon had, many times, had to intervene between myself and a superior I'd insulted, thus, if only temporarily, saving my future.

"He did not do it, Sergeant," I said.

Pomeroy shrugged. "That's as may be. But it's my duty to

take in a man to face the magistrate. If you believe you can get him off, then I leave you to it. I won't hinder you."

He would not. Pomeroy liked getting convictions, because he would receive the reward money, but if a man were proved innocent, well then, the gent had had a bit of luck, and who was Pomeroy to rob him of it?

"I will certainly try," I said.

"Best to you," Pomeroy said cheerfully. "I'll be off then. Done all I can do here."

"What about Turner?" I asked. "If the coroner's been and gone, what is to become of his body? You cannot leave him in Lord Gillis's spare bedroom."

"Already taken care of, sir. Lord Gillis sent for Turner's man, who will trundle it back to Turner's ma and pa." He tugged his forelock. "'Night, sir. Mr. Grenville."

Grenville murmured his good night, and Pomeroy trudged out, whistling a tune.

"Who is Turner's father?" I asked Grenville.

"Retired MP, lives in Epsom. Cousin to the Earl of Deptford."

As always, Grenville had everyone's pedigree in his pocket. "I would like to speak to him."

"I would, as well," Grenville said. "I will fix an appointment. But what about tonight? Will you speak to this Mrs. Harper?"

"Not yet," I said. I did need to visit her—she was key to this matter, but I had an even greater need to see someone else. "I must go to Louisa."

Grenville shot me a look. "She is with Lady Aline."

"I know. But I want to reassure her."

I broke off, uncertain of how I could reassure her. I wanted Louisa to know I would pursue this inquiry and find out what had truly happened. Brandon might well be guilty, and, if so, I had to make the shock easier for her. If he were not guilty, I would work to get him free. I had to.

"Do you want me along?" Grenville asked.

I shook my head, and he cleared his throat. "Very well then, I'll leave you to it. I need to look in at Clarges Street."

He meant he would visit Marianne Simmons, an actress who had lived upstairs from me in Grimpen Lane until recently. Grenville, whether wisely or not, had taken her to live in luxury in a house he owned in Clarges Street. Their relationship thus far had been stormy, any progress made usually followed by a painful regression.

"Greet Marianne for me," I said. "And send me word when you've obtained an appointment with Mr. Turner's father. It might be decent of us to attend the funeral."

"I will," Grenville agreed, and we parted.

Lord Gillis's quiet and efficient footmen let me out of the house. Berkeley Square was wet with rain, but the bitter chill of winter had gone, and my breath did not hang in the air.

I had expected to have to hike a long way to find a hackney, but another carriage already waited at the door, and a footman I recognized as Brandon's hopped down and approached me.

"Good evening, Captain," he said. "Mrs. Brandon said we was to have the town coach to fetch you to her. Will you get in, sir?"

CHAPTER 2

The Brandon house in Brook Street was a pale brick edifice inside which I'd endured many an evening with the hostile Colonel Brandon. When we'd returned from the war, Louisa had seemed to think we could resume our easy companionship in suppers and chatter, but the days of laughing in the Brandon tent late into the night had gone.

I missed that life. I missed it sharply. Even with the ever-present danger of battle and death lurking over us, my existence in the king's army had been good. I had been a whole man, fit and vigorous, enjoying my friends and comrades.

The footman assisted me from the coach and opened the door to the house. He took my greatcoat and hat and gloves but left me my walking stick.

"She's upstairs, sir," he told me.

I knew the way. I climbed the stairs, noting the house was dark, cold, and silent. If the servants were up and awake, they were staying out of sight.

I found two maids in the room with Louisa, both looking upset and alarmed. Lady Aline Carrington, a stout, white-haired woman with a booming voice, was seated on a divan with Louisa.

Louisa reclined next to her, a blanket over her knees. Her maids had loosened her hair, and it hung down one shoulder in a golden swath. Despite that, she looked tired and old, well beyond her forty-three years.

When she saw me, she exhaled in relief. "Gabriel."

Lady Aline creaked to her feet. "Lacey, my boy. Dreadful business, this. You will find out what really happened, won't you?"

"That is my intention," I said.

"Louisa was a bit worried you wouldn't trouble yourself," Lady Aline said, always frank.

Louisa flushed. "Aline, will you please allow me to speak to Gabriel alone?"

"Of course. Come along," she told the maids. "Your mistress will not crumble to dust without you. At least not for ten minutes."

The maids, who had been straightening Louisa's blanket and holding a cup of tea for her, made every show of reluctance as they left the room. Lady Aline drove them out before her, then she shut the door.

"Louisa," I began, preparing to launch into my speech of comfort.

Louisa pushed aside the blanket and left the divan to fling her arms around my neck.

This was so unusual for Louisa, that I stood still, nonplussed, before I closed my arms around her and pulled her close.

Once, three years ago, Louisa had come to me for comfort. On that rainy, hot night in Spain, her husband had told her of his plan to end their marriage. She'd come, weeping, to my tent in the middle of the night, and I'd held her as I held her now, stroking her golden hair and giving her words of comfort.

"I will do everything I can, Louisa. I will help him. Never fear that."

She laid her head on my shoulder. It was unlike her to crumble, but tonight she had endured much. I wondered whether she had known about Mrs. Harper before this, and I silently cursed Brandon for raining everything upon her at once.

I held her for a time. The coal fire flickered quietly on the hearth, and rain pattered against the dark windows.

At last, Louisa lifted her head and wiped her eyes with her fingertips. "Forgive me, Gabriel. But I feel as if I cannot breathe."

I smoothed her hair. "Louisa, I know magistrates; I even know a man whom magistrates fear. Your husband will be released and brought home to you. I swear this."

Her gray eyes, luminous with tears, contained resignation and a strange finality. I realized with a jolt that she believed Brandon guilty.

"Louisa," I began, and then I felt a draft on my cheek.

The door had opened, and Lady Breckenridge stood on the threshold.

The widowed Viscountess Breckenridge was thirty years old. She was slender but not overly thin and had thick black hair and dark blue eyes. She was quite attractive and knew it, and I had let that attraction entrance me quite often of late.

Lady Breckenridge was outspoken and acerbic, but she could show touches of kindness, such as when she had purchased me a new walking stick when my old one had been ruined. She also enjoyed bringing up-and-coming artists and musicians to the attention of society, and she lived well in her status as widow of a wealthy and titled gentleman and only daughter of another wealthy and titled gentleman.

She had claimed once that she wanted friendship from me, but I never quite knew how to take her overtures.

Lady Breckenridge paused for one silent moment on the

threshold, taking in Louisa in my arms without changing expression. Then she swept into the room, gesturing for the tray-bearing footman behind her to follow.

"Lady Aline suggested drink stronger than tea, Mrs. Brandon," she said. "I sent your servant to find your husband's cache of brandy and whiskey."

Louisa stepped away from me and moved back to the divan.

Lady Breckenridge instructed the footman to leave the tray on the tea table. She was still in her ball gown, a creation of deep blue velvet. The hem was lined with a stiff gold lace that rose in an inverted V in the front to be topped with a bow somewhere near Lady Breckenridge's knees. Her sleeves were long, but the ensemble left her shoulders bare. She'd draped a silk shawl over her arms, but did not bother to pull it up to warm her skin.

Lady Breckenridge gave me a sharp stare, as though daring me to ask what she was doing there. I was grateful to her for helping Louisa home, but I wondered at her motives.

I was grateful also to Lady Aline for suggesting the brandy. I poured a dollop into Louisa's teacup and pressed it into her hands. "Drink this."

Obediently, Louisa lifted the cup to her lips. I sloshed whiskey into one of Brandon's precious cut crystal glasses for myself, and sipped. The liquid burned a nice warmth through my body.

"Brandy, nothing better," Lady Aline said, coming back into the room. "Lacey, pour me some of that whiskey, and do not look shocked, I beg you. I am much older than you and can drink what I like."

I hid a smile as I obliged her and poured the whiskey. "May I give you tea, Donata?" I asked Lady Breckenridge. "Or will you be daring and drink whiskey as well?"

Lady Breckenridge hesitated, then made the smallest negative gesture. "Nothing for me, thank you."

Louisa gave me an odd look. Lady Aline raised her brows and drank her whiskey.

I realized after a moment that I'd betrayed myself. I called very few women by their Christian names; to do so was to acknowledge an intimate friendship. I addressed Louisa by her Christian name, and Marianne Simmons, who'd filched my candles when she'd lived upstairs from me. I should properly address Lady Breckenridge as *my lady*.

I decided that trying to correct myself would condemn me further, so I said nothing.

Lady Aline tossed her whiskey back as well as any buck at White's and told Lady Breckenridge to go home.

"I will stay with Louisa tonight, poor lamb," she said. "I will call on you tomorrow, Donata, dear."

"Thank you, my lady," Louisa said to Lady Breckenridge from the divan. "It was kind of you."

Lady Breckenridge raised her brows. "Not at all. Good night, Aline, Captain." She made a graceful exit from the room.

I could not leave it at that. I excused myself from Louisa and Lady Aline and followed her out.

When I caught up to Lady Breckenridge at the head of the stairs, she gave me a faint smile. "I am capable of finding the front door, Captain. Mrs. Brandon's servants are most obliging."

She began to descend, not waiting for me. She'd dressed her hair tonight in tightly wound curls looped through a diamond headdress. The coiffure bared her long neck, which I studied as I followed her down the stairs.

At the door, one of the maids helped her don a mantle, a heavy velvet cloak with a hood.

"Thank you," I told Lady Breckenridge. "For helping Louisa. It was kind of you."

"You are wondering why I did," she said as she settled the hood. "I am not known for my helpfulness."

"I know you can be kind, when you wish to be."

A smile hovered about her mouth. "High praise, Captain. I helped her, because I knew she was your friend. And Lady Aline's." Her eyes were a mystery. "Good night."

I touched her velvet-clad arm. "May I call on you tomorrow? I would like to hear your version of events, if you do not mind discussing them. You were there and likely much less agitated than Mrs. Brandon."

"Of course." She inclined her head. "I will tell you all I can. Call at four o'clock. I intend to laze about tomorrow and be home to very few. Good night."

I released her arm and bowed. Lady Breckenridge acknowledged the bow with a nod, then swept out into the strengthening rain under the canopy the obliging footmen held over her.

BY THE TIME I RETURNED TO THE SITTING ROOM, LOUISA had regained some color. The blanket was tucked around her again, and pillows cradled her back. Lady Aline sipped a full glass of whiskey, her rouged face now bright pink.

"I should have been more gracious," Louisa was saying.

"Nonsense," Lady Aline said. "Donata Breckenridge is a woman of sense, despite her ways. She enjoys playing the shrew, and who can blame her? Her husband was appalling to her from beginning to his very nasty end. She has a good heart, but she hides it well."

"All the same," Louisa murmured. I realized she was embarrassed. A viscountess, a member of the aristocracy, had witnessed her husband's humiliating arrest and confessions.

"She will say nothing, Louisa," Lady Aline assured her.

Louisa sank into silence.

I pulled a chair close to the divan. "Louisa, I will have to ask you questions about tonight," I said. "Can you bear to answer now? Or would you rather wait?"

"She needs her rest, Lacey," Aline said.

I looked at Louisa's drawn face, and my heart bled. I'd spent most of my adult life wanting to make things better for her, and I never had been quite able to do so.

"I would rather tell you at once," Louisa said. "I want to put it behind me."

I glanced at Aline, who gave me an almost imperceptible nod.

"Let us start from the very beginning, then. Why did you attend Lord Gillis's ball?"

"We were invited. I received the invitation a week ago. I decided to accept because we could fit it into our night." Louisa paused. "No, that is not entirely true. I was flattered to be asked. Aloysius had met Lord Gillis during the war. I was pleased Lord Gillis remembered us."

"And he was willing to attend?" Colonel Brandon went to social occasions because of a sense of duty, not pleasure. When he reached the gatherings, he immediately sought the card room or his circle of friends and left Louisa to enjoy the event on her own.

"As willing as he usually is," Louisa said with the ghost of a smile.

"Tell me every detail you can remember," I urged. "Begin with leaving your house tonight. What was Brandon like? Did he behave in any way out of the ordinary?"

"Much as usual, I think." Louisa sighed. "I admit I was not paying attention. I was much more worried my gown would be not quite right, and what would Lady Gillis think of me? It seems so silly now."

I could not imagine Louisa looking anything but radiant, but I did not say so. The way ladies viewed other ladies, I had come to learn, was much different from the manner in which gentlemen viewed them. A woman would notice whether the braid on another woman's bodice was two years out of date; a man would note how the color of the braid brought out the blue of her eyes.

"You looked splendid, Louisa," Lady Aline said. "I told you so, I believe."

Louisa gave her a wan smile. "You were very kind, I remember."

"What time did you reach the Gillises' home?" I asked.

"About ten o'clock, I think. Many others arrived at that time, as well. I remember that the square was packed with carriages."

"When you walked into the house, did you note who was around you? Who went in before and after you did?"

Louisa's brow furrowed. "I am not certain. I cannot remember, Gabriel. It seems as though it took place in another lifetime."

"Why is it important, anyway, Lacey?" Lady Aline interrupted. "Surely it's only important whether Brandon went near the Turner fellow."

"I am thinking along the lines of the knife. Brandon said he did not even know he had it with him. Perhaps he is lying, perhaps not. In either case, what if someone picked his pocket and obtained the knife that way? In the crush at the front door, with people milling about trying to enter the house all at once, a hand could easily slip into Brandon's pocket and purloin the knife."

Aline gave me an incredulous look. "Do you mean to say a guest of Lord Gillis was an accomplished pickpocket? All of Mayfair would swoon."

"Not necessarily a guest. Footmen and maids surround their masters and mistresses. Lord Gillis's own servants usher in the guests and take their wraps."

"Well, good Lord," Lady Aline said. "Then everyone in the house, from the master to the scullery maid and everyone in between, could have murdered Mr. Turner."

"Yes," I said, feeling gloomy. "They all *could* have. We need to pare down the number to the ones most likely, and from there we will find the culprit."

"You make it sound alarmingly simple," Aline said, a wry twist to her lips. "How can we?"

"By asking rude and impertinent questions. Something I excel at."

Lady Aline looked amused. I was not known for my patience, especially in situations with dire consequences, like this one.

I returned to the question. "Do you remember, Louisa? To whom did you speak when you first entered the house?"

She sat in silent thought for a moment. I knew it would be a difficult task for anyone to remember what they did every minute of one particular evening. The events that followed would make it doubly difficult for her, but I had to try.

"Mrs. Bennington, the actress," Louisa said at last, naming a young woman who had recently taken the crowned heads of Europe by storm.

From what I'd heard, Claire Bennington had an English father but had been raised on the Continent, taking the stage in Italy about five years ago. She had become a success there, and recently returned to London, where she had quickly won over audiences. She was still quite young, only in her early twenties, and married to an Englishman whom she'd met on the Continent. This season, it was quite popular for hostesses to have Mrs. Bennington attend one of their events and give a short performance for the guests.

"She seems a rather vague young woman," Louisa went on. "I have seen her perform and enjoyed it very much. I remember remarking on the contrast, how brilliantly she plays a part, to her blank stares when anyone greeted her tonight."

"I noted that, myself," Lady Aline said. "Probably she plays others so well because she has no thoughts of her own."

"I can hardly imagine her picking my husband's pocket, however," Louisa said.

"Who else was nearby?"

Louisa closed her eyes, as though shutting out the room to remember the streams of guests entering Lord Gillis's house. "I suppose I remember Mrs. Bennington because she is so famous. Oh, yes, Mr. Stokes was behind us. He is rather loud. I could not mistake him."

I glanced at Lady Aline. "I do not know Mr. Stokes."

"Basil Stokes," Aline answered. "Knew him since I was seventeen. Always tried to look up my skirts then—said he only wanted to see my ankles. I boxed his ears. Still likes to look up a lady's skirt, the devil."

"Would he have a motive for murdering Mr. Turner?" I wondered.

"I have no idea. Don't see why. I could ask him, I suppose."

Lady Aline's idea of investigation might be more like inter-rogation by enemy soldiers. "That might not be necessary," I said quickly. I turned back to Louisa. "What happened when you entered the house?"

Louisa plucked at the blanket's edge. "The usual sort of thing. The footman took my wrap. My maid and I went to a retiring room, where she brought my slippers from their box and helped me put them on. Then she re-pinned my hair. Lady Breckenridge was in the retiring room with her maid, as well. We greeted each other."

"Where did you rejoin Colonel Brandon?"

"Near the entrance to the ballroom. He was speaking to Mr. Grenville and looking impatient. Aloysius so dislikes the ceremony of balls. I have no idea who else spoke to him while I was in the retiring room."

And Brandon was not the sort of husband to say breezily to his wife, *Oh, my dear, I've just been talking to Mr. Godwin and Lord Humphreys about our ride in the park the other day.* Brandon kept his mouth closed unless asked a direct question. Louisa had by this time mastered the technique for prying information from him when she needed to, but she'd have had no reason to on that occasion, unfortunately.

"No," I agreed. "Go on."

"I entered the ballroom with him. We were announced, though no one took much notice. Not of an obscure colonel and his wife."

Lady Aline patted her hand. "But we know your true worth, Louisa."

Louisa tried to look grateful, but I could see her struggling with exhaustion.

"I dislike to ask you about everyone you and Brandon talked to after that," I said, "but I am afraid I will have to. Did Brandon stay with you or flee as soon as the formalities were over?"

"Fled, of course," she said with a tired smile.

"To the card room? Or the billiards room?"

"Neither. I had stopped to speak to ladies of my acquaintance, and when I turned around again, Aloysius was approaching Mrs. Harper." Louisa faltered. "I did not know who she was. I remember feeling surprised because he began speaking to her as though he knew her and did not have to be introduced."

"They stood alone?"

"No." Louisa's lips tightened. "Mrs. Harper appeared to be with Mr. Derwent and Lady Gillis. Mr. Turner was also nearby, and he joined them."

"What did you think?" I asked as gently as I could.

"I did not think anything, not then. I did not know the lady was Mrs. Harper—I'd never seen her before. But when Aloysius turned and walked away with her, I wondered if she might be the woman called Imogene Harper. You see, Mrs. Harper had been sending Aloysius letters."

My brows rose. "Had she? Did he tell you that?"

"Goodness, no. One morning at breakfast, I'd finished and started to leave the table while Aloysius was still reading his correspondence. I paused to kiss his cheek, and I happened to see the signature on the letter he was reading. *Imogene Harper.* I knew no one of that name. I must have startled him, because he immediately turned the paper facedown. He looked relieved when I merely wished him good morning and continued on my way."

What sort of man read letters from his mistress at breakfast with his wife? Knowing Brandon, I would assume the woman had simply written him a letter about some business interest—except Brandon had admitted to being Mrs. Harper's lover.

"She wrote more?" I asked.

"Yes. Several days after that, I saw a letter by his plate at breakfast, written in a woman's hand. Aloysius had not yet entered the room, so I picked it up." Louisa flushed, as though ashamed of herself. "It smelled of a woman's perfume. It was then I began to suspect."

Tears swam in her eyes. I rested my hand on hers. "Louisa, I am sorry."

"If the connection were innocent," she said, "why should Aloysius not mention it? Mrs. Harper's husband, it seems, was a major who died at Vitoria. Why not tell me, or ask whether I remembered her?"

Why not, indeed? The evidence and admission were there. And yet, it still seemed unbelievable for Brandon. His sense of moral exactness had always been strong. Or had he simply been moral because he'd never been tempted? It is easy to reject sin when one has no interest in it.

"When he walked away with Mrs. Harper tonight, where did he go?" I asked.

"To an alcove. There were several such niches that opened around the ballroom where the guests could adjourn to talk."

"So he walked into a private alcove alone with Mrs. Harper for everyone in the ballroom to see? The bloody idiot."

"Yes." Lady Aline nodded. "He does not seem to be gifted in the ways of discretion."

Louisa put her hand to her mouth. "Forgive me. Gabriel, I cannot speak of this any longer."

Lady Aline's grim look softened. "You poor darling. You must be put to bed. Captain Lacey can ask his questions in the morning."

Tears slid down Louisa's face and pooled on her lips. I itched to know everything immediately, to run through the streets of London putting everything aright, but I knew that Lady Aline was correct. Louisa was exhausted and upset and needed to rest. I had rarely seen her this wretched.

I silently vowed that when I saw Colonel Brandon, I would make him pay for every one of Louisa's tears.

CHAPTER 3

*A*line signaled me to wait for her as she led Louisa into
her bedchamber, so I paced Louisa's feminine sitting
room while she and a maid tucked Louisa into bed.

The room reminded me of Louisa. She liked yellow,
because she said it brought the sunshine to her and made her
feel cheerful even on the gloomiest days. Tonight, the cheerful-
ness did nothing for me. The cream and yellow striped wallpaper, the white drapes with gold tassels, and the matching gilt
and yellow silk chairs and sofa could not chase away the
darkness.

I had known Louisa Brandon for twenty years. She'd been
a fresh young woman of twenty-two when Brandon had
proudly introduced her. I, already married at twenty, had
marveled at her forthrightness and good sense, as well as her
prettiness. My own wife, Carlotta, had been an ethereal beauty,
all gold ringlets and soft white skin. Louisa had a wide smile, a
crooked nose, and shrewd gray eyes that noted everything.

I hadn't understood that Carlotta, shy as a mouse, had been
intimidated by her, and I had not helped by holding up Louisa

as a model for Carlotta to follow. Carlotta, after we'd been married six years, had left me, deserting me for a French officer. I had been furious and blamed her entirely at first, but then I'd shifted the blame to myself. I'd been an appalling husband.

Lady Aline returned through the white and gold door that led to Louisa's bedchamber and closed it behind her. She was shaking her head. A pure white curl came loose from her coiffure and fell to her shoulder.

"She's overset." Aline wiped a tear from her eye, smearing the kohl she'd applied liberally around it. "I am not certain what has horrified her more, the fact that her husband has been arrested for murder or the fact that he betrayed her with another. *All gentlemen take mistresses, she said to me, a wife must learn to bear it.* What rot. Men fill women's heads with that nonsense so they can do what they like. Don't you think so, Lacey?"

"I agree," I said.

She gave me a look of surprise. "Well, well. If that is the truth, then you are the most remarkable gentleman I have ever known. Ring for the maid, please. We need more tea."

I crossed the room to tug a bell pull.

"I've given Louisa a drop of laudanum," Aline said. "That and the brandy should ensure she sleeps well into the morning. I will stay with her until she's stronger. I do hope you clear up this mess quickly, Lacey."

"I appreciate your faith in me."

Lady Aline folded the blanket Louisa had used and drew it onto her lap. "You have impressed me so far. You cleared up the murder at the Sudbury School in Berkshire, discovered who killed Lydia Westin's husband and that barrister's wife, not to mention put up with Lady Clifford and her blasted missing necklace. I much prefer having you look into the matter than Bow Street. So unsavory."

"It is unsavory no matter who looks into it," I said. I gathered up the tea things to give my hands something to do.

"Perhaps, but this is Louisa's life. Her husband. Their secrets. You can at least be gentle."

"I can be gentle with Louisa, true. I'm certain I'll throttle Brandon when I see him. As far as I can discern, he's been a complete idiot."

The maid entered with a fresh pot of tea on a tray. She removed the dirty cups and saucers and departed. I noted the maid's eyes were red with tears.

Lady Aline poured tea in a businesslike manner. She sloshed a dollop of brandy into mine without asking me before handing me the cup.

"Now then," she said, lifting the teapot to pour for herself. "I will tell you the entire nasty tale. I arrived at the Gillises' ball not long after the Brandons did. I entered, in fact, in time to see the damn fool colonel lead Imogene Harper from her friends to a private alcove. Louisa watched them go with a look of dismay. Tongues around me began to wag on the instant. Mr. Bennington, the husband of the actress, drawled to me, *I say, he's no model of discretion, is he?* He sounded delighted to be entertained. Others speculated about who this Harper woman truly was. She is a friend of Lady Gillis's, I gather, though Mrs. Harper claimed to me she'd known the Brandons during the war."

"And yet, Louisa says she does not remember her."

"Precisely. At any rate, Louisa's friends took her under their collective wing and went on as though nothing had happened. Colonel Brandon and Mrs. Harper stayed in that alcove for a very long time. They did not emerge, in fact, until the dancing began. Brandon stood near Mrs. Harper after that, and whenever I happened to glimpse him, he did not look best pleased. I saw Mr. Turner approach Mrs. Harper, possibly to ask her to dance. Colonel Brandon more or less shooed him away. Mr. Turner looked unhappy, but he went. But later on, I happened to be standing near when he approached again.

"Mr. Turner claimed Mrs. Harper had promised him the waltz. Mrs. Harper looked a little confused, then she said, *Oh yes, of course.* Colonel Brandon turned bright red. He said, *Mind your manners; the lady does not wish to waltz.* Mr. Turner said, *You are mistaken, sir. She promised.* Then Colonel Brandon said, rather loudly, *If you do not cease pestering her, I will thrash you.* People began to stare at that, I do not have to tell you. Mr. Turner smiled a bit and said, *No, you won't.* He bowed to Mrs. Harper and wandered away."

"Damn," I said, exasperated. "Brandon appears the very picture of a jealous rival."

"Yes, it was not well done. Soon after that, supper was called. Leland Derwent escorted me in, sweet boy. Colonel Brandon immediately stuck out his arm to Imogene Harper. Never mind Louisa was standing near to them. I know it's not the thing for a husband to always escort his wife, but the snub was apparent. Brandon was red and uncomfortable. He knew what it looked like."

"And Mrs. Harper? Was she uncomfortable as well?"

"Not a bit of it." Lady Aline clicked her cup to her saucer. "She smiled sweetly at him and took his arm. He led her to the supper room and seated himself next to her, stayed glued to her throughout the meal. Louisa was not far from him, trying not to look mortified, poor lamb."

"What the devil was he thinking?"

"Precisely what Mr. Bennington asked me. He was seated on my other side. *My wife runs about where she pleases,* he said with a cynical smile. *But she pretends to be the very picture of devotion. Of course, that is what makes her a celebrated actress. Perhaps the colonel could take lessons from her.*"

"Dear God," I said. "Brandon's made himself and Louisa a laughingstock."

"I know," Lady Aline replied sadly. "That was not the worst of it."

I drank down my tea, the bitter liquid burning my tongue. "Go on," I said.

"After supper, Colonel Brandon led Mrs. Harper out of the dining room again He monopolized her in her ballroom, kept her near him. They did not dance, but neither did she dance with anyone else. When Mr. Turner approached again, Brandon snarled at him. Mr. Turner laughed and walked away. I heard Mr. Turner say, *Soon, sir. Very soon.* What this meant I have no idea, but Mrs. Harper looked distressed, and Brandon grew even redder."

"Did anyone else approach them?" I asked. "Or Mr. Turner, for that matter?" I knew I needed to tamp down my anger at Brandon in order to decide what had happened. Anyone near Brandon might have stolen his knife, including Mrs. Harper herself.

"Basil Stokes spoke to them. I saw him laughing about something in that loud way of his. Colonel Brandon and Mrs. Harper endeavored to be polite. Leland Derwent spoke to them, but then, young Mr. Derwent is a stickler about making the polite rounds. He is too shy to be much of a conversationalist, but he knows to ask about one's mother or ailing sister and to remark upon the weather." Lady Aline put her forefinger to the corner of her mouth. "Let me think. Lady Gillis herself approached them. The irritating Rafe Godwin. He is an annoying young man, tries to imitate Grenville, but Grenville has nothing to do with him, and so he should not."

"What about Mr. Turner? To whom did he speak?"

"Oh, a good number of people. He circulated the room, danced with a few debutantes—whose mothers ought to have known better, but he is an earl's cousin, after all. He spent much time with Leland Derwent. I believe they knew each other at school, though I would not think innocent Leland was much Henry Turner's type. But Leland suffers from over-politeness and doesn't have the bad manners to tell Turner to go to the devil."

I thought about the people Lady Aline had named, some of whom I knew, some I did not. I would have to discuss them with Grenville later, to obtain his opinion. One person, I noted, Lady Aline had not mentioned. "What about Lady Breckenridge?"

Lady Aline opened her mouth to answer, then she closed it again and eyed me shrewdly. "Lacey, my boy, what is exactly between you and Donata Breckenridge?"

I stopped. "Between?"

"I am not blind. I know you're not courting her, and yet . . ."

She left it hanging. My face heated as I touched the handle of the walking stick Lady Breckenridge had given me. "We are friends," I said. But I had kissed her lips on more than one occasion, and she had helped me when I'd needed it. I had not liked her when I'd first met her, over a billiards game in a sunny room in Kent. I'd found her abrupt, abrasive, and overly forward. "Perhaps more than friends," I finished.

"She had a wretched marriage to Breckenridge," Lady Aline said, a rather unnecessary statement. I had met Lord Breckenridge and knew exactly what kind of man he'd been. "Marriage to him would have killed a woman with a lesser strength than Donata's."

"I have no desire to make her wretched," I said.

That was the truth. On the other hand, I had not the means to marry her, either. My own wife, I'd discovered, was still alive, and in France, with my daughter. I had been given her exact whereabouts a few weeks ago, and I had been contemplating traveling across the Channel to find her.

I would go sooner or later, but I was having difficulty steeling myself to meet her again. The only thing that drove me to do it was the thought of seeing my daughter again. Gabriella would now be seventeen.

Even if I came to some arrangement with my wife, even if Grenville helped me with a divorce or annulment, I'd have little to offer Lady Breckenridge. I was a poor man, though I was a gentleman born. Lady Breckenridge marrying me would be a sad misalliance for her.

"And *I* have no desire to see her wretched either," Lady Aline said. "But you treat her kindly, and she is grateful for that."

I raised my brows. "She said so?" I could not imagine Lady Breckenridge expressing such a tender thought.

"Of course not," Lady Aline said. "She does not need to. But I've known her since she was in leading strings. Her mother is a great friend of mine."

"I am pleased she has such an ally in you. But you haven't answered my question. To whom did Lady Breckenridge speak this evening?"

Lady Aline gave me a smile. "Not to Colonel Brandon and Imogene Harper. Donata spoke to me and to Lady Gillis—although she does not like Lady Gillis very much. She finds her too washed out and tiresome. She danced much, of course. She always does. She even danced with Mr. Derwent, who asked her out of painful politeness. She seemed most amused."

I imagined she had. Leland Derwent was the epitome of innocence, and Lady Breckenridge had a rather worldly outlook. I hoped she had not shocked Leland too much.

I studied the head of my walking stick, which was engraved with the inscription *Captain G. Lacey, 1817.* "Now, we come to the event of Turner's death. Take me to that and tell me what happened, exactly."

"I remember very precisely that I was talking to Lady Gillis. We both had seen a patterned silk at Madame Mouchand's and admired it. I was explaining it would look fine on her, but not me, because I am too stout to carry it off. All at once, we heard a horrible scream. It pierced the air, cutting over the music. Everyone stopped, of course, even the musicians, as we looked for the disturbance. And there was Imogene Harper, near the stairs with the anteroom door open behind her, screaming frantically."

"Did you see Colonel Brandon? Was he near her?"

"No. At that moment, I saw him nowhere in the room. He did reappear, however, when I made my way to Mrs. Harper. The colonel came from behind me and shoved his way through. We reached her at about the same time."

"What did he say?"

"Nothing very much. In general, men are useless in a crisis. Except Grenville. He very sensibly took Mrs. Harper by the hand and led her to a seat and called for brandy. Then he entered the room with Lord Gillis. The rest of the guests could only gape. I stayed with Louisa, who took it very well, until Lord Gillis sent for Bow Street. Then she nearly swooned. Louisa believes her husband truly did kill Mr. Turner, you see."

I recalled the resigned look in Louisa's eyes. "Pomeroy obviously thinks he did also. But is there anything that points concretely to Brandon having stabbed Turner? Two gentlemen can exchange sharp words without one murdering the other. Or if they do, they call each other out and make a formal show of it."

"Ah, Lacey, the problem of it is, there were so many people in the ballroom. Who knows who entered that room with Mr. Turner, or who was there already when he entered it? Had he slipped inside for peace and quiet, or did he mean to meet someone? No one saw. We were concentrating and dancing and gossip and disparaging other ladies' gowns, you see. The usual thing."

"One does not expect a member of the *ton* to be murdered at a ball," I agreed. "And yet, these are violent times."

"The rioting, you mean?" Lady Aline asked.

Since March, with the hanging of a seaman called John Cashman for the crime of getting drunk and stealing a few weapons, the people of London had rioted. Some protested the unjust killing of Cashman, some the fact that British soldiers, back from the war, often had no money, no employment, and no prospect of payment for the blood they'd given in battle. Others rioted simply because it focused their anger and disgust at something other than the tediousness of their lives.

"Rioting, and the men who put down the riots," I said. "Murder in general. It is as though the war allowed us some measure of venting that side of man's nature, but now that avenue is gone."

Lady Aline's plucked brows rose. "Surely the threat of Napoleon's invasion and the loss of ten thousand men at Waterloo is not better than a few riots."

"No, of course not. Never mind. I am melancholy about this entire business."

"As am I. Poor Louisa."

She glanced at the closed door, behind which Louisa rested.

"Is there anything more you can tell me?" I asked. "Anything else you might have noticed?"

"I will think on it. I admit, Lacey, I am rather stunned by it all. When Mr. Pomeroy arrived, he was inclined to believe Mrs. Harper had killed the man. She may have. I don't know. But then Colonel Brandon stepped forward to protect her, and Pomeroy switched his attentions to him." She shook her head. "This will be scandal. Vicious scandal."

"Perhaps Louisa would be better off somewhere other than London," I said.

"Indeed. I could take her with me to Dorset. That is sufficiently distant, for now, I think."

"She will refuse, of course."

"I will persuade her. If nothing else, I'll feed her laudanum and drag her off while she sleeps."

I smiled at the thought, but I knew Lady Aline was capable of doing just that.

Lady Aline sighed. "Tonight Louisa came face to face with

the idea that her husband might be in truth a very dreadful man."

"Yes," I said. I was nagged by the feeling that Brandon's vice in this was mere pigheadedness, not evil. Something did not make sense. I, who should have been ready to believe the worst of Brandon, could not now it had come to it.

Behind the door, Louisa cried out in her sleep. I sprang to my feet, jolted by the heart-rending sound. She must have awakened herself, because we heard a muffled moan, and then the unmistakable sound of weeping.

I was halfway to the door before Lady Aline stopped me. "Not you," she said sharply.

I halted, my heart pounding. The need to comfort Louisa struck me hard.

Lady Aline shook her head at me. Then, gathering her skirts, she strode past me to the door of Louisa's bedchamber and let herself inside.

I QUIT THE HOUSE. I COULD NOT BEAR TO STAY ANY LONGER, listening to Louisa cry and knowing I could not help her. I took a hackney coach across rainy London and arrived at my lodgings in Grimpen Lane, near Covent Garden, just as dawn broke the sky.

Bartholomew waited in my rooms for me, awake and as fresh as though he'd slept all night, which he hadn't. He had warmed the sitting room and bedchamber, and he helped me to bed.

I closed my eyes, but I could only see Louisa, pale and drawn, her gray eyes full of conviction her husband had committed murder and adultery. More than that, I could feel Louisa's soft body against mine as she clung to me, needing me. I was not quite certain how I felt about that.

I did doze a few times only to dream of Henry Turner's still, dead body and the sound of Imogene Harper's screams.

Bartholomew woke me at ten that morning. Pomeroy had told me last night that Brandon would be examined by the Bow Street magistrate at eleven o'clock, and I intended to be there. I bathed my face and let Bartholomew shave me.

"Do you think the colonel did it, sir?" Bartholomew asked as he scraped soap and whiskers from my chin.

"I do not know, Bartholomew. He certainly was not very helpful."

"Want me to come along, sir?"

"No. I have the feeling trying to keep Colonel Brandon out of Newgate will take much time. No need for you to waste your day in the magistrate's office."

"Mind if I poke around a bit? Get chummy with Lord Gillis's servants, I mean. See if they witnessed the event?"

He sounded eager, ready to begin the game of investigation.

I told him to enjoy himself. Bartholomew could be a mine of information on what went on not only below stairs, but above stairs as well. He had certainly helped me solve crimes before, even getting himself shot during one adventure. The incident had not dampened his enthusiasm the slightest bit.

Before I left my rooms, I wrote a short letter to Sir Montague Harris, the magistrate of the Whitehall Public Office, informing him of my thoughts on the death of Turner.

Bartholomew agreed to post the letter for me, and I walked from the narrow cul-de-sac of Grimpen Lane to Russel Street. I turned left onto Russel Street and traversed the short distance to Bow Street, my knee barely bothering me this morning.

The spring day was warm, and people thronged the lanes. Women with baskets over their arms and shawls against the damp threaded their way among the vendors, working men hurried about with deliveries or on errands, and middle-class women strolled arm-in-arm with their daughters looking into shops.

Bow Street was crowded. Rumor of a murder in elegant Mayfair had reached the populace, and many waited for a glimpse of the murderer Bow Street had apprehended. I had not looked at a newspaper yet, but I imagined their stories would be lurid. As time went on, every snippet of Brandon's life would be splashed across the pages of the *Morning Herald*.

I let myself into the magistrate's house and asked one of the clerks for Pomeroy.

"Ah, there you are, Captain," Pomeroy bellowed across the length of the house. He shouldered his way down the corridor, pressing aside the assorted pickpockets and prostitutes who'd been arrested during the night. "Come to see the colonel committed, have you?"

CHAPTER 4

I became aware that every person in the vicinity turned to watch us. "He must be examined, first," I said.

"Oh, aye, him and the witnesses. I called in Lord Gillis and Mr. Grenville. Lord Gillis because it was his house and he'd likely know what went on in it, and Mr. Grenville because he makes a decent witness. And he was first on the spot when it happened. I wanted to call Mrs. Harper, but the magistrate said wait until she's a bit less distressed." He shrugged. "He's the magistrate."

I wanted very much to meet Mrs. Harper myself, but I agreed that traveling to Bow Street and enduring the scrutiny of last night's crop of prostitutes might be beyond her. "Lord Gillis is coming?" I asked.

"Not the thing for an earl to come to the magistrate, Sir Nathaniel says," Pomeroy said, naming Bow Street's chief magistrate, Sir Nathaniel Conant. "Sir Nathaniel will go to him later today. But Mr. Grenville should be arriving at any time."

Grenville liked to be in the thick of things. I knew he would not mind walking among the muck of Bow Street in his perfectly shined boots if he could indulge his curiosity. I would be happy to see him, though. He'd been on the spot, and he was quite good at noticing things out of the ordinary. A decent witness, as Pomeroy had called him.

Grenville arrived as Pomeroy and I started for the stairs. His fine phaeton stopping in the street caused some commotion as those inside craned to look out windows at the most elegant horses and rig in town. Grenville leapt down and handed the reins to his tiger, a young man whose sole purpose in life was to look after Grenville's horses when he was not driving them.

Grenville swept inside, removing his hat, and was instantly bombarded by a mass of humanity.

"A farthing in me palm, milord. Wouldn't say no," an elderly man with few teeth breathed at him. "Spare a penny for an old man?"

"Yer a fine one. Remember sweet Jane when she's done with the magistrate, won't you?"

Grenville blushed but he sprinkled pennies among the others until Pomeroy lumbered forward and shouted, "Clear off. Let him through."

"Good morning, Lacey," Grenville said with his usual politeness. We might be meeting at his club. "Mr. Pomeroy."

Grenville looked as though he'd not slept much the night before. His face was impeccably shaved, but his cheeks were pasty white and dark smudges stained the hollows beneath his eyes.

We did not speak further as Pomeroy took us up the stairs and to the room where the chief magistrate waited.

Sir Nathaniel Conant, an elderly gentleman who'd presided over the Bow Street court for the last four years, sat behind a table upon which waited a sheaf of paper and a pen and ink. The room felt damp and smelled faintly of unwashed clothes, an inauspicious place to decide a man's fate.

Colonel Brandon sat near Sir Nathaniel, but he got abruptly to his feet when he saw me.

Brandon looked terrible. His usually crisp black hair was disheveled, although he'd made some attempt to smooth it. His chin was covered in black stubble, and his dark and elegant suit was rumpled and stained. He gazed at me with blue eyes that resembled cold winter skies and were just about as friendly.

"Good, Pomeroy," Sir Nathaniel said. "We can begin. These are your witnesses?"

"Mr. Grenville is." Pomeroy introduced him. "He was at the ball when the murder took place. This is Captain Lacey."

Sir Nathaniel peered at me, his watery eyes taking more interest. "I have heard Sir Montague Harris speak of you. He regards you as intelligent. Why have you come? Are you also a witness?"

"I was not at Lord Gillis's ball, no," I said. "But I know Colonel Brandon. He was my commander in the army."

"Ah, a character witness. Sit down, if you please."

"Sir Nathaniel," Brandon said stiffly. "I do not want Captain Lacey here."

Sir Nathaniel looked surprised. "Do not be foolish, sir. At this point, you need all the friends you have. Sit."

He pointed his pen at the chair Brandon had vacated. With another belligerent glare at me, Brandon resumed his seat.

Colonel Aloysius Brandon was a handsome man. At forty-six, he had black hair with little gray, a square, handsome face, and an athletic physique that had not run to fat. I had often wondered why he seemed oblivious to the attentions women wished to bestow on him, although, as evidenced with this business, perhaps he was not so oblivious after all.

I took a straight-backed chair next to Grenville. Pomeroy sprawled across a bench, and we waited for the procedure to begin.

At least, I thought, as Sir Nathaniel scratched a few words on his papers, Brandon did not have to suffer the indignity of standing in the dock before the sitting magistrate downstairs, with thieves and prostitutes and other poor unfortunates awaiting their turn. Sir Nathaniel had obviously kept Colonel Brandon's standing in mind, as well as the fact that murder was a bit more serious than pickpocketing or laundry stealing.

"Colonel Brandon," Sir Nathaniel began. "This is an examination, not a trial, in which I will determine whether you should be held in custody for trial for murder. Do you understand?"

Silently, with an angry glint in his eye, Brandon nodded.

"Excellent. Now, Mr. Pomeroy, please present the evidence that made you bring in this man for the murder of Mr. Henry Turner."

Pomeroy climbed to his feet and plodded forward. He took from his pocket a wad of cloth, and unwrapped the dagger that had killed Turner. He clunked the knife to the table.

"This was plunged into the chest of Mr. Henry Turner, coroner says near to midnight last night," Pomeroy said. "The body was found at twelve o'clock, and witnesses saw the deceased alive and well at half past eleven, so there's not much doubt about the time of death. When I arrived, I asked who the knife belonged to. Colonel Brandon told me that the knife was his. His wife, Mrs. Brandon, said she could not remember whether the colonel had such a knife, but he was pretty certain."

"It is mine," Brandon said, tight-lipped. "I never denied that."

Sir Nathaniel gave him a sharp glance then made a note. "Any other evidence?"

"No, sir. I examined Colonel Brandon's gloves and found them clean. The colonel denied having killed Mr. Turner, and denied having gone into the anteroom where he was found at all. But a few witnesses, Mr. Grenville included, saw Mr. Turner and Colonel Brandon enter the room together at eleven o'clock. However, they emerged after about five minutes and went their separate ways. No one I can find remembers either

Mr. Turner or Colonel Brandon entering the room after that, but Mr. Turner must have done, because there he was, dead, an hour later."

"I must ask you, Colonel," Sir Nathaniel said, "why you lied to Mr. Pomeroy about entering the anteroom at all?"

Brandon looked uncomfortable. "Because it was none of his affair. And it had nothing to do with Turner being killed."

"That remains to be seen," Sir Nathaniel said. "Please tell me the nature of your conversation with Mr. Turner in the anteroom."

Brandon sat up straighter. "I do not wish to."

Sir Nathaniel raised his gray brows. "Colonel Brandon, you might well be tried for murder. Were I in your place, I would try my best to establish that my business with Mr. Turner had nothing to do with his death. Now, what did you discuss?"

Brandon's neck went red. "I called him out."

"Called him out. Do you mean you challenged him to a duel?"

Brandon nodded.

Sir Nathaniel made another note. Even the scratching of his pen sounded disapproving. "Dueling is against the law, Colonel."

"I know that. But Mr. Turner was being offensive to Mrs. Harper. He needed speaking to. In any event, it is a moot point now."

I stifled my dismay. Brandon might as well build the scaffold and tie the noose around his own neck.

"Indeed, it is," Sir Nathaniel said. "And you were annoyed with Mr. Turner's behavior, because Mrs. Harper is your mistress?"

Brandon hesitated. I saw his eyes swivel to the paper, above which Sir Nathaniel's pen poised. It was one thing to say the words to Pomeroy, quite another to have them written down in black ink.

"Yes," he said slowly.

This was nonsense. It had to be. And yet, what had Brandon to gain from protecting Mrs. Harper?

"Very well." Sir Nathaniel's pen moved. "After you and Mr. Turner made an appointment to meet, what did you do next?"

"We never made the appointment," Brandon said. "He refused me. I told him he was a coward and left him."

Grenville glanced sideways at me, and I gave him a grim look in return. If Brandon could convince the magistrate he'd planned to meet Turner honorably, he might have a chance to prove he'd never kill him *dis*honorably. But Brandon's words put paid to that defense.

"I see." Sir Nathaniel redipped his pen. "Well, then, Colonel, please go on. Tell me what you did from the time you left Mr. Turner until his body was discovered."

"I've told Mr. Pomeroy," Brandon said in a hard voice.

Sir Nathaniel looked at him with deceptively mild eyes. "Now tell me."

Brandon's shoulders sagged the slightest bit. "I walked out of the anteroom, as I told you. I went back to find Mrs. Harper, and we adjourned into an alcove so I could speak privately with her. I told her what Mr. Turner had said. She was naturally upset that I had challenged him, and it took some time to calm her down. She asked that I find her some sherry, and I went in search. I could not find a footman with a tray—never about when you need one, footmen—so I was obliged to leave the ballroom. I searched the supper room and found all the decanters empty, so I went out to the hall to find a servant. I had no success and was about to tramp down to the kitchens myself, when I heard Mrs. Harper screaming. I pushed my way through the crowd and saw her standing outside the anteroom, and Turner dead inside."

Sir Nathaniel scribbled away. Presently he asked, "Did you see anyone in the supper room or the hall outside who can be a witness that you were there?"

"No," Brandon growled. "As I said, I found no sherry and no servants. God knows where they all were. When I came back inside, everyone was watching Mrs. Harper. I do not think anyone noticed me."

I broke in. "That does corroborate what Lady Aline Carrington told me. She said Colonel Brandon came from behind her."

Sir Nathaniel made a note without thanking me. "Even better," he said, "would be a witness who saw you in the alcove with Mrs. Harper between the time you left Mr. Turner and twelve o'clock."

Brandon shook his head.

"Mr. Pomeroy?" Sir Nathaniel asked. "Have you found any witnesses to swear where Colonel Brandon was at the time?"

"No, sir," Pomeroy said. "Most unhelpful, that."

"Indeed," Sir Nathaniel said. "Now then, Mr. Grenville, what can you add or subtract from Colonel Brandon's statement?"

Grenville cleared his throat. "I did see Colonel Brandon and Mrs. Harper enter the alcove after Mr. Turner emerged from the anteroom. I cannot say when they departed it. I was dancing after that, giving all my attention to my partners. I was very near the anteroom, however, when Mrs. Harper entered it. I saw her go in. After a minute or two, she rushed out, screaming at the top of her lungs. I looked inside and saw Mr. Turner slumped against the table. I settled Mrs. Harper on a chair and made her swallow some brandy, then I entered the room with Lord Gillis. Lord Gillis pulled Mr. Turner upright. I saw the knife in Mr. Turner's chest and knew he was dead."

Sir Nathaniel wrote. The quiet scratch of his pen made a strange contrast to the violence Grenville described.

"Did you see Colonel Brandon come back into the ball-room?" Sir Nathaniel asked when he'd finished.

Grenville shook his head. "I did not see him, no."

"Well, he wouldn't, would he?" Brandon broke in. "He was looking at Turner, not searching the ballroom for me."

Sir Nathaniel gave him another sharp look. "Quite so, Colonel. Captain Lacey. What evidence do you have to add?"

Brandon glowered at me. He did not want me to speak, did not want me there at all. I wondered at his resistance. He might not like me, but he ought to at least realize I could help him.

"I served under Colonel Brandon from the time I was twenty years old until the time I was thirty-eight," I said. "The fact that Colonel Brandon stands accused of this crime surprises me very much indeed."

"Not accused," Sir Nathaniel said quickly. "This is a preliminary examination, as I said."

"I am astonished he is under suspicion at all. Colonel Brandon has always acted with the utmost honor." At least, he'd acted with honor except where I was concerned.

"You were in the wars together," Sir Nathaniel said. "A man learns to kill during a war. Otherwise, he'd make a poor soldier."

"Fighting a battle and cold-blooded murder are two different things," I said.

"I concede that." Sir Nathaniel nodded. "I know some officers who are the gentlest of men. That does not mean your colonel has not done murder. Though I commend your loyalty."

Brandon's face had gone a bright, cherry red. The last person he wanted to stand up for him was me.

But if I could save the wretch for Louisa, I would. I still had difficulty believing he'd stabbed Turner. Brandon was guilty of something here, but of what, I was not yet certain.

Presently, Sir Nathaniel ceased writing. "I would like to speak with the ladies who were present. Mrs. Harper and Mrs. Brandon."

"No," Brandon said at once. "I do not want my wife involved in this."

"My dear sir, this is murder. Did you believe it was a private matter?"

"As a matter of fact, I do," Brandon said stiffly. "This is not France, where the police survey our every action. Our committees call for police reform. We shall all be scrutinized whenever we leave our houses, if that happens."

His speech did not please Sir Nathaniel, whose nostrils pinched. "That's as may be, Colonel. At present, I need to investigate a murder and determine whether or not you should be tried for it. Your wife, in fact, may be able to produce evidence that you did not do it. You would like me to find that, would you not?"

Brandon said nothing. His eyes glittered with stubborn fury.

I wondered what the devil was the matter with him. He behaved as though he did not want to be proved innocent.

Perhaps he was throwing himself to the wolves, knowing Mrs. Harper had killed Turner. But why on earth should he feel so compelled to go to the gallows for her? Brandon was, all in all, a selfish man. Why he'd suddenly become heroic for another person was a mystery to me.

Sir Nathaniel straightened his papers. "Very well, I have made my decision. Colonel Brandon, I am committing you to trial for the murder of Mr. Henry Turner on the night of the fifth of April. The evidence against you is stronger than the evidence for your innocence. You will go to Newgate prison and remain there until your trial. Thank you, Mr. Pomeroy. Please have Colonel Brandon escorted to the prison."

Pomeroy looked slightly taken aback. I imagined he'd regarded arresting his former colonel as a good joke, assuming I'd quickly get him off. But Sir Nathaniel looked severe, in his understated way.

Pomeroy rose. Grenville and I stood up with him.

"Sir Nathaniel," I said. "Must he stay in the prison? It will be a blow to a man of his standing."

"I am sorry, Captain Lacey, but there are laws. Colonel Brandon will live in Newgate until he stands in the dock. The wait will not be long, and he will have a private room. He will not live in the common cells with the rabble."

No, Brandon was wealthy enough to afford a room with furnishings and good meals. His physical comfort would not be impaired, but he'd be a ruined man.

"Colonel," Pomeroy said reluctantly.

The only one who did not argue was Brandon. He rose, his face set, and let Pomeroy lead him from the room.

NEWGATE PRISON STOOD AT THE INTERSECTION OF NEWGATE Street and Old Bailey, north of Ludgate Hill and not far from Saint Paul's Cathedral. The dome of the cathedral hung against the leaden sky as Grenville stopped his phaeton in the crowds of Ludgate Hill at my request.

"I can drive you all the way," Grenville offered.

I declined. "Your high-stepping horses and polished rig are for Hyde Park, not the gallows yard at Newgate."

Grenville nodded his understanding. He'd certainly draw attention if he went down to the prison. He held the horses steady while the tiger hopped from his perch on the back and assisted me to the ground.

"I am sorry for all this, Lacey," Grenville said. "I was not much help, was I?"

"You told what you saw. Not your fault Brandon is so damned stubborn." I adjusted my hat. "Will you take a message to Mrs. Brandon? Tell her what happened at the examination, and that I am here to settle Brandon's needs. Tell her I will come as soon as I can."

Grenville regarded me a moment, as though he wanted to

say something more. But already people were taking notice of
him and the elegant phaeton. Grenville took the hint, tipped his
hat, then signaled his horses to move on. I walked the rest of
the way to the prison.

Newgate prison itself was a depressing building of gray
block stones. Windows, barred and forbidding, lined its walls.
In the open area outside the gate was the gallows, empty today.
Hangings took place on Monday for the public; those waiting
their turn inside could watch. Today was Sunday. The
condemned would attend chapel and emerge tomorrow to their
dooms.

When I'd been a lad, the hangings had taken place at
Tyburn near the end of what was now Park Lane. Once when
I'd come to London with my father, I'd sneaked away to
witness a hanging there. I still remembered the fevered press of
bodies, the excitement and dismay radiating from the crowd,
the buildup of frenzy as the prisoner rolled past in his cart,
ready to face the gallows.

Thinking back, the hanged man must have been less than
twenty years old, though he'd seemed older to me at the time.
He'd stood straight in the cart, nodding to the crowd like an
actor pleased by his audience. The guards with him had led
him up the steps to the scaffold, where he'd stood and
addressed us all.

"Friends, today I die for the crime of being honest. I
honestly stole those clothes from me master's shop."

The crowd had laughed. He'd grinned along with them.
"Do not cry for me, I go to a better place." He'd looked
around. "Any place is better than Newgate in the damp."

Again, they'd laughed. The hangman had cut off his words
by jamming a hood over his head and a noose around
his neck.

I'd crept to the very edge of the scaffold while he'd joked
with the crowd. I'd seen the young man's face before the hood
had gone down. He'd been gray, his lips trembling. He might

have made light of his punishment to others, but he was terrified.

When they hauled him from his feet, he gave a startled cry, which was cut off in mid-breath. I watched in fascinated horror as he kicked and struggled mightily to live, then just to breathe, while the crowed cheered or mocked him.

They'd cut him down, stone dead, and sold his clothes to the people there.

I'd run back to the townhouse my father had rented and was sick all night.

I'd witnessed hangings since then, in the army, in India, and deaths more terrible, but the hanging I'd seen as a child of six had seemed the worst terror I could have faced. I'd dreamed for weeks I was that man, having my vision cut abruptly off by the hood, feeling the burn of the rope about my neck, hearing the crowd laughing and cheering.

Passing the gallows now, I felt a qualm of old dread, the ghost of the noose that had killed the young thief.

Pomeroy and Brandon had already arrived. I caught up to them as they passed beneath the gate, following them into a courtyard that smelled of urine.

Pomeroy went to the keeper's room, a square office with a bench and a table and a window giving onto the courtyard. The keeper was alone with another turnkey, the two men portly from beef and ale.

Pomeroy released Brandon officially, then said, "He's a posh gent. He'll want the finest rooms you have."

"Oh?" the keeper guffawed. "A duke, is 'e?"

"He's a colonel and a gentleman," Pomeroy said severely. "He's to be treated fine, or I'll hear of it."

The keeper seemed a bit in awe of Pomeroy, probably with good reason. Pomeroy was a powerful and strong man, not shy about using his fists when necessary. In addition, he was a Bow Street Runner, and keeping on the friendly side of a Runner was always wise.

The keeper told Brandon, in a slightly more respectful tone, "Aye, if you pay me well, sir, you'll have no troubles here. Send for one or two of your own servants, and you'll live as well as you would at home. A gentleman is always welcome."

Brandon looked from the keeper to Pomeroy in fury. "Do you mean, Sergeant, that you wish me to bribe this man?"

"You have to pay for room and board, sir," Pomeroy said in a patient tone. "And buy your bedding and fuel and things. Stands to reason. The more you pay, the better you live."

"For God's sake," Brandon began. "I do not even have much money with me."

"I will settle his affairs," I broke in as the keeper took on a belligerent expression.

"No you will not," Brandon retorted.

"I do not believe they will let you visit your man of business on the moment," I answered impatiently. "I will visit on your behalf. Or would you rather bed down on hay with a flea-ridden street girl?"

Brandon blanched. Street girls made him nervous in any case. "I take your point, Lacey. I only wish to God I had someone else to help me."

I knew he did. The turnkey grinned at me and led us into the bowels of the building.

CHAPTER 5

The room Brandon obtained was not elegant by any means. A tall tester bed stood in one corner, with a heavy mahogany cupboard on another wall and a table and chairs in the middle of the room. A small fireplace, cold, lay opposite the door.

The turnkey barked at a lackey to build a fire. Gloom-faced, the servant looked neither at me nor Brandon while he worked, then he shuffled out. Pomeroy, with a cheerful "Good day, sirs," left us alone.

Brandon looked out of a barred window to the courtyard three floors below. He remained silent, his stance still and sullen.

"Sir," I said. Even after all the years I'd known him and all we'd been through, I still could not bring myself to address him in a way other than as an officer who outranked me.

"I suppose," Brandon said coldly, addressing his words to the window, "that as soon as you heard what had happened, you went immediately to my wife."

"Of course I did. I knew Louisa would be distressed once I learned what a pig's breakfast you'd made of everything."

"How fortunate she has a friend as kind as you," he said, biting off every word. "A friend who will stay with her in times of trouble."

"Lady Aline Carrington stays with her."

Brandon swung around. His face was carefully neutral, but his eyes glittered. "You must be delighted, Gabriel. Watching me be arrested and tried for murder. My wife will need much comfort during this ordeal, and there you will be. Perhaps the turnkey will allow me to hang a pair of horns above my door, so all who pass will know that herein lies a cuckold."

I was tempted to march out of the room and leave the idiot to his fate, but I knew Louisa would never forgive me if I did. "You are a fool and a bloody hypocrite. Your wife has never betrayed you. Yet you claimed, with Louisa standing next to you, this Mrs. Harper was your mistress. If Louisa leaves you, it will be as much as you deserve."

"Ah, yes. I can learn from you how to be an abandoned husband."

I stared at him in astonishment. In all our quarrels, he had never cast up to me that my wife had deserted me, as though the topic were impermissible. Now he glared at me, defiance in his very breathing.

Through my anger, I had a hint of understanding. "Why are you deliberately provoking me?" I asked. "You know you need my help. Why are you tempting me to tell you to go to the devil and stay there?"

"Because this is none of your affair!"

"It hurts Louisa. And is therefore my affair."

"Affair," he sneered. "A fine choice of words."

"Your word, sir." I stepped close to him. "Do you *want* to die in ignominy? Hanging is a nasty death, and you know it. Louisa will have to live her life as the wife of a condemned murderer."

"Lacey, for God's sake, stay out of this."

"Why?" I asked him. "Never tell me you really did kill Turner."

He avoided my gaze. "I do not wish to speak of it."

"Did Imogene Harper kill him? Why are you protecting her?"

"I will not answer."

"I will ask her," I said.

"You will leave her alone," he snapped in reply.

"You are no longer my commanding officer. Your own actions made that so. I no longer must obey you."

I expected him to argue, to rage, to bluster. But Brandon said nothing. After a time, he turned away, his shoulders slumped in defeat.

"You are a fool, sir," I repeated.

He turned back to me, a strange light in his eyes. "No, Gabriel. *You* are the fool."

I knew I would gain nothing more from him, so I turned away and left him alone.

I VISITED BRANDON'S MAN OF BUSINESS BEFORE LEAVING the City to explain Brandon's situation and tell him to send money to the prison. The man of business was distressed, with good reason. A respectable solicitor wants a respectable clientele, and a client held in Newgate to await trial for murder was a most distressing thing indeed. However, he put in motion the errands needed to ensure Brandon spent his time in prison in the most comfortable accommodations possible.

I returned to my lodgings and ate a hasty meal of bread at Mrs. Beltan's bakery below my rooms. I bathed and changed my clothes, giving them over to Bartholomew to clean, but I could not shake the stench of Newgate from me.

I took a hackney back to Mayfair and to Brook Street.

Lady Aline met me at the door to Brandon's house. Grenville had been and gone, she said, and had broken the bad news.

Louisa was up, pacing her sitting room in agitation. Her face was white, her eyes sunken into hollows. She held herself rigid when I went to take her hands and kiss her cheek.

I explained I'd seen Brandon settled and that he could have a servant or two to look after him. Lady Aline said she'd dispatch Brandon's valet at once and bustled off to do so. As soon as the door closed, Louisa's hands clamped down on mine.

"What will happen now, Gabriel?"

"Pomeroy and his patrollers will try to gather evidence against Brandon. If they find nothing that firmly points to his guilt, then he will be acquitted."

"His knife in the man's chest is not firm evidence?"

"Anyone may steal another's knife and use it. Were I to murder someone, I would use a weapon easily identified as belonging to another man. Why bring suspicion to myself?"

"If you were angry, you would not think of that," Louisa said. "You would snatch up the first thing you saw and stab."

"Perhaps."

Her observation gave me an idea. What if Brandon had left the knife in the anteroom when he was in there earlier with Turner? Why he should, I didn't know, but he might have done. The murderer could have quarreled with Turner, noticed the knife, and in a fit of pique, snatched it up and driven it into Turner's chest.

"Louisa, your husband is being stubbornly cryptic, but I will discover the truth," I said. "I will bring him back to you. I promise you that."

Louisa released my hands and walked away from me, her eyes bleak. "Gabriel, have I been deceived all my life? I stuck by him through thick and thin. Through everything he did. Even after . . . When he came looking for me in your tent that night, I went back to him. He tried his best to harm you over that incident, and even then I stood by him."

I remembered. Colonel Brandon had decided one day soon after Vitoria he no longer wanted a wife who could not give him children. He'd told Louisa he would find some way to annul the marriage so they could be parted without scandal. Then he'd left camp for who knew where.

Louisa, her world crumbling around her, had fled to my tent and told me the entire tale. I'd been furious at Brandon and tried to comfort Louisa the best I could. Brandon had returned the next morning to find Louisa sitting on my lap in a camp chair, her head on my shoulder.

He'd assumed the worst.

Not long later, Brandon had sent me out with false orders into a pocket of French soldiers, who had caught and tortured me. I'd managed to escape and survive with the help of a Spanish farmer's widow, who'd dragged me the long way back to camp.

I remembered lying on the bunk of the surgeon's tent, hideous pain leaking through the haze of laudanum, my body sweating with fever and infection. When Louisa had come and discovered what Brandon had done, she'd shouted at him long and hard. I had lain in my stupor and laughed.

"I recall you telling him quite firmly what you thought of him when you found out what he'd done to me," I said.

"Oh, yes, I was furious. You might have died because of him. I could have left Aloysius, then. I should have."

"There was not much you could do, Louisa." When a woman left her husband, she could only return to her family or elope with another man—one was a recipe for shame, the other, complete ruin.

"I know. But I remained his wife, in all ways. I wanted to prove, I suppose, that I had not betrayed him. I saw the good in him, still. I loved him." Louisa lifted her arms in a limp gesture. "This is my reward."

"And it is decidedly odd," I said. "I am not saying your husband is guiltless in the matter of Mrs. Harper, but the situation seems wrong somehow. I would think if Brandon were pursuing another woman, he would not be so bloody obvious. He prides himself on being the perfect gentleman, the perfect husband, the perfect officer."

Louisa gave me a tired look. "Well, he isn't, is he?"

"But would he let the world see that? There is something very wrong, Louisa. Can you tell me nothing more of this Imogene Harper?"

"No, I cannot. When I dared ask him, Aloysius grew angry and told me to mind my own damned business. In those words. He has never been that harsh to me."

"No, he usually saves that for me. I ask your leave, Louisa, to go through his desk and his papers. I want to read what Mrs. Harper wrote, if he has not destroyed the letters. She is key to this murder; perhaps she even killed Turner herself."

"She never went into that anteroom. At least, not until she found Mr. Turner. Believe me, Lacey, I had my eye on her. The only time she disappeared from view was when she went into private corners with my husband." She trailed off bitterly.

"And I am going to find out why she did," I said.

Louisa stood rigidly, her face gray, her eyes holding exhaustion. "I have resigned myself to the fact that Aloysius was having an affair with her. You do not have to try to prove he was not."

I went silent a moment, then I said, "Do you know, I believe I am the only person in London not happy to believe in Brandon's guilt."

Her eyes flashed. "*Happy?* Do you believe I am happy to know my husband has been betraying me?"

"Ready to believe his guilt, then. Perhaps I used the wrong word. But it seems as though everyone wants him to be guilty, including Brandon himself."

The muscles of Louisa's delicate neck were tense, as though she strained to hold up her head. "You are kind to try to give me hope."

"And I do wish both you and your husband would stop trying to assign me motives," I said in irritation. "I am looking into this problem because it distresses you and because I do not believe Brandon killed Turner. I believe he *could* have killed him, but I will be quite glad to find evidence to prove otherwise."

Louisa sank to the sofa. "Perhaps I simply want it to be over. I do not want to wait and wonder and hope you find something. I want it to be over, even if it means I lose him forever."

"Have you so little faith in me?"

"I know you, Gabriel. You believe a thing is so, therefore it must be so. You stubbornly burrow through things to prove yourself right, no matter who you hurt."

I stilled. "And I've hurt you?"

"No." She smiled a little. "But you are so impetuous, and you will run afoul of the wrong people. It would hurt me so to lose you. I never would have survived all these years without you."

We looked at each other. I knew, as well, my life would have been much harsher without Louisa Brandon in it.

I could have said something then that might have changed everything between us. I think she wanted me to say it, waited for me to say it. Perhaps I was foolish to keep my silence. But I kept it.

"Louisa, I will do everything in my power to help your husband. And you. I swear this."

A light went out of her eyes. Louisa looked away from me, and then she nodded. "Ask Aloysius's valet for the key to his desk. Tell him he has my permission to give it to you."

"Thank you," I said quietly.

Louisa looked up at me again, but her eyes held no hope. I bowed to her briefly and left her.

I found Robbins, the harried valet, and requested Brandon's key. He went off to find it, seeming relieved to escape Lady Aline's strident demands. Louisa was always gentle with her servants; Lady Aline must seem like an unexpected hurricane.

"Lacey, my boy, I do wish you luck," Aline said as she passed me on her way back to Louisa's sitting room. "If you can find an answer to this murder, I will bow before you."

The thought of Lady Aline bowing her tall bulk amused me somewhat. I told her I could only do my best, took the key Robbins brought running back, and let myself into Brandon's private study.

I'd been in this room only a few times before, because Brandon rarely invited me into it. He put up with me in his dining room and drawing room at Louisa's request, but he disliked me in the more private rooms of the house.

A screen of gold-leaf and ivory he'd obtained in Spain decorated one corner. I'd always wondered where Brandon had found the screen, and if it had in fact been looted. Wellington had declared looting to be a hanging offense. The English army had gone to liberate the Spanish from French rule, not to rob from them, he'd said. Brandon had claimed he'd purchased it, but his belligerence whenever he spoke of it always aroused my suspicion.

The desk, a secretary with a closed bookcase, stood near the screen. I sat down in the desk chair, put the key in the lock, and pulled down the sloping cover that formed the base of the desk. Two pieces of wood slid out of slots to support the desk's top.

Inside I found neat ledgers and folded papers and small

drawers full of letters. None of the letters were from Imogene Harper.

I searched the drawers and the ledgers, then unfolded all the letters to see if another had been tucked between their pages. I found nothing. I hadn't thought I would.

I remembered Grenville showing me a secretary he'd purchased in France, a beautiful piece of golden satinwood with rosewood inlay. Grenville's delight in it, however, was its secret drawers. He'd made me try to discover the drawers myself, while he'd hovered gleefully at my side, watching.

I had found two, but he'd showed me four others I'd missed.

I lifted the small drawers out of the middle of Brandon's desk and felt the recesses behind them for catches. I found one rather easily, which extruded a drawer from the left side of the desk. Rather obvious, I thought. Many desks had such drawers.

I found no letters in the drawer, only a stray button. Perhaps Brandon had no use for secret drawers, and perhaps he'd simply burned Mrs. Harper's letters.

I found a second secret drawer that again had nothing inside it. I searched for the catches Grenville's desk had, but either I missed them entirely, or the designer of this desk had given up after he'd created two.

I slid the main drawers back in place and was about to shut the first secret drawer, when I noticed its bottom did not fit correctly. I picked up the button and found its shank just fit into the slight gap. I worked the button back and forth, and suddenly, the entire bottom of the drawer lifted away.

Three letters lay inside it.

I lifted unfolded each of them. Written in a woman's hand, they were signed *Imogene Harper*.

The letters were not dated, but I made sense of the timing as I read them. The first was hesitant, as though Mrs. Harper had been timid about contacting Brandon after so many years.

I learned your direction from Colonel Singleton, whom my husband also knew during the Peninsular campaign, and I make so bold to write to you. Perhaps I am the last woman on earth from whom you wish to receive correspondence, but I find it necessary. If you would speak to me, I will be riding in Hyde Park at five o'clock on Wednesday next. I will wait near Grosvenor Gate for you to come. I have need to see you, my dear A. Please come.

She'd signed without any closure.

The second letter opened with relief. *How glad I was to see you! You are a gentleman of honor, and I have always known you to be. To see you riding to me, as tall and strong and handsome as you were four years ago, brought pleasure to my heart. I did not know how much I longed to see you again until that moment. The friendship we shared returned to me, with a warmth I will never forget. I hope when we meet again on Saturday, I will have good news for you. Until then, God bless you..*

The tone of the third letter was quite different. *My dear A. What shall you do? You refer to your wife, but shall I suffer alone? If I must pay, then you must. We are both guilty, and I cannot take the blame alone. He said he would be at the Gillises' ball on Saturday night, and that he would ensure you were invited—with your wife. I have played upon my connections of friendship and wheedled an invitation for myself from Lady Gillis. We will meet there and decide what to do. He must not reveal all. And if he does, he will reveal your sins as well as mine. You know this. You must come.*

This letter was signed simply, *Imogene.*

Who was *he?* Henry Turner? Had he threatened to reveal Mrs. Harper's affair with Brandon? In any event, Brandon had betrayed his guilt at the Gillises' ball; he'd not needed Turner to do it for him.

The letters read very much like those of a woman wanting to rekindle an affair, then growing angry when Brandon indicated he did not want the relationship to resume. The threat in the last letter was blatant. Mrs. Harper refused to face Turner alone. If she were to be exposed, she would expose Brandon as well.

Had Mrs. Harper killed Turner before he could go through with the blackmail? Mrs. Harper had gone into the anteroom and found Turner's body. She'd gotten blood on her glove, and according to Grenville, it was a minute or two before she screamed. Time for her to snatch up the knife—which Brandon might have left for her—stab him, then rush out and begin her fit. Her horror at the blood on her glove had no doubt been real.

Was it that simple? That Brandon and Mrs. Harper feared Turner's knowledge and so conspired to kill him?

Louisa had been right about one thing. Many gentlemen took mistresses after they were married. It seemed almost expected. Society marriages often occurred because two families wanted to increase their power or wealth. A poor aristocrat married a rich nabob's daughter; the daughter of an impoverished baron married a wealthy merchant. Even better, wealthy nobility married each other.

Once the nuptials were complete, the ladies busied themselves setting up their nurseries and hosting parties, and gentlemen adjourned to their clubs, horses, and mistresses. Husband and wife might live very separate lives, seeing each other only occasionally.

Brandon's marriage had been different. He'd married Louisa by choice, not for gain. Brandon came from a wealthy gentleman's family in Kent. Louisa's family had been as gently born, but poorer. Her father had considered a cavalry captain with a personal income to be a good catch for Louisa.

I understood perfectly well why Brandon had married her. Louisa at twenty-two had been a beautiful woman. Not only did she have golden hair and brilliant gray eyes, but she had fire, an adventurous spirit coupled with grave intelligence that would make her a fine life companion. I'd regretted from the moment I'd met her I'd not found her before Brandon had.

But until this business with Mrs. Harper, I never believed
Brandon had sought another lady's bed. Now I wondered.
Mrs. Harper's husband had been killed at Vitoria. Shortly after
that, Brandon had declared his intention to end his marriage
with Louisa, because she could not give him children.

I wanted very much to meet Imogene Harper. I wanted to
know what sort of woman could draw Brandon from Louisa's
side.

I folded the letters together and tucked them into my
pocket. I carefully reassembled the drawer, dropped the button
back inside it, and slid the drawer into its recess.

I grimaced as I locked the desk. Brandon, as usual, was not
making things easy.

AFTER TAKING LEAVE OF LOUISA AND LADY ALINE, I MET
Bartholomew in the tavern in Pall Mall where I often conferred
with Grenville when I investigated things. Bartholomew was
there before me, enjoying an ale with his brother, Matthias.

I had hoped Grenville would join us, so we could talk
things over together. Grenville would have a more objective
sense of this case than I could. But Grenville had another
appointment, and I was just as curious to hear what the two
brothers had learned from speaking to the Gillises' servants.

Bartholomew and Matthias looked much alike, both big
and broad-shouldered and blond-haired. The pair of them had
been footmen for Grenville for a time before Bartholomew had
announced his intention of becoming a valet, and Grenville had
sent him to train with me. The bargain was that I got someone
to wait on me while Grenville paid his wages. I had a wardrobe
that would make the best valet shudder, but Bartholomew kept
my few pieces of clothing and my regimentals cleaner than
they'd been since new.

The brothers jumped up when they saw me, and I waved them back to their seats. The landlord brought me an ale, and I sat down and joined them.

"An interesting morning I've had," Bartholomew said. "The servants of Lord and Lady Gillis, though a bit high and mighty, were glad to give me a meal and a bit of a gab. Didn't hurt I'm slavey to Mr. Grenville."

Being employed by Grenville carried much weight in Bartholomew's world. The higher the master, the higher the servant could hold his head.

"They didn't mind talking about the night of the ball," Bartholomew said. "The thing is, Captain, several of the servants said Lady Gillis was in a rare state most of the day. They admitted to hearing a flaming row coming from the private rooms early in the afternoon. Lord and Lady Gillis were arguing about someone who was invited to the ball that Lord Gillis did not want there."

"Turner?" I asked.

"The servants could not say, in fact. None of them heard a name."

That disappointed me, but there was nothing to be done. I asked Matthias, "During the ball that night, did you by chance chat with Mr. Turner's valet?"

"I did, sir," Matthias answered. "Name of Hazelton. When he was brought the news his master was dead upstairs, you would have thought Mr. Turner died just to upset him. Hazelton was quite mournful about it, saying didn't he have enough to do already without Mr. Turner up and getting himself killed?"

"That is interesting," I said. "You don't happen to know where Mr. Turner's rooms are, do you?"

Matthias started to answer, but Bartholomew broke in cheerfully, "In Piccadilly, sir. Near the Albany. In fact, Matthias says once Hazelton realized his master was gone, he was keen we should come and help him drink up Mr. Turner's claret."

"I believe you should oblige him," I said.

Bartholomew winked. "Right you are, sir. You would like to come along?"

"Please," I rose, took up my walking stick, and let the lads lead the way out.

CHAPTER 6

$\mathcal{W}$e took a hackney coach around St. James's Street to Piccadilly. Mr. Turner had lived in rooms near Burlington House and the Albany. The Albany was the former residence of the Duke of York, which had been sold and converted into flats for the very rich man-about-town. I noted Henry Turner had taken lodgings as close as he could to the house without having to pay the exorbitant rent to live there.

Turner's rooms consisted of a sitting room and a bedchamber, one room in the front, one room in the rear. I lived in similar accommodations, but Mr. Turner's rooms held a comfort and warmth mine would always lack.

Mr. Turner, in fact, lived in a bit of decadence. His furniture was either made of costly satinwood or had been thickly gilded. I noticed Bartholomew and Matthias look around in some distaste. Working for Lucius Grenville had given the two of them experience with the best money could buy, plus the taste and moderation that made a thing worth having. Mr. Turner seemed to have been the sort of young man more interested in what a thing cost than in taste or moderation.

We found Mr. Turner's valet, Bill Hazelton, in the bedchamber, where he'd emptied the armoire and spread Turner's clothes over the bed, chairs, and every other available surface. Hazelton wore drab black pantaloons that bagged around his knees and ankles in preposterous wrinkles. His coat was of good cut in last year's style, probably one of Turner's castoffs. His long chin was covered with stubble, and his brown eyes were morose.

"Oh dear," he said upon seeing us. "What now?"

Matthias reminded him they'd had a chin-wag at the Gillises' ball, and that he and his brother worked for none other than Lucius Grenville. He introduced the man to me.

Hazelton glanced at me, categorized me, and dismissed me. I would not be likely to hire an out-of-work valet, and he knew it.

"I would like to ask you a few questions about your master, if I may," I began.

Hazelton looked sorrowful. "Why? I never killed him, and I don't know who did."

"Mr. Grenville and I are simply curious," I said.

Hazelton regarded me dubiously, but he nodded as he continued folded linen cravats.

"How long were you Mr. Turner's manservant?" I asked.

"Seven years." Hazelton sounded depressed. "All through his long Oxford years I looked after him. It was me what had to lie to the proctor when Mr. Turner had been out all night, me what had to roll him out of bed in the mornings and get him to lectures. And what did he do? Wagered my pay on horses, he did. And any other thing he could think of. Always kept good drink, though."

He trailed off wistfully. Servants' posts were difficult to obtain, and no matter how irritating the master, most preferred employment to the prospect of having to look for work.

"And then," Hazelton continued, "he went and got himself done in and left me high and dry. Typical."

"Getting himself killed is typical?" I asked.

"Leaving me to bear the brunt of his problems is. After all I've done for him."

I pondered my next questions with care. A manservant could know more about his master than his master did himself. But a manservant could also have fierce loyalty to his gentleman and never reveal that man's secrets.

"Was Mr. Turner ever hurting for money? If he had to wager your pay on the horses, that must mean he was short of blunt from time to time."

"He got an allowance from his pater, but he was always in need of more funds. Had to be, hadn't he? He had to dress and keep rooms and go to White's and Tattersall's. Spent all his pater's money, but he would win on his wagers. Sometimes quite a lot, but then the money would be gone again, to high living." Hazelton glanced at his master's clothes strewn about the room. "Little good it's done him now, though, eh?"

I ran my hand over one of the coats. The cloth was fine; the coat as costly and elegant as what Grenville might wear. Indeed, Turner probably had many of his clothes made to imitate Grenville's. Most young men-about-town did.

"His father continued to give him money?" I asked. "He did not cut him off with a shilling over his gaming, as angry fathers sometimes do?"

"No, no. Mr. Turner's family are quiet people. Too respectable for the likes of my master. Must have been an embarrassment to them, he was. His father kept up the allowance but sent him pleading paternal letters to mend his ways."

I wondered whether Hazelton knew this because he'd read his master's mail. Or perhaps he'd known Turner well enough to guess exactly what the man's father would say to him.

"Had he recently received more money than usual?" I looked out of the window as I asked the question, as though only half-interested in the answer.

"Not that I know of, sir. Leastwise, I saw no sign of it. Of course, Mr. Turner would not be likely to give anything spare to me."

I wondered what Turner would have done with any money Brandon or Mrs. Harper had given him. Would he hoard it or pay his tailor and his gambling debts? Was he experienced at blackmail, or had he simply seized upon an opportunity?

I sent Bartholomew a meaningful look. I wanted to have a look at Turner's rooms without Hazleton hovering over me.

Bartholomew took the hint. "Well then, Hazleton, what about this claret?"

Hazleton perked up, at least as much as Hazleton would ever perk up. His mournful mouth smoothed the slightest bit. "Ah, yes. His pa told me to put his things together and send them home. But a bottle of claret wouldn't travel very well now, would it?"

I thought it would make no difference to the bottle, but I welcomed the chance to clear Hazleton out of the way for a few minutes. Bartholomew told him to lead the way, and he and Hazleton and Matthias clattered out.

Left alone, I searched the bedchamber but found very little. I went through the pockets of the coats strewn on the bed and chairs and then checked the cupboards. I found nothing but shirts and undergarments and other accoutrements of a gentle-man's wardrobe in the armoire, but nothing tucked inside any of them. Turner, or perhaps Hazleton, had kept his things very neatly.

I left the bedchamber and entered the front room, where I went through the small writing table. Remembering Brandon's secret drawer, I went carefully through the desk, but I found no hidden drawers and nothing very helpful in the ordinary ones.

Turner had kept no correspondence, no dunning notices from his creditors, and none of the tearful letters from his father Hazelton had mentioned. In short, Mr. Turner seemed to have no personal papers in his rooms at all.

As I closed the last drawer, I was startled by the sound of the front door opening behind me. I knew how long Bartholomew and Matthias could linger over a glass, and they'd both understood I'd wanted time to search the rooms.

But when I looked around I found neither the tall footmen nor the long-faced Hazleton. Instead, a woman I did not know entered the room. She did not see me until she'd walked well inside, then she froze, the color draining from her face.

She swung around and reached for the door. Moving with a speed I'd not known I had, I made it to the door and pressed my hand against it. The woman looked up at me with startled brown eyes that were rather too small and sparsely lashed.

We stared at one another for a full, silent minute. The room was chill, because Hazleton had not bothered to start a fire. The woman had wrapped a cashmere shawl around her, but the skin on her neck stood out in gooseflesh, and her lips were thin and almost bloodless.

"I beg your pardon," she said stiffly. "I seem to have entered the wrong room."

I did not think so. In wild surmise I said, "Mrs. Harper."

Her eyes widened, but to her credit, she did not faint or grow hysterical. Her assessment was one of surprise, not fear.

"Who are you?" she asked.

"My name is Gabriel Lacey."

If she'd heard of me, she hid it well. "Yes, I am Mrs. Harper. Mr. Turner . . ." She broke off. Perhaps she'd prepared a story for the servants but not one for the likes of me.

I answered for her. "You were looking for a letter or paper that belonged to you that you thought Mr. Turner had."

Now, some fear did enter her eyes. "Why do you say so? Exactly who are you?"

"I am a friend to Colonel Brandon."

She looked me up and down with new scrutiny, her lips

tightening. I saw she was not sure whether to categorize me as friend or foe. A friend of Colonel Brandon could be for him and against her.

I returned her look with the same curiosity. Brandon might have been having an affair with this woman; indeed, he might well have tried to leave Louisa for her, but she was not beautiful. Her brown dress was trimmed in black braid, with black buttons making a neat line down the bodice, and the cashmere shawl was also a rich brown. She knew how to dress tastefully, and her bonnet, brown straw trimmed with cream silk ribbons, was of a very late fashion.

The hair that straggled from under the bonnet was brownish yellow, the color to which some blond women find their hair turning as they grow older, much to their despair. Her face was round, her nose straight, and her eyes, as I had observed, were small, though a pleasing shade of brown. She was not by any means a radiant beauty, although she was not ugly. I would describe her overall as pleasant.

I gestured to a rather gaudy crimson damask sofa. "Shall we sit down, Mrs. Harper, and talk about Mr. Turner?"

Mrs. Harper searched my face, her eyes wary, but at last she inclined her head and moved to the sofa. She sat down, adjusting her skirt and her gloves, not looking at me as I limped across the room.

"You knew Colonel Brandon," I said, sitting next to her, "on the Peninsula."

Mrs. Harper nodded. "He was very helpful to my husband and to me."

A gratitude any woman might express toward a friend who once had lent assistance. "Your husband was killed at Vitoria, I believe," I said. "I was there. The battle was devastating. We lost many."

"Yes, my husband had often been praised for his valor. He died trying to save others." She made the statement flatly, as though she had said it so many times it no longer had meaning.

"Quite heroic of him. Brandon had been a friend of his?"

"Yes." Mrs. Harper had a quiet confidence about her, something I might admire under other circumstances. Her apparent ease at dealing with me, someone she had not expected, made me wonder. If she were this cool-headed, why had she become so overwrought at the sight of Turner's blood?

"If you are a very close friend of Colonel Brandon, Mr. Lacey . . ."

"Captain. And yes, I am quite close to the Brandon family."

"Captain," she said. "Then you must know more about me than you appear to at present."

"I do not wish to be rude, Mrs. Harper, but it will help me if you tell me exactly what your relation was and is to Colonel Brandon."

Mrs. Harper regarded me with calm eyes. "I believe you've already guessed. We had a brief liaison when we were on the Peninsula. When my husband died, I was alone and afraid, and Aloysius helped me. Small wonder I turned to him." Again her voice held that flat indifference.

"Not surprising under the circumstances. I know from your recent letters to Brandon that Turner somehow found out about the affair and threatened to expose you."

She flushed. "You are quite well informed, Captain."

"You came to London and wrote to Brandon for help. Turner told you to meet him at Lady Gillis's ball, and you asked Brandon what to do. What did he suggest?"

"That we meet him. That we try to persuade him it was all in the past and did not matter anymore."

"Then I take it you had no intention of resuming the affair?"

She hesitated. "I'm not certain what my intentions were. At the moment I was worried about Turner and his revelations."

"What did you fear? That Turner would go to Brandon's wife with the information? She already knew. Brandon's manner when he received your letters at home shouted it loud and clear, not to mention his obvious actions at the ball. He has been most tactless."

"I cannot help Colonel Brandon's behavior," Mrs. Harper said, tight-lipped. "I'm afraid I was quite agitated last night, or I might have noticed we were making cakes of ourselves. My only concern was speaking to Mr. Turner."

"And Turner, very conveniently, turned up dead."

At last, Mrs. Harper looked distressed. "I do not know why you say *convenient*. It was the most horrifying thing that has ever happened to me."

"More horrifying than the casualties of the battlefields?"

"Yes," she said defiantly. "I followed the drum long enough to expect the carnage. Even when my husband died, I cannot remember feeling terribly surprised. I think I knew it was only a matter of time before *his* body was brought back from a battle. But last night was different. You certainly do not expect to find a corpse sitting in a chair in your friend's house. It frightened me. More than that, it appalled me. London is supposed to be civilization. To see something like that in such an elegant little room was unnerving."

"More than unnerving," I said. "In fact, witnesses say you screamed quite a lot. You were so upset you had to be taken home—leaving Brandon to face arrest by himself."

She reddened. "I am not stupid, Captain. You believe I killed Mr. Turner then feigned hysteria in order to gain sympathy and let Aloysius take the blame. But I assure you, I did not murder Turner. He was dead when I entered the anteroom."

"How quickly did you realize he was dead?" I asked.

"I didn't right away. I thought him drunk. He'd been quite foxed when he'd spoken to us earlier, so I was not surprised to find him unconscious. But when I touched his shoulder, I saw that his face was gray. It was quite horrible. Then I saw the knife, and lost my head. I did scream. I cannot remember much after that."

"How did the blood come to be on your glove?"

She looked startled. "On my glove?"

"Mr. Grenville told me you stared at your glove in horror, and that it was crimson with blood. But if you touched Turner's shoulder, you could not have gotten blood on your glove. You could have done so only if you'd touched the knife or the wound."

Mrs. Harper stared at me, her lips parted. I sensed her thinking rapidly, considering arguments and discarding them before she chose her answer. "I believe I touched the back of the chair, where he'd been leaning," she said at last. "I rested my hand on it. The blood must have been there."

I had not seen blood on the chair, dried or otherwise. She lied, but I was not certain why.

One thing I did notice was she'd not suggested Brandon did not murder Turner. I said, "Colonel Brandon was committed to trial for killing Turner, and now he is in Newgate prison."

"I know."

Mrs. Harper looked neither angry nor distressed. She spoke in the same calm voice and looked at me in the same resignation.

"You do not defend him?"

She made a gesture that was almost a shrug. "What would you have me say? Colonel Brandon was quite upset last night. He was livid with Turner. I had never known him to be in so much of a temper."

"But you had not seen him in a long time."

"No, not I since I left Spain four years ago. Do you believe me?"

"More unsettling to me is you believe he killed Turner."

"I really have no idea what happened," Mrs. Harper said in a hard voice. "When I walked into that room, Turner was dead. I did not see Colonel Brandon actually kill him, but I have no idea who else would want to."

"Colonel Brandon seems to believe you killed him."

She flushed. "He said that?"

"No, he has done his best to incriminate himself and spare you. Which makes me realize he believes you killed Turner. If he'd thought a passing footman had done the deed, he would have said so loudly and expressed outrage to be arrested. Instead, he let Pomeroy's patrollers take him away without much fuss."

Mrs. Harper looked astonished. "He truly believes I would do such a thing?"

"You believe *he* would. In either case, it will be Brandon who pays. He is being gallant, and you are condemning him to hang."

She pressed her hands together, gloves sliding over very thin fingers. "You have not told me what *you* believe, Captain Lacey."

"I believe the colonel is innocent. I have not yet decided who else would want Turner dead. There were quite a few people at that ball. One of them may have been Turner's mortal enemy, who knows? I only know you are ready to send Brandon to the gallows, and I do not want him to go there."

For the first time since she'd entered the room, Mrs. Harper looked at me in real fear. Her lips trembled, and I saw her strive to keep them steady. "Do you plan to give me to the magistrates? Without knowing me, without proof I went into that room and stabbed Mr. Turner?"

"There is the blood on your glove," I said.

"Which I have explained. I touched the back of the chair."

"What I think you actually did, Mrs. Harper, was put your hand inside Mr. Turner's coat. You checked his pockets, did you not? You were looking for the letter or whatever evidence he had of your affair with Colonel Brandon. I conclude you did not find it, because you came here today to look for it. So did I."

She stared at me, eyes wide, and I saw her reassess my

character. She must have first thought me simply a hanger-on of Colonel Brandon's, an acquaintance left over from the war. Colonel Brandon was a man who did not always think before he acted. He was brisk and determined but sometimes did not bother with critical thought. Imogene Harper must have thought I would be much the same.

"You have found me out, Captain." She met my gaze, her voice steady. "Yes, I looked for the letter. I must have gotten the blood on my glove when I did so. I searched Mr. Turner's pockets, but I found nothing. At least, not the letter. He had a snuffbox, a few coins, and a scrap of lace, but no letter." She opened her hands. "You are correct that I came here to look for it."

"A scrap of lace," I said.

She blinked. "What?"

"The scrap of lace. What sort of lace? From his handker-chief, perhaps?"

Not the question she expected me to ask. "I don't know. It looked as though it had come from a lady's gown."

"Interesting. Could you happen to tell me which lady?"

She shook her head. "I am afraid I paid very little attention to the lace. I cared only for the letter."

"I will assume Pomeroy took all effects from Turner's pockets." I would certainly ask him to let me examine them. "What puzzles me, Mrs. Harper, is why you and Brandon were so afraid of Turner. Your affair ended four years ago. Brandon moved back to England and went on with his life, and that was that. I read the letters you wrote to him. You were not certain he would remember you or even would want to remember you."

I saw her try to remember exactly what she had penned to Brandon, but she spoke briskly. "It is hardly something one would wish to see made public."

"Is that what Turner threatened? To make it public?"

"I do not know what he threatened. I only know he had a letter and would make us pay to have it back."

"But how easy it would have been to dismiss his threat," I said. "You could claim the letter a forgery, written by Turner himself. Louisa Brandon would be hurt by the revelation — indeed, she *is* hurt — but she would hardly take her husband to court over it. Mrs. Brandon prizes discretion and privacy."

Mrs. Harper flexed and closed her hands. "We did not think. How could we? When Mr. Turner approached me about the letter, it was horrible. In panic, I wrote to Colonel Brandon, and he suggested we do whatever Mr. Turner said in order to get the letter back."

"Have you considered the possibility Turner did not have a letter at all? That he somehow got wind of your affair and, always liking cash, decided to capitalize on it? I have searched these rooms thoroughly, but I found nothing."

Relief flickered through her eyes. Perhaps she'd worried I might blackmail her as well, or perhaps she simply did not want me to read a love letter she'd written to Aloysius Brandon.

"The idea had not occurred to me," Mrs. Harper said. "Why should Mr. Turner say he had the letter if he did not?"

"He did not show it to you?"

"No."

"You and Colonel Brandon have behaved like a pair of fools," I said in exasperation. "You took it on faith Turner had a letter that would betray you. If you were experienced at being blackmailed, you would know to insist the blackmailer show you what he has to sell first."

The curls on her forehead trembled. "Perhaps we were fools, Captain. But we did not want to chance he did not have the letter. We did not think of that possibility, I confess." She looked at me a moment, clearly unhappy. "What will you do with the letter if you find it? Give it to the magistrates?"

"I have not yet decided. It is possible I will burn the foul thing. I do not intend to let Brandon hang for this crime."

"I know you will not believe me, Captain, but I wish no harm to come to him, either. Colonel Brandon was good to me. He helped me when I could turn to no other."

"You knew he was married," I said flatly.

"I did." Her defiance returned. "I needed him. At the time, that was all I could consider."

Mrs. Harper got to her feet and I did as well, because that was the polite thing to do. She said, "I admire you for standing by your colonel."

She did not offer me any help to save him. Perhaps Mrs. Harper still believed Brandon had killed Turner, or perhaps she was pushing the blame on Colonel Brandon to save herself.

"May I call on you if it proves necessary?" I asked.

"Can I stop you, if you think I can bring evidence to bear?"

"I am not a magistrate, nor am I a Bow Street Runner. I simply wish to clear Brandon's name, so his wife does not have to watch him hang by the neck until dead."

At last, Mrs. Harper looked ashamed. "Please tell Mrs. Brandon I am deeply sorry for the trouble I have caused her. I never realized how much grief a person can bestow when they are fixed on one course."

She did not elaborate on what that one course might be. I imagined loneliness, but looking back later, I realized the entire conversation seemed wrong somehow. Imogene Harper did not tell me much more than I'd already known. Unfortunately, I was not to realize that fact until other things emerged. I did not know then how murky things would become for me and for Brandon.

I ushered Mrs. Harper to the door and closed it behind us. I stood at the head of the stairs, watching her descend, in order to discourage her from returning to search the rooms again. I had found no letter—Turner's rooms had presented nothing but innocence and badly matched furniture — but she might be willing to try again.

Mrs. Harper glanced back at me once, her expression veiled, then she walked out of the house and into the rain.

~

I COLLECTED MATTHIAS AND BARTHOLOMEW FROM THE kitchens below stairs. Hazleton, the valet, held up his glass and slurred a greeting to me. One bottle was on its side, empty, a second, upright but half-empty. By the look of things, Matthias and Bartholomew had stuck to one or two glasses each, allowing Hazleton to imbibe the rest. I imagined he'd already partaken of a bottle or two before we arrived.

Bartholomew and Matthias said farewell to him, wishing him luck, and we departed.

Imogene Harper had long since vanished. Matthias took leave of us to return to Grenville's house. He said goodbye to his brother, touched his forelock to me, and trotted off in the direction of Green Park.

Bartholomew and I took a hackney back across London to Covent Garden. The going was slow, the traffic thick. Whenever I rode in a private conveyance, such as Grenville's carriage, things went faster, because people and wagons would move aside for a fast team and a shouting coachman with a long whip.

But at last we reached Covent Garden. The hackney stopped there, and I walked on alone to Grimpen Lane, while Bartholomew lingered among the vendors in Covent Garden to scare together our next meal.

Therefore, he was not present to help me when I was attacked in my rooms.

CHAPTER 7

The attacker was not waiting for me; he followed me up the stairs at a dead run, as though he'd been pursuing me through the streets. He was a man of my height with a wiry build, a thin face, dark eyes, and close-cropped hair.

I started to ask him who he was and what he thought he was doing, when he hurtled into me and pushed me back inside my rooms.

Many men have made the mistake of thinking me feeble because I hobble about with a walking stick, but I was still fit and strong. I brought up the walking stick, slammed it into the man's chest, and shoved him away from me.

The man was strong, his slim build disguising powerful muscles. He also knew how to fight, and fight dirty. He kicked my bad knee, hard. As pain knifed through my leg, he took advantage of my weakness and punched me in the face.

I fought back. We struggled, each of us emitting only the occasional grunt as we vied to best one another. I dropped my walking stick and got my hands around his throat, my thumbs going for his windpipe. He kicked my bad leg again, scooping my feet out from under me.

I went down, trying to take the fall with my shoulder. He kicked me again in the ribs. He snatched up my walking stick and struck me repeatedly across the chest and shoulders. I tried to roll away, but the pain in my leg swallowed my strength.

As I rocked on my back, trying to shield my face, he let off on the blows. He thrust his hand inside my coat, searching my pockets. Before I could stop him, he found and drew out the three letters from Mrs. Harper I'd taken from Brandon's desk.

I snatched for them. The man punched me across the jaw. In fury and in pain, I lunged at him. He brought up the walking stick and again beat me thoroughly and deliberately. My father, an expert at beating his son, would have admired him.

At last, I could only lie there, groaning and cursing. As soon as he thought me no longer a threat, he flung away the walking stick and began to open all the drawers and cupboards in the room, searching as I'd searched Henry Turner's rooms.

"It is not here," I croaked. "I could not find it, either."

The man ignored me completely. He sifted through the contents of my chest on frame and dumped everything onto the floor.

While he worked, I got painfully to my hands and knees and begin to crawl toward my walking stick. Inside the stick was a sharp sword, and I was anxious to begin poking it into my intruder.

He saw me. He swung around, took a pistol from his great-coat and trained it on me. I froze.

"I will not be long, Monsieur," he said. His accent was thick.

I wondered in the back of my mind why he'd bothered to beat me if he might have simply shot me dead, or at least threatened me with the pistol from the start.

"Tell me who you are and what you want," I said. "Or are you taking revenge for San Sebastian?"

He did not answer. He flung open a final drawer and tossed aside the expensive snuffboxes Grenville had given me. One box broke open, and fragrant snuff drifted through the room. The Frenchman, with a snarl, threw the empty drawer to the floor.

I heard a gasp from the hall. "Lacey, what the devil?"

Marianne Simmons stood in the doorway, her eyes wide.

"Get out!" I cried to her.

The Frenchman trained his pistol on me again. "Tell her to show her pockets."

Marianne would have none of that. She began screeching obscenities that would make the most hardened soldier flinch. I shouted at her to hold her tongue, fearing the Frenchman would shoot her in his impatience.

The Frenchman strode to Marianne and slapped her across the face. Marianne screamed in rage, grabbed his hand, and sank her teeth into it.

I struggled to my hands and knees, finally reaching the walking stick. The Frenchman struck Marianne again. I wrapped my hand around the walking stick and withdrew its sword.

The man fumbled at Marianne's dress, trying to search her, while she screamed and batted at him. I got shakily to my feet and came at the Frenchman with my sword.

He realized finally he could not fight us both. He took a step away from Marianne and pointed the pistol at her head.

I stopped. She tried to kick him.

"Be still, Marianne, for God's sake!"

The Frenchman, his face scratched and bruised, gave us both a look of fury, then he turned and ran out of the room. Marianne started after him. I shoved her aside, told her to stay put, and followed him.

The man hurtled down the stairs and out of the house. I

gave chase as quickly as I could. Outside, rain and mist
shrouded the tiny cul-de-sac of Grimpen Lane. I heard the
Frenchman running away toward Russel Street, then he disappeared into the fog.

I knew I'd never catch him. Angry and hurting, I made my
way back upstairs.

Marianne helped me inside. "Who the hell was that?"

"I don't know. I have never seen the man before." Whoever
he was, he'd just run off with Imogene Harper's letters.

"Well, he made bad work of you." Marianne gave me a critical look. "Sit down. You look terrible."

"Thank you very much." I obeyed her and sank to a chair
before the hearth, where this morning's fire had died to a
smolder.

Marianne took out a handkerchief and touched it to my
face. I winced as she found abrasions. "I should ask what you
are doing here," I said.

Marianne now lived in luxury in Grenville's Clarges Street
house, but she could not bear the confinement. She liked to
confound Grenville as much as she could by leaving the house
without a word and returning when she pleased. At first,
Grenville had tried to restrict her, but he'd not counted on
Marianne's pride and her love of freedom.

In the end, she'd worn him down. Last month, after she'd
disappeared to Berkshire without warning, he'd wearily told
her she could do as she liked.

"I came to talk to you," she said. "To ask your advice." She
bit her lip. Marianne so hated to ask for advice.

"About your son?" I asked.

I'd found out about Marianne's son by accident when I
stayed in Berkshire. I'd told her to confide the entire story to
Grenville, but I knew she had not.

Marianne gave me a hard look. She had an almost childlike
face, with a pointed chin, big blue eyes, and curls made more
golden by artifice. Her pale silk gown was the finest I'd ever

seen her wear, though it was now mussed and torn from the fight.

Her looks had kept her employed on the stage at Drury Lane, but her little girl prettiness belied a shrewd mind and a very sharp tongue. Marianne had learned to live by her wits, and she took a severe and cynical view of the world.

"No, not about David. And I will thank you keep that to yourself."

"I promised to keep silent, and I will keep my promise. But if you came to ask my advice, you should be a little more polite to me."

"That's a fine thing to say from someone I just found brawling." Her voice softened as she spoke, and she dabbed blood from my face. "You had no idea who he was? He could not have been here to rob you. You have nothing to steal. He must have been looking for something."

Marianne, as I said, was too shrewd for her own good. "I believe I know what he was looking for. But for the life of me, I do not know why."

"Has it to do with your Colonel Brandon getting himself committed to trial?"

"Very likely. Did Grenville tell you about it?"

She gave me a sour look. "No. I heard it in the usual way — gossip among the servants. I have not seen *him* in many days."

I looked at her in surprise. "But last night he said . . ."

She shot me a cynical look. "It was not me he visited last night. If he told you that, he lied. That is why I came to see you, his dearest friend. He tells me nothing, but you will know what is what."

Marianne cleaned my cuts in silence for a few moments, her nostrils pinched and white. I recalled Grenville telling me the previous night, with a self-deprecating smile, that he'd go to Clarges Street from Lord Gillis's. I wondered whether he'd lied or simply changed his mind, and in either case, why he'd done so.

"Grenville does not answer to me," I said. "I did not see him today. Possibly something happened that prevented him from visiting you as he planned."

"Of course," Marianne said in a hard voice, "The *something* was Mrs. Bennington."

I stared. "Mrs. Bennington?"

"Mrs. Bennington, the celebrated actress."

"Yes, I do know who she is."

"*He* has become quite fascinated with her," Marianne said. "He has seen many of her performances since his return from Berkshire. He cannot say a bad word about her. Now, he has taken to visiting her."

I listened in growing disquiet. Mrs. Bennington had been at Lord Gillis's ball, but I'd heard of her presence from Louisa and Lady Aline; Grenville had not mentioned her at all.

"She is a fine actress, Marianne. You know Grenville is fond of patronizing the best artists."

Marianne gave me a pitying look. "She is already so popular she has no need of *his* patronage. And I know he is fond of lady violinists and actresses and dancers. His interest in me is rather unusual."

I could not argue with her. I had seen Grenville with his previous mistresses, all of whom had been famous in some way or other. Marianne had never landed parts larger than a chorus or a short walk-on, and she was by no means well known. I did not believe even Grenville understood what had brought about his fascination with Marianne.

"He has expressed no particular attraction to Mrs. Bennington," I said. "And he has told me of no special visits to her."

"That confirms it then. If he had nothing to hide, he would have confided in you."

"Or, he has nothing to confide," I said.

"For God's sake, Lacey, I am not a fool. I know when a gentleman is tiring of me. Usually I am wise enough to leave when I see the first signs. This time, I've held on and hoped. I do not know why." Her words slowed, grew sad. "Perhaps because he is so wealthy."

I knew that was not her reason. Marianne's relationship with Grenville was complex, and I by no means understood it, but I sensed that beneath her hard-bitten cynicism, Marianne cared for him. I had seen evidence of that when Grenville had been hurt in Berkshire. Marianne had come to me, anguish in her eyes, and begged me to let her see him. She'd sat at his side, holding his hand, until he'd awakened.

I also knew Grenville was a man easily bored. He might have grown tired of Marianne's willfulness and unpredictability and decided to find a less complicated woman with whom to amuse himself.

I took the now-bloody handkerchief from her—a fine piece of lawn Grenville must have given her—and dabbed at the abrasions myself.

"Have you given him a chance, Marianne? You are keeping secrets from him, and you never let him give you what he wants to give you."

"What he wants to give me is an entirely different life, without asking if that is the life I want. Without so much as a by-your-leave."

"Many a penniless actress would be pleased by the prospect."

"And many a penniless captain would be pleased at his offer to let you share his house or travel with him. And yet you decline."

I could not deny that. I was as proud as Marianne was. "I do have my own income, tiny as it is. But you have even less. Perhaps you had better reconsider."

"You mean I should let him make me into the woman he wants me to be."

"I mean you should stop antagonizing him. Grenville helps

you because he feels charitable, and yes, he does pity you. And you punish him for it."

She snorted. "I am extremely grateful to you, Lacey. You have made me realize you men will always defend one another, no matter what. You say he is looking to Mrs. Bennington because I am angering him. Of course, it must be all my fault."

"I said nothing of the sort. You will drive me mad. The fault lies in both of you. You both have stubborn pride." I touched my face, feeling the bruises. "Grenville has said nothing to me about leaving you for Mrs. Bennington. And if he does try to cast you into the street, I will stop him."

Marianne cocked her head and observed me with her child-like gaze. "What can you do against him, Lacey? He is a powerful man. When he makes a pronouncement, even royalty listens. You may hold his interest now, but when you lose that, you will be nothing to him."

I knew the truth of this, but perhaps I had more faith in Grenville than she did. "I have seen evidence of his kind heart. He is not as callous as you would have him be."

Her eyes were as cool as ever, but I knew Marianne well, and I sensed the hurt in her. I could reassure her until my breath ran out, but both she and I knew Grenville did what he liked for his own reasons.

"If I discover anything, I will tell you," I promised. "I agree he should not keep you in the dark about Mrs. Bennington."

"Well, thank you for that anyway."

"I cannot blame him if he grows exasperated with you. You are a most exasperating woman."

"He has power," she said. "I have none. I am only getting back a little of my own."

The door banged open. I leapt to my feet, and so did Marianne, both of us expecting the return of the Frenchman. But it was only Bartholomew, balancing a covered dish and two tankards. He caught sight of me, and his jaw sagged.

I sprang forward and rescued the plate. "Do not drop my

dinner, Bartholomew, for heaven's sake. I am hungry." I put the platter safely on a table and took the tankards from him.

"Good Lord, sir." He looked me up and down then glanced at Marianne. "Did she have a go at you?"

Marianne looked affronted. "Of course not, you lummox."

I quickly told Bartholomew about the Frenchman. Bartholomew, growing excited, wanted nothing more than to dash out and scour the city for him then and there.

I stopped him. "He did not find what he came to find, so he will no doubt show himself again. He has a distinctive appearance. We will find him."

I did not say so, but I had the feeling Imogene Harper would know good and well who this Frenchman was. If he'd stolen her letters to Brandon, he must have had good reason to do so. He could be her friend or a lover—even her husband. Mrs. Harper had left the Peninsula four years ago, after all, and had only recently come to London. She could have done many things during that time.

"Do run to Bow Street," I told Bartholomew as I uncovered the beefsteak he'd brought me. "Tell Pomeroy to watch out for a lean Frenchman with close-cropped hair. The man may next try to search Mrs. Harper's rooms, or Turner's, or even Turner's father's house in Epsom."

"Of course, sir." Bartholomew's eyes were animated. He tugged his forelock and ran off, leaving me with Marianne and a quickly cooling dinner.

~

I SHARED THE BEEFSTEAK WITH MARIANNE. NEVER ONE TO forgo a free meal, she ate but did so in silence. We did not mention Grenville or Mrs. Bennington again.

Marianne departed before Bartholomew returned. She did not tell me where she was going, and I did not ask. She was angry and worried, and somehow, I did not blame her.

Marianne was correct when she said Grenville could wash his hands of me whenever he wished and I could do nothing against him. But I did not care. The threat of losing his patronage would not hold my tongue if he had been betraying Marianne. I had seen men change mistresses before, but I felt protective of Marianne, perhaps because I knew how vulnerable she truly was, despite her hard-nosed approach to life.

I finished my meal and, as it was nearing four o'clock, remembered my promise to call upon Lady Breckenridge.

I looked at myself in the dusky mirror above my washstand and winced. The left side of my face was puffed and bruised, and a cut creased my right cheekbone. My lip had split, and dried blood stained my chin. I was sore and stiff, and my knee felt as though it were wrapped in bands of fire.

I was in no fit state to visit a lady. I soaked a handkerchief in water and continued to clean my face. It was a slow, tricky business, every touch stinging.

I made myself ready for the visit anyway. I very much wanted to put together the pieces of Turner's murder before Brandon could be tried. When the wheels of justice turned, they turned swiftly. Brandon's trial could come up before a week was out, and only days after that, he could be hanged or transported. Louisa would be shamed and disgraced, and likely abandoned by everyone she knew, excluding myself and Lady Aline.

I refused to let Brandon bring that sorrow upon his wife. I would find the killer and release Brandon, whether he liked it or not.

My other reason for resolving to visit Lady Breckenridge as planned was I simply wanted to see her.

Since our first discordant meeting in Kent, Lady Breckenridge and I had become friends of a sort. She had helped me during the affair of the Glass House and the problem of Lady Clifford's necklace, and she'd had given me a new walking stick when my old one had been lost.

She'd taken to inviting me to gatherings at which she launched musicians or poets into society and made it clear I could add her to my list of afternoon calls. I rarely made calls, but since my return from Berkshire I had several times sat in her drawing room sipping tea while other members of the *ton* stared at me and wondered why I'd turned up.

I bade Bartholomew accompany me back to Mayfair, and we made our way to South Audley Street and Lady Breckenridge's home. I used Bartholomew as a scout to discover whether Lady Breckenridge had received anyone else that afternoon. If she had guests in her drawing room, I would take my battered face away.

Bartholomew returned with the news the lady was alone. Relieved, I descended from the hackney coach and went inside.

Lady Breckenridge's butler, Barnstable, looked at me in shock. "Sir?"

I gave him a smile that pulled at my sore face. "Will I frighten her ladyship, do you think?"

"No, sir." He continued to stare at me. "Her ladyship is made of stern stuff. I have just the thing to put on those bruises, sir. Take them down in no time."

Barnstable, it seemed, had remedies for everything. He had, a few months ago, treated my sore knee with hot towels and a penetrating ointment, which he'd graciously sent home with me. I'd begun to believe in Barnstable and his remedies.

One of Lady Breckenridge's footmen, looking no less dismayed at my state than the butler, led me up the stairs. He did not take me to the drawing room, but led me up another flight to Lady Breckenridge's private rooms. When he opened a door and ushered me inside, I realized I'd been shown to her boudoir.

Lady Breckenridge's entire house was very modern, and this room was no exception. A Roman couch faced the fire-place, and windows were elegantly draped in light green silk to complement the cream-colored walls. Thick carpet under my boots warmed the room.

Lady Breckenridge entered only a few moments after the footman left me. Today she wore a peignoir of gold silk and had threaded a wide, ivory-colored bandeau through her dark hair. When she saw my bruised face, her reaction was predictable.

"Good God," she said, stopping on the threshold.

"Forgive me," I said. "I decided to participate in a boxing match before making my calls today."

She came all the way into the room and closed the door behind her, but her expression did not alter. "Whom did you anger this time, Gabriel?"

"A Frenchman searching for something he could not find."

Lady Breckenridge raised her brows, and I explained the incident. As I spoke, Barnstable bustled in with a steaming bowl on a tray. He politely waited until I finished then bade me to sit on the Roman couch.

I did so and stretched my aching leg to the fire. Barnstable dipped a cloth in the liquid and touched it to my face. It hurt like fury and at the same time soothed.

"You ought to be a physician, Barnstable," I said.

"Indeed, no, sir." He sounded affronted.

Lady Breckenridge watched the proceeding without speaking. She wandered to a small rosewood table, pulled a black cigarillo from a box, and lit it with a candle.

"Are you certain this robbery was connected with Turner's death?" she asked as thin smoke wreathed her face.

"I am certain of nothing." I inhaled the heady-smelling steam Barnstable waved beneath my nose. "If he were a mere robber, he would have taken the snuffboxes, which were costly. But he held on to the letters he found in my pocket."

"Why would a Frenchman be interested in letters written by Mrs. Harper?"

"That I do not know. I do not know anything." Colonel

Brandon was being uncommonly stubborn, I had only vague accounts of what had happened at the ball, and both Louisa and Mrs. Harper had convinced themselves Brandon had murdered Turner.

"If your line of thinking is that Mrs. Harper stabbed Turner before she screamed, you will be wrong," Lady Breckenridge said, breaking my thoughts. "She did not. At least, not then."

"How do you know?"

She took a pull of the cigarillo. "Because I saw her. When Mrs. Harper went into the anteroom at twelve, she left the door ajar. I could look right in and observe her."

I sat up straight, pressing Barnstable's hand aside. "Why did you not say so?"

"I did not have the chance. Your Mr. Pomeroy turned his attention to Colonel Brandon very quickly, and I had not the time to explain."

Yes, Pomeroy could fix on one purpose and ignore everything else in his path.

"Tell me what Mrs. Harper did," I said as Barnstable calmly returned to patting my bruises and cuts.

"I saw her bend over Turner, then she gave a little start. I suppose that's when she realized he was dead, but of course I had no idea yet that he'd been killed. She moved her hands over him or inside his coat, I could not see exactly. Then she straightened up. She looked at her glove, which was red with blood. She recoiled from it, and that was when she began to scream."

"If you could not see exactly, how do you know she did not press the knife into Turner's chest when she bent over him?"

"Because I did not see a knife in her hand when she went in, nor did I notice her picking one up from the desk. She went nowhere else in the room. Besides, she would have had to put quite a bit of strength behind the blow, would she not? She did not raise her arm or strike out, and in any event, it's likely

Turner would have seen her and fought her. Unless Turner were drunk and senseless." Lady Breckenridge shook her head. "No, I do not believe Mrs. Harper stabbed him. It was as though she searched him for something—love letters perhaps? Although I cannot imagine her writing love letters to Turner. But supposing he had letters from her to someone else?"

She was a perceptive woman. "Perhaps," I said cautiously.

Lady Breckenridge glanced at her butler. "Barnstable, will you leave us?"

Barnstable rose and handed me the linen pad. "Of course, my lady. Keep that pressed to the wound, sir. It will take the ill from it."

I promised I would see to it. Barnstable bowed and took himself from the room, closing the door behind him with every show of deference.

"He looked a bit disappointed," I said.

"Of course he is. He is as interested in this business as I am. But he will not listen at the door. He considers that beneath him."

I gave her a smile. "I am certain my man, Bartholomew, will tell him all he wants to know below stairs."

"I sent him away so we might speak frankly. Because your colonel was arrested for the crime, I assume Mrs. Harper was looking for letters she had written to Colonel Brandon, or he had written to her. This would explain their mutual antagonism toward Mr. Turner."

"You guess well," I said.

She sank to the sofa next to me, crossing her legs in a graceful move. "You must remember that I was there last night. I observed the very strange behavior of Colonel Brandon and Imogene Harper. Did they forget how much the *ton* gossips? Believe me, today the polite world is grateful to Lord Gillis for providing them with something new to discuss. We were growing tired of who would race what horse at the Derby and what an appalling frock Lady Jersey wore last

Thursday. Mind you, it would be much more interesting if Colonel Brandon were one of us, but it will have to do."

She spoke with her usual acid tones, but I took no offense. She was directing her sarcasm at her own circle, not Colonel Brandon.

I removed the linen pad from my face, defying Barnstable's instructions, and laid it across my knee. The warmth of it felt good there. "And what is the *ton* saying today?"

"I will know more about which way gossip is directed when I go out, but I have already received several notes from my acquaintances regarding the matter. Lady Seville, a girlhood acquaintance who attended the ball, is terribly excited at having been at a gathering where something actually *happened*, even something so low as murder. Lord Gillis is to blame, she says, for having so many military men among his acquaintance. They are violent, she believes, and do not always have the right connections. Lady Seville puts much store on pedigree."

"Colonel Brandon comes from a fine family."

"But not a peerage." She emphasized her words with a jab of the cigarillo. "And that is the only thing that counts with Lady Seville. She is a horrible snob. She would approve of you, however."

I looked at her in surprise then glanced at my threadbare trousers, made worse by my scuffle with the Frenchman. "Would she? Why?"

"Because you have pedigree of the right sort. Your family is older and more connected than your colonel's."

"I would be interested to learn how you know all this."

Lady Breckenridge took another pull from the cigarillo then laid it on the edge of the table. "You are not the only person who likes to investigate things. Your family was quite important during the time of Charles the Second, I discovered. They were given land, and even offered a title, one declined by your proud ancestor. Later a Lacey married a peeress, rendering you quite respectable."

"Until my father and grandfather impoverished us," I said.

She waved that away. "Money is not as important as breeding. You know that, my dear Captain. That is, until someone sets their sights on marriage. Then money is quite important, but it would never do to let on, would it?"

"You are a most cynical lady."

"Indeed. I learned very early in life that the world is not a kind place. Your position in it determines all. For instance, were I born into the servant class, my sharp tongue would earn me many blows. As it is, I am smiled at because I am the daughter of an earl and the widow of a viscount."

I had to concede the truth of this.

"And so Colonel Brandon suffers," she concluded. "If he were a peer, there would be much scandal and sensation, but I doubt he would be cooling his heels at Newgate."

"He might be," I said. "He is mostly there because of his pigheaded stubbornness."

Lady Breckenridge hung her arm over the back of the sofa, a dangling well-shaped hand near my head. Slim gold rings, one embedded with a topaz, the other with twinkling sapphires, hugged her fingers.

I found myself thinking I could never afford to give her jewels. For instance, if I wanted to give her a strand of diamonds for her slim wrist, I could not do it. It stung a man's pride not to be able to give a lady a gift.

I drew my thumb across the inside of her wrist where the bracelet would lie.

Her eyes darkened and grew quiet. I waited for her to drawl sarcasm or to snatch her hand away, but she did neither. I rubbed her warm skin, comforting myself in the small feel of softness. Lady Breckenridge moved closer to me and rested her fingers against my chest.

I had kissed her before, once in her private box at Covent Garden Theatre. She had not minded. I leaned to her and kissed her now. My sore lip pulled a little, but I did not care.

She kissed me well, then she lifted my hand and pressed a long kiss to my fingers.

Donata Breckenridge was a lovely woman, and I needed comfort. We were alone in her private rooms, and only her servants would know what we did here. I wondered how loyal they were to her or whether they would give the *ton* something new to talk about tomorrow.

"Stay for a time, Captain," she said, as though reading my thoughts. She smoothed her palm across my chest. "Your heart tells me you wish this."

Indeed, my heart was beating swiftly. I kissed her again, tempted, so tempted to take her hand and lead her to her bedchamber, despite the pain in my body. Her eyes were moist, her lips soft.

I smoothed back a strand of her hair. "It would cause great scandal if you had a liaison with me."

She studied me with a mixture of curiosity and resignation, as though she'd made a wager with herself as to my reaction to her offer. I wondered whether she'd won or lost.

"It is not only scandal you think of," she said.

"Indeed, it is," I answered, surprised.

"No. You forget. I saw exactly how you looked at Louisa Brandon last night when you comforted her in her sitting room."

I sat up, and her hand dropped away from me. I remembered Lady Breckenridge entering the room while I'd held Louisa in my embrace. At the time, I'd tried to dismiss her shrewd glance, but she had seen all and forgotten nothing.

"Louisa Brandon and I have been friends for twenty years," I said. "She loves her husband, and I will help restore him to her."

Lady Breckenridge folded her arms across her silk peignoir, assuming a neutral expression. "So that is the way of it."

"The way of what?"

She did not move, but I felt a distance grow between us. "Do you know, Captain, I am trying to decide whether I am too proud to take another woman's leavings."

I looked at her, uncertain how to respond.

"I know what I saw," she went on. "You love Louisa Brandon, but you are a man of honor. You would never stoop to offering her the shelter of your arms while her husband waits in prison. You would never violate your honor, or hers, in that way." She drew a breath. "And so, you seek solace elsewhere."

Her voice shook a little, but she lifted her chin. Lady Breckenridge had her own code of honor. She would never let me see her hurting.

"No," I replied in a hard voice.

"Why not let him hang? Mrs. Brandon will no doubt turn to you once the deed is done."

Brandon had said much the same thing. The devil of it was, Louisa *would* likely turn to me for comfort were Brandon hanged—at first. Eventually, she would want to put all reminders of the sordid business behind her, including me, no matter how many years of friendship we'd shared.

I realized my compulsion to clear Colonel Brandon might have more significance than my trying to discover the truth. Perhaps I believed Brandon innocent because I needed him to be innocent. If I could not save him, I knew I would lose Louisa's friendship—forever.

Lady Breckenridge was wrong, however.

"It is not solace I seek from you," I said. "I would not insult you so."

"What do you seek, then?" She sounded curious, not offended.

I touched her cheek with the backs of my fingers. "What you said you sought from me."

She looked at me for a moment with her dark blue eyes, but she did not pull away from my touch.

"You put me in a difficult place, you know," she said. "Your heart is already beyond reach. Any victory I have with you must be hollow. If I lose, you lose nothing. If I win, I will never win you completely."

She stood. "Please go now, Captain. I am attending the theatre tonight, as well as an at-home, where I and the rest of London will talk incessantly of the murder. I need time to prepare myself."

I rose, surprised to find myself shaking a little. "Donata."

"Go, Lacey. While I can still cling to the shards of my dignity, please."

I wanted to admonish her or take her into my arms and prove she was wrong, but my common sense told me that, at this moment, neither course would be wise.

I buttoned my coat, took up my walking stick, and crossed the room in silence.

At the door, I turned back. "You are not completely correct as to where my heart is engaged." I bowed, while she watched me speculatively. "Good afternoon."

Lady Breckenridge held herself stiffly, watching me go.

CHAPTER 8

The next afternoon, Grenville and I journeyed to Epsom to attend the funeral of Henry Turner.

Grenville drove his phaeton, the weather being fine. His larger traveling coach followed us, bearing our servants and bags southward. The phaeton was light and fast, and we soon drew clear of the metropolis and headed across green downs for Epsom.

Grenville's persona today was that of horse-mad dandy. He sat upright, his gloved hands competently holding a complex configuration of reins. He occasionally touched his whip to the horses, encouraging them to hold a smart pace. In his black suit, knee-high boots, and fine hat, he was the epitome of the fashionable gentleman. His horses were perfectly matched grays, the phaeton nearly new and shiny black, the wheels and points picked out in gold.

Grenville navigated us swiftly through other vehicles and over the rutted roads. I held tightly to my hat with one hand and the seat with the other.

Remembering his motion sickness inside carriages on

previous journeys, I remarked, "The movement does not bother you when you drive?"

"No." Grenville kept his gaze on the horses and the road beyond. "Don't honestly know why. Probably because I must concentrate on something other than my stomach."

Grenville evidently liked to focus on obtaining the speediest journey possible. I braced my feet on the footboard and concentrated on holding on.

When I'd mounted the phaeton this afternoon, Grenville's reaction to my bruised face was not as severe as could be, because Bartholomew had already told him the tale. He quizzed me on the particulars, however, as we rode south.

"Are you certain the Frenchman had connection with the Turner murder?" Grenville asked. "Perhaps he was looking for something else entirely."

"He had an inordinate interest in Mrs. Harper's letters," I said over the noise of our passage. "Why take them otherwise? No, depend upon it, he has something to do with Mrs. Harper, and probably with Turner."

We rode silently a few minutes, the rattle of the wheels over the road and the thudding of the horses' hooves making talking impractical.

"What I most wonder," Grenville said, when he slowed to drive through a village, "is why Marianne was there."

"She'd come to talk with me," I said. "She happened to get in the way of the Frenchman's fists, which she would not have if she'd run away like a sensible woman."

"She was hurt?" Grenville gave me a look of alarm. "Bartholomew did not tell me that."

"She was not much hurt. I made certain. And Marianne gave back as good as she received."

Grenville rarely grew angry, but he grew angry now. "Why the devil was she there to get in his way at all? If she wanted to speak to you, why not send for you to visit her?"

"She still feels a bit confined."

His mouth set. "I have told her she can come and go as she pleases. She can do what the devil she likes. I have ceased trying to hold her."

"*Constrained*, I should have said. Your servants would no doubt mention a visit from me to you, possibly telling you what they heard us discuss."

"Dear God," Grenville shouted at the countryside in general. "The woman will drive me mad. It is my own fault; I remember you warning me against her. I wish I had listened."

"You wanted to help her. It was kind of you."

He gave me a sideways glance. "Helping her was not my only reason, and you know it. Well, I suppose I have paid the price for my folly."

If Grenville had imagined Marianne would be forever grateful for his charity and fall into his arms, he had certainly read her character wrong.

I wanted to ask him about Mrs. Bennington, and Marianne's speculations, but we exited the village and picked up speed, and I did not fancy bellowing such questions to him on the road. Time enough for that later.

I did tell him, when we slowed again near Epsom, about my encounter with Imogene Harper in Turner's rooms and the rest of my investigation until this point.

I had imagined we'd put up at an inn at Epsom and journey to Turner's father's home for the funeral the next day, but to my surprise, Grenville drove to a red-brick, Tudor-style manor a little outside the town.

When the phaeton finally rattled to a halt, a groom came out to greet us and hold the horses. Grenville said, "When I wrote to Mr. Turner to express my condolences, he invited me to stay at the house. You are welcome, as well."

A footman appeared at the front door and led us inside into a narrow, dark-paneled hall lined with doors. At the end of this hall, a staircase, its wood black with age, wound upward to a gallery.

We did not meet Mr. Turner, but were taken upstairs to bedchambers that were low-ceilinged and dark, though warm and comfortable. The footman brought us hot coffee and hock and left us alone.

"I've stayed here several times," Grenville said. "Turner does fine house parties for the Derby. They are quite popular, and Turner is a good host."

I looked out the window across green hills toward the dusty road on which the Derby race was held. I had no doubt that house parties here were filled with gaiety and excitement. Sad that such a place would now have to be the site of so dismal a scene as a young man's funeral.

Not long later, our host sent for us, and Grenville and I descended to meet Mr. Turner in his study.

Large windows here overlooked a lush back garden where spring flowers pushed themselves up in the beds. The sun shone hard, rendering it a lovely landscape. On any other occasion, I would have stopped to enjoy the sight.

Henry Turner's father, Mr. Allen Turner, looked much like his son. His hair was straight and close cropped, but he had the same rather soft features as Henry and had probably been quite handsome in his youth. Mr. Turner was not very tall, standing only about as high as Grenville, and he had to look up at me. He shook my hand politely, showing no resentment of my intrusion.

"You are the captain who sometimes works with the magistrates, are you not?" he asked.

I admitted I was. "My condolences on the loss of your son, sir."

Turner nodded in a resigned manner. "It came as a bit of the shock. When your only son dies, it is as if you lived your life for nothing. All this . . ." He gestured to the room, and I took him to mean the entire house and the estate as well. "Henry will not have any of it now. It will go to my second cousin and his son, and that will be the end of it."

His eyes were sad, but his back was straight, as though Mr. Turner determined to face the future, no matter how bleak it was. I remembered the frustration Brandon sometimes expressed that he had no son to carry on his name and his line, no one to inherit his money and his houses. I personally was happy not to bestow the ruin of the Lacey house in Norfolk on a son, but Brandon and Mr. Turner had much more to lose. An Englishman without a son was almost like a man without an appendage.

Brandon had been disappointed at Louisa's failed attempts to produce his hoped-for heir, but I believe Turner suffered worse. He'd had a healthy and robust son, who'd been cut down in the prime of his life. No matter what Henry Turner's character had been, he might have lived a long time and produced many children so his father might see his line stretching to eternity. Now that possibility was gone.

Mr. Turner placed his hands behind his back. "I've offered a large reward for the conviction of the felon who killed my son. I understand from Grenville that you believe there is doubt the colonel who's been arrested actually committed the murder."

"I'm trying to ascertain whether he did, but I am skeptical," I answered. "This might seem a strange question, sir, but could you tell me if there is anyone who could have been angry enough at your son to want him dead?"

Turner shook his head. "If Henry had been called out and died in a duel, I would understand it. This—the senseless killing—while he sat in a chair, at a society ball of all places, confounds me. No, Captain, I do not know whether he angered anyone in particular. My son had a wide circle of acquaintances, and he was not always the most polite young man, unfortunately. The young seem to find extreme rudeness to be fashionable."

He glanced once at Grenville, as though debating whether

Grenville's famous disdain were to blame for the rudeness of young people today.

"Did he speak of anyone with particular emphasis?" I asked. "Or did he fear anyone? What I mean is, he must have known the person who killed him. He died without much struggle. The only comfort I can offer you is that he died almost instantly. It took him by surprise. He certainly would not have had time to feel fear or pain."

Mr. Turner's eyes were moist, but his mouth was tight. "I am afraid Henry did not speak much to me about his acquaintance. His friends will attend his burial, tomorrow. Perhaps they will know whether Henry was afraid of anyone."

Mr. Turner excused himself before long, and Grenville tactfully suggested he and I walk in the garden since it was such a fine day. We strolled along the flower beds, and the head gardener, who looked as morose as his master, pointed out the garden's more unique characteristics. The entire landscape had been laid out by Capability Brown, the brilliant garden designer from a century ago.

By the time we'd walked to the folly at the end of the grounds and back again, the dinner hour had arrived. Mr. Turner joined us for the meal, although his wife did not appear. Turner was still quiet and apologized for his lack of conversation, and Grenville and I assured him we understood.

It was not until Grenville and I had returned to Grenville's bedchamber to drink brandy alone that I could mention Mrs. Bennington.

When I ventured surprise that Grenville had told me he would be visiting Marianne when in fact he had gone to see Mrs. Bennington, his dark brows furrowed. "Does it matter?"

"It mattered a great deal to Marianne."

"My visit to Mrs. Bennington is my own business, Lacey."

I knew he resented my intrusion, but I did agree with Marianne on one point. Grenville had far more wealth and power than either of us, and if he chose to use us ill, there was not much we could do to stop him. However, I intended to prevent him from using Marianne ill if I could.

"I doubt it meant anything to Marianne," Grenville said, trying to sound offhand. "She was simply trying to plague you. I suspect she does not care whether I live or die."

"Not true. She was quite distressed when you were hurt in Sudbury."

He scoffed, an inelegant noise.

I tried another tack. "I remember when you took me to Covent Garden to see Mrs. Bennington perform. You did not sing her praises as everyone else in the theatre seemed to."

"What are you talking about? I said much that was complimentary."

"No, you simply did not disagree with what others said. That is a different thing."

Grenville gave me a tense glance. "Why this sudden interest in my opinion of Mrs. Bennington?"

"I am merely curious. She was at the Gillises' ball, and afterward, you sought her company. At her house?"

"Very well, Lacey, if you must know the entire story, no. I fully intended to visit Clarges Street, but as I journeyed home, I happened upon Mrs. Bennington's carriage—it had broken an axle, and she was wild to get home. I let her ride to her house in my carriage, and I stayed with her until she'd calmed down. Then I went home. That is all."

I drank brandy in silence, while he grew red in the face. He was annoyed, and trying to stifle it.

"I would like to meet Mrs. Bennington," I said.

"What the devil for?"

"If nothing else, to ask her what she observed at the Gillises' ball. If she saw something that would point to solving Turner's murder, I certainly want to hear it."

"I tried to ask her," Grenville said in a more even tone. "She noticed very little. She believes she saw her husband speak to Turner, but she cannot be certain."

I pushed my feet closer to the fire. "Who is this Mr. Bennington? Is he known for anything but marrying a famous actress?"

Grenville seemed to relax. "Bennington is one of those Englishmen who enjoy living most of the time on the Continent. Both she and Bennington are a little vague about how they met, but from what I understand, Bennington saw Claire perform one night in Milan and asked her to marry him the next day."

"A love match?"

"No, I do not think so," Grenville said. "The marriage was sudden, but I cannot believe love had anything to do with it. Bennington is sardonic about Claire if he speaks about her at all, and Claire never mentions her husband or even notices when he's in the room with her. I imagine they came together for mutual convenience."

"Money?" I asked.

"That is the usual reason, but who knows? Bennington seems well off. Perhaps she needed money, and he wanted something pretty to look at." Grenville's mouth twisted in distaste. "Although he does not dance attendance on Claire, nor does he seem inclined to be possessive of her."

"Is it an open marriage, then?"

"I do not know why you should think so," Grenville began, then he caught himself. "Admittedly, they live almost separate lives. I imagine they appeared at the Gillises' ball at the same time entirely by accident."

I had begun to construct a scenario in which Mr. Bennington killed Turner in a fit of jealousy when Turner had made up to his young wife, but at Grenville's answer, I discarded the idea. If they'd married for convenience and lived separate lives, Bennington might simply look the other way at his wife's affairs, and she at his.

"Did Mrs. Bennington know Henry Turner?" I asked.

"She says not," Grenville answered. "She has no reason to

lie about that."

"But he was found murdered, and she is an actress. Perhaps her first instinct would be to lie."

Grenville gave me an unfriendly glance. "I know what you are doing, Lacey. You need a suspect other than Brandon. Do you plan to suspect everyone at the ball?"

"Every person in that house had the opportunity to murder Henry Turner. Including you."

"True. I was close to the room when he was found. I could have slipped in and out without anyone noticing. Although most people notice what I do. *Some* person usually has their eye on me, which makes things dashed difficult at times. I cannot take a private walk across a remote country meadow without it being reported in full in every London newspaper the next day."

"The curse of fame," I said.

"You wonder why I travel to the corners of the earth. Escaping newspapermen is one motive. But you are correct, I could have killed Turner. I had no reason to murder him, however, except his cravat knot was appalling. But I am reasonable enough to simply look away and swallow when I see such abuse of a cravat."

He spoke lightly, but I sensed his tension. I also noted that he'd turned the conversation neatly away from discussion of Claire Bennington.

"Who else would have reason to murder him?" I asked. "Either because of his cravat, or something else?"

Grenville at last began to show interest. He dropped his dandy persona and went to the writing desk to search for paper and pen and ink.

"Suppose I make a list of all present at the ball who knew Turner and who might have reason to dislike him?" He began writing, his pen scratching softly. "The most obvious person, of course, is Imogene Harper. She found Turner, she admitted she searched his pockets for her love letter to Colonel Brandon, and Lady Breckenridge confirms she saw Mrs. Harper doing so. Turner was apparently blackmailing Mrs. Harper about the letter, which gives her quite a strong motive."

"Yes, but why kill him in so public a place as a ballroom?"

Grenville waited, pen poised. "Because she was angry and frightened, and in such a crush, there would be a chance someone else would be accused of the crime. As indeed, happened."

"Yes," I said. "Who besides Mrs. Harper?"

"Lady Breckenridge?"

I raised my brows. "She did not know Turner well."

"So she says. And she was quite close to the room when Mrs. Harper went in. I remember seeing her standing very near the door. Not speaking to anyone, just looking about."

"Donata is an unlikely murderess. If a gentleman angered her, she would dress him down, in no uncertain terms, no matter who listened."

Grenville chuckled. "The lady has a sharp tongue and a sharper wit. I include her only because she was so near the room. And she told you she'd seen Mrs. Harper bend over Turner—Lady Breckenridge might have invented the story to make you more suspicious of Mrs. Harper. However, I admit such a thing seems unlikely."

"We are looking for people who knew Turner well," I said.

"Indeed. Lord and Lady Gillis, then. They invited him."

"Lord Gillis says he knew Turner only in a vague way. The friend of a friend of his wife's, he told me."

"Yes, Lady Gillis is the connection there," Grenville said, writing. "You did not meet Lady Gillis. She can be a charming woman when she wishes, and she is very much younger than Lord Gillis. About Turner's age, I put her."

"Hmm," I said. "And Bartholomew puts her arguing with Lord Gillis earlier that day about someone she'd invited. I wonder who the object of this argument was."

"We can but ask her."

"Any other names?" I said.

"Leland Derwent," Grenville said. "He and Turner were at Oxford together. Leland often mentions this, usually in a tone of apology."

"I doubt Leland Derwent would commit murder." Leland was one of the most innocent young men I'd ever met. He looked upon life with the unworldly eyes of a puppy and had the enthusiasm to match. I dined regularly with his family, where Leland listened to my stories of the war in the Peninsula with flattering eagerness.

"I would agree with you," Grenville said. "The thought of Leland Derwent as a murderer stretches credulity. I saw Leland speak to Turner at length that evening, however, angrily, and he was quite troubled when Turner left him."

"I see." I didn't like that. "Very well, write his name, and we will ask him about this conversation with Mr. Turner. Mr. Bennington next, I think."

Grenville hesitated, looking annoyed, but he nodded and wrote again.

"You said it was accidental he and Mrs. Bennington were there together," I said. "Were they invited separately, or together?"

"I do not know, but thinking it over, I wonder why Bennington came at all. He tends to sneer at social gatherings. *Where we stand about and pretend interest in the cut of Mr. Teezle's coat and whether Miss Peazle's come-out will be a success,* he says."

"And yet, he arrives at a grand ball and stays most of the night."

"Precisely," Grenville said. "I must wonder why."

"Very well, make a note of him. Any others?"

Grenville tapped his lips with the end of the pen. "It is difficult to say. Turner was not well liked. Snubbed people at Tattersall's and so forth. But he always paid his debts at White's when he lost and everywhere else for that matter, and always stopped short of mortally insulting a fellow so that he would not be called out. Not very brave, was our Mr. Turner."

I half listened to him, while I contemplated what I'd learned from Lady Aline, Louisa, and Lady Breckenridge. "What about Basil Stokes?" I asked. "Louisa and Lady Aline mentioned him, but I know nothing about him."

"Stokes?" Grenville raised his head in surprise. "Why would you suspect him?"

"Because Louisa said he stood very close to Colonel Brandon when they entered the house. I am looking at the possibility of someone stealing Brandon's knife—picking his pocket. Louisa said the closest persons to them in the crush were Mrs. Bennington and Basil Stokes."

Grenville shrugged and made a note. "Very well, then, Basil Stokes. We will easily find him at Tatt's or the boxing rooms—he is mad for sport."

"In all frankness, I cannot imagine why Mr. Stokes would murder Turner, but I hate to leave any stone unturned."

"If nothing else, we'll get good tips on what horse will win at Newmarket or which pugilist is likely to be a champion this year. Now, what about this French gentleman who assaulted you?"

I took a sip of brandy, letting the mellow taste fill my mouth. "I had not forgotten him. He had a rather military bearing, an officer, I would say, not one of the rank and file."

"He was not at the ball," Grenville said. "I would have noticed a lean man with close-cropped hair, a military bearing, and a thick French accent. I knew everyone there. There were no strangers."

I cradled my brandy goblet in my palms. "Lord Gillis likes military men, which was why he invited Colonel Brandon and the Duke of Wellington. Supposing this Frenchman had been a guest in the house but did not come down for the ball. Suppose he was someone Lord Gillis had invited to stay so they could discuss old military campaigns. The Frenchman spies Turner entering the house for the ball and kills him—for reasons of his own. The French officer took Imogene Harper's letters, but if he had not looked at them closely, he would not know what they were. Perhaps he thought they were something of his Turner had taken."

"Or the Frenchman has nothing to do with Henry Turner at all. You are only guessing he does."

"True. But he followed me, after I'd finished searching Turner's rooms, and he was looking for something. Pomeroy is now scouring the city for the Frenchman, and I hope to question him before long." I touched my face gingerly. "And complain of his very hard fists."

If anyone could find the man, Pomeroy could. He had a tenacity greater than the Russians who'd driven Bonaparte out of Moscow. Also, the Frenchman would not remain hidden for long. A French officer of such distinctive appearance walking about London would be noted and remembered.

There existed another reason a Frenchman might profess interest in me. My wife, Carlotta, had eloped with a French officer. I had never met the man or even seen him. Why Carlotta's lover would come to London and ransack my rooms, I had no idea, but I could not dismiss the fact that the connection might be along those lines.

I kept this to myself, however, as Grenville and I continued our discussion. Grenville brought up names and wrote them down or rejected those who'd left the ball long before Turner's death. Grenville's circle of acquaintance was vastly greater than mine, so I let him speculate on the characters of gentlemen of whom I knew nothing.

By the time we parted to seek our beds, we had come up with a lengthy list. But I focused on only a few of those as most likely: Imogene Harper, Mrs. Bennington, Mr. Bennington, Basil Stokes, my mysterious Frenchman, and possibly Leland Derwent.

I felt grateful Grenville did not suggest listing Brandon, but

I knew, glumly, that I could not rule him out altogether. He and Mrs. Harper still had the strongest motives thus far.

I went to sleep in the soft bed in my chamber and dreamed of Lady Breckenridge and her blue eyes.

THE FUNERAL FOR HENRY TURNER WAS HELD THE NEXT morning. The day dawned clear and fine, the air soft, the sky an arch of blue overhead. It was a day made for hacking across the downs on a fine horse, not for standing in a churchyard while a vicar droned the burial service.

"Man that is born of a woman hath but a short time to live, and is full of misery. He cometh up, and is cut down, like a flower; he fleeth as it were a shadow . . ."

I stood next to Grenville, both of us in somber gray. Nearer the tomb stood Mr. Turner and his wife, several young men I took to be Turner's friends, and a few older men, who must be Turner's father's cronies. People from the town of Epsom also attended, working people who had given Mr. and Mrs. Turner respectful words of condolence when they arrived.

Henry would be buried in a rather private corner of the churchyard where, Mr. Turner had informed me, his family had been buried for generations.

"I thought the next person there would be me," Mr. Turner said.

I'd had little comfort to give him. Grenville spoke the right phrases, but I, whose mentor was even now waiting in prison to be tried for the murder, could think of nothing to say.

One of the mourners was Leland Derwent. He had seen me when we all arrived at the church and had given me a nod of greeting. Now he stared down at the grave, his young brow furrowed.

Next to him stood a young man called Gareth Travers. I'd met Travers during the affair of Colonel Westin last summer.

He was Leland's closest friend, but he lacked the complete innocence of Leland and had a bit more worldly intelligence.

The vicar launched into the Lord's Prayer. I heard Grenville murmuring along, although most of the attendants remained silent. A soft spring breeze carrying the scent of new earth touched me.

The service finished, and we turned away from the grave-side. In tacit agreement, Grenville and I hung back while Mr. Turner led his wife away.

Leland and Gareth Travers waited for us at the gate to the churchyard. "It was kind of you to come, Captain," Leland said as he shook my hand.

"I am afraid my motive was not entirely kindness," I said. "I came to obtain an idea of Turner's character, and to find out who would want to kill him."

Leland looked puzzled. "I thought your colonel had been arrested."

"He has, but his arrest does not mean he is guilty. I intend to bring forth evidence that he is not guilty before his trial."

I had expected, if anything, for Leland to look interested, but his expression became troubled. "You think someone else committed this crime?"

"Yes, but I'm damned if I know who. You went to school with Henry Turner, I believe."

"Yes, but he was two years ahead of us." As Grenville had indicated, Leland sounded apologetic.

The other mourners had dispersed, leaving us alone. "Will you tell me about him?" I asked.

Leland fell into step beside me on a path that skirted the edge of the churchyard and swung out across the downs. Travers and Grenville came behind.

"There is not much to tell," Leland said. "I do hate to say anything bad about Mr. Turner, now that he's lying in the ground."

"I assure you, I will repeat nothing that is not relevant to my problem. But I need to know everything I can if I'm to discover who killed him."

Leland settled his curled-brimmed hat against the breeze. "I admit he was a bit of a bully. I didn't fag for him, but I knew the lads who did. He put them through their paces and was never happy with anything."

"Was he—forgive me for putting this bluntly—a blackmailer?"

Leland looked startled. "A blackmailer? No. No, I do not believe so. I never heard anyone say anything like that."

"Did he ever seem desperate for money?"

"He liked money, that is true, but I do not know whether he was *desperate* for it. His allowance was plenty for him, I would think."

I stifled my impatience at his nicety. "Anything you can tell me will help us, Leland. I need details. Did he have lovers? Did he keep to himself? Did he seem to have more money than could be accounted for from a father's generous allowance? Was he a gambler?"

"Yes, he did like to gamble." Leland seized on my last question in seeming relief. "But he generally won. Chaps always owed him money for some wager or other."

"And they paid him?"

"Oh, yes. Well, you have to, don't you? Pay up your wagers. All in good sport."

"He played cards? Dice?"

"He was not so much a gamer," Leland said. "I do not think he had a head for cards or hazard. No, he would wager on other sorts of things. Something as simple as a horse winning at Newmarket or as obscure as whether an ill housemaid would get well on Wednesday or Thursday. He had an uncanny knack of always being right."

"If he won so often, why did the other chaps wager with him?"

"Couldn't resist." Leland flashed me a smile. "One always

wanted to best him. And betting whether or a cat would walk to the left or right around the quad seemed safe. But he still managed to win."

"Perhaps," Grenville said behind us, "he enticed the cat with a bit of chicken or put ipecac in the maid's tea."

Leland gave him a horrified look over his shoulder. "Cheated?" He sounded as though we'd accused a heroic a man of being a traitor. "I do not think he would have cheated, Mr. Grenville. He was simply lucky."

"Perhaps," I conceded, more to calm him than because I agreed. "Aside from his great fortune at games, was Turner particularly liked or disliked?"

Leland shrugged. "Not particularly disliked—or liked, I suppose. He had his friends, his circle."

"Did you particularly like or dislike him?" I asked.

Leland started. "Why do you ask that?"

"You turned up for his funeral," I said. "Is that because he was a great friend, or did you wish to make certain he was buried?"

Leland gaped at me. "How can you say that? I came out of respect, Captain. I was at the ball where he died. I thought it well that I come to show his father how sorry I was." His face had gone white, his lips, tight.

"I should not have said such a thing, Leland. I'm sorry. I am simply trying to ascertain why someone would want to kill him. You say he had no particular friends but no particular enemies, that he usually won at wagers but those he bet against paid up without fuss. You paint a picture of a young man with a gaming streak but of rather neutral temperament. But this does not bear out what others have told me, nor does it explain his appalling rudeness to Mrs. Harper at the ball."

"Well, I cannot help that," Leland said weakly.

"What I am getting at is that someone might have killed Turner because he owed Turner a great deal of money. Suppose the Frenchman who attacked me was not looking for a letter, but a note of hand, perhaps a ruinous gambling debt. My bruises attest to the fact that the Frenchman was capable of violence."

"I saw no Frenchman in the Gillises' ballroom," Leland said, bewildered.

"I know." I sighed. "The man seems to have been inconveniently invisible at the critical moment. What did *you* see, Leland? Did you observe anyone trying to corner Henry Turner, perhaps leading him to that little anteroom?"

Leland shook his head. "I am sorry, Captain. I saw nothing out of the ordinary."

I hadn't thought he would have. "What is it about Turner you do not wish to tell me?"

Leland stopped walking, his walking stick arrested in midair. "I beg your pardon?"

"Mr. Grenville says you had a conversation with Turner at the ball, in which you became angry with him. What did you argue about?"

"Nothing. Nothing in particular. I'd lost a bet with him on a London-to-Brighton race recently, and perhaps he gloated a bit."

"But you paid up your wager, without fuss?"

Leland flushed. "Of course I did. Why would I not?"

I knew I was being hard on the boy, but I was frustrated, and Leland was holding something back. "You knew Turner in school, but you did not like him, that is obvious. Why not? What is it about Henry Turner that would drive someone to murder?"

Leland looked at me with wide eyes, disconcerted. "Please, I cannot answer any more questions. The air is too warm, and I am tired. I—" He broke off, flushing. "I must rest. Good day."

He spun on his heel and set off back the way we'd come. His long and hurried stride belied his claim that he was tired. He would quickly cover the three miles back to the village at that pace.

Grenville watched him go, brows raised. "Good Lord."

I feared I might have spent my last pleasant evening at the Derwent's home. Leland would tell his father, Sir Gideon, that I was a bully, and gone would be the lovely meals and warm conversation I enjoyed once a fortnight. Worse, I feared Leland's nervousness meant he had something to do with Turner's death, and I desperately hoped I was wrong.

I expected Gareth Travers to rush after him, or to berate me for browbeating his friend, but Travers simply stood and watched Leland go. He leaned on his walking stick, the April breeze stirring the brown curls beneath his hat.

"Do not mind Leland," he said. "He is embarrassed, that is all."

"Embarrassed?" I looked after the retreating figure. Leland was putting all his strength into getting away from us as fast as he could.

"There are certain things Leland does not like to speak about. It is no great secret; most chaps at Oxford knew, although one never said anything, of course."

"Knew?" I queried. "About Henry Turner?"

"Indeed. What Leland does not wish to tell you, Captain, is that Henry Turner did not keep the company of women. He preferred young men, if you understand me." He smiled. "I trust that little *on dit* will go no further than the three of us? One does not like to gossip about the dead."

CHAPTER 9

*W*ell, Gareth Travers has given us quite another motive," Grenville said as we rode back to London in his phaeton that afternoon. "Perhaps Turner was killed by a lover, one who did not want him to reveal the true nature of their liaison."

"Or a lover jealous of another," I said. "Or a man who felt threatened by him."

"Leland himself? He and Mr. Travers are very close. Perhaps Turner concluded they are closer friends than seems. Perhaps Turner even made advances to Leland, possibly threatened to expose Leland if he refused. Leland claimed Turner wasn't a blackmailer, but Turner was certainly trying his best to blackmail Mrs. Harper and Colonel Brandon. Leland seemed to protest too much. Of course, he'd not dare to admit anything, true or not. Far too dangerous if someone got hold of the wrong idea."

True. Sodomy was a hanging offense, though difficult to prove. Penetration had to be witnessed. But a man could be accused of buggery and sentenced to stand in the pillory, left to the mercy of the mob. A sodomite in the stocks at Charing

Cross could be killed by an angry enough crowd. Leland, the son of a well-respected gentleman might not suffer the stocks, but his and his father's reputations would be ruined, his sister's chances at making an advantageous match spoiled.

"I have difficulty imagining Leland killing Turner to shut him up," I said. "He would try to appeal to Turner's better nature, whether Turner had one or not. Leland is very much in the same mold as his father."

Grenville shook his head. "I sometimes pity Leland. It must be difficult being the son of so moral a man."

"I cannot say. My father was a man of rather confused morals." I stretched my leg, which had become sore, trying to find comfort on the small seat.

I thought of the bedchamber Turner's father had let me see that afternoon. Mr. Turner was not certain why I wanted to see where his son had lived when he was at home, but he'd led me to the chamber without fuss.

Inside, Mr. Turner had stopped, as though realizing all at once that his son would never inhabit the room again. Numbly, he'd straightened a chair in front of a desk, then he'd turned around and walked out without a word.

I'd wandered the cold, still chamber, not certain what I was looking for. It was not a terribly personal room. Turner's flat had been filled with his own things, as tasteless as some of them had been, but they'd been what he liked. This room had been a mere place to sleep when he visited his family. I found no indication Turner might have had male lovers, no love letters from people of either sex. In fact, I found no letters at all.

The few books in the small bookcase near the fire had been treatises on botany, one on rose gardens with colored plates. The rose garden book was nicely bound but did not look as though it had much been read. I also found several volumes of *The Gentleman's Magazine* from years past bound together. I thumbed through them, but saw little of interest, except an article on the house of one Lucius Grenville in Grosvenor Street. Sketches of his drawing rooms and ballroom were presented.

Now, as I held on to the seat while Grenville let his phaeton fly over the roads, I said, "I keep returning to that damned Frenchman. What did he want, and what has he to do with Turner?"

Grenville steered his phaeton through a ford of a small stream. Such was his skill that water splashed from the wheels but did not so much as touch our boots.

"Perhaps it is not Turner who interests him," Grenville suggested. "But Mrs. Harper and Colonel Brandon. Hence he went after Mrs. Harper's letters."

"Mrs. Harper, perhaps, but I cannot see Brandon having dealings with him for any reason. Brandon will not speak to anyone French, even émigrés who have lived in England for thirty years. *Damn all French,* is his motto."

"I did not say he and this Frenchman were friends. Perhaps they encountered one another during the war."

"I very much doubt it," I said. "Although I will not out-and-out disregard the idea. Brandon refused to have anything to do with anyone French, even when he and I and Louisa lived in France during the Peace of Amiens. Brandon talked only to Englishmen and ate only English food. He was quite a bore about it. And I never remember seeing the fellow who invaded my rooms."

Grenville smiled a little. "I encounter such Englishmen abroad. Cannot abide foreign ways, they say. Give them the *Times* and a joint of beef, and they are happy. I wonder that they bother to leave home at all."

"Travel broadens the mind, I have heard tell," I said.

Grenville barked a laugh. "You are in a cynical mood today, Lacey. But let us return to France. Did Mrs. Brandon have the same prejudice about all things French? Or did she make friends with French persons?"

"She did make friends. She simply neglected to mention them to her husband."

"Perhaps Mrs. Brandon is the connection. Could she have met this Frenchman?"

"I never heard of it. She did not mention her French friends to Colonel Brandon, but she told me of them. She never spoke of meeting a French military man, and I never saw her speaking to anyone who looked like him."

"Perhaps she simply did not tell you. I don't wish to be indelicate, Lacey . . . I know the lady is a great friend of yours . . ."

"If you are hinting Louisa Brandon she had an affair with him . . ." I broke off. "It is unlikely, but truth to tell, I have no idea."

I hadn't thought Brandon capable of betraying Louisa, but now he was in prison, trying to defend the woman who was, or at least had been, his mistress. I'd thought myself Louisa's greatest friend, that there was nothing Louisa Brandon would not confide in me. But I had to concede that if she decided to keep a liaison secret from me, she could. She was wise enough and discreet enough to hide it well.

"I will have to find this Frenchman and squeeze the truth from him," I said.

We had reached the outer limits of London, rolling fields giving way to houses with gardens and increased traffic of drays and wagons and carriages.

"Do you think your Mr. Pomeroy will have found him by now?" Grenville asked as we closed in behind a chaise and four.

"Pomeroy is nothing if not thorough. However, if he has not, then I know a gentleman who will definitely be able to put his hands on the Frenchman."

Grenville glanced sideways at me. "You mean Mr. Denis."

I nodded once. "I do."

James Denis was a man who found things, and people, for

others for an exorbitant price. The methods with which he found them were not always legal — stealing artwork and other valuables was in his line as well as punishing those who disobeyed him with death.

He and I had lived in an uneasy truce since the day a year or so ago when he'd had me kidnapped and beaten to teach me manners. The event had, in fact, *not* taught me manners, but we'd each learned exactly how far we could push the other.

Earlier this spring, I had found the culprit who'd murdered one of his lackeys, and Denis had expressed gratitude. In return, he'd told me where in France my wife lived, leaving it up to me whether I sent for her or sought her out or left her alone. I was still a bit annoyed with him over his dealings in the affair of Lady Clifford's necklace, but I couldn't say I'd been surprised.

Grenville never approved of my visiting Denis. He knew of my uncertain temper and was convinced that one day I would go too far and induce Denis to rid himself of a troublesome captain once and for all. Grenville was likely right.

"He has told me he will own me outright," I said. "If so, I might as well make use of him."

"The more favors he does you, the more favors he can call in," Grenville said.

"It has gone far beyond that already." James Denis had said he would snare me, and I already felt that web closing about me.

Grenville drove me all the way to Grimpen Lane. Bartholomew joined me there, descending from Grenville's coach and making his determined way toward the bake shop and my rooms, as though resolute that I'd not be assaulted today.

"Come to the theatre tonight," Grenville said as he gathered his reins. "My box at Covent Garden."

I felt tired, wanting to stretch and yawn. "I'm not certain

I'm in the mood for frivolity. Funerals tend to dampen my spirits."

"Come anyway. I have invited Mr. Bennington and Basil Stokes. I will introduce you, and you can interrogate them."

"That puts a different complexion on things." I tipped my hat. "Thank you I will attend."

Grenville told me goodbye, turned his phaeton in a complicated move, and signaled his team on.

Bartholomew had already lit a fire by the time I entered my rooms. Mrs. Beltan brought me my post and some coffee. She'd been quite distressed at the attack on me, but she informed me no suspicious person had come near the place while I'd been gone. She'd kept watch specially.

Certainly, nothing had been disturbed. I thanked her, read my post, and wrote my letters for the day. Sir Montague Harris had written that Brandon's trial was scheduled for the fourteenth of the month, one week from now. I gritted my teeth. I needed to find firm information that would acquit Brandon, and soon.

Sir Montague had also fixed an appointment to meet me the next day. I looked forward to discussing things with him, because too many questions swam in my head. I wrote a note accepting the appointment, then I wrote to James Denis asking if he knew anything of my Frenchman, and if not, could he find out?

Denis had an uncanny way of being aware of everything involving me, so I would not be surprised if he already knew the Frenchman's name, where he came from, and whether he enjoyed fishing in the Seine.

I posted the letters, ate the bread and butter Bartholomew had procured for me, and took a hackney to Newgate prison.

Brandon was not best pleased to see me. His cheekbones looked sunken, and untidy bristles covered his chin.

"What do you want?" he growled as I was shown in.

"To save your hide," I answered. "Sit down and let me ask you questions."

He would not sit. Brandon stood stiffly in the center of the room, ever the officer, and eyed me with chill dislike. "If you have come to further impugn Mrs. Harper, you may leave at once."

I dragged a chair in front of the meager fire and sat. If he wanted to freeze in the center of the chamber, that was his own business. "I have met Mrs. Harper. I believe you are both fools."

His eyes widened. "You met her?"

"Yes. She was attempting to search Turner's rooms for whatever letter he had of yours and hers. I am trying to decide how the letter came to be in his possession at all."

"I have no idea," Brandon shot back.

His indignation was so prompt and so adamant that I believed him.

"What I wish to know," I continued, "is why you and Turner entered the anteroom at eleven o'clock and left it together a few minutes later."

"I told you. I called him out. He refused."

"No, that was your lie for the magistrate—you claimed you resented Turner's intentions to Mrs. Harper. But we both know Turner's only interest in Mrs. Harper was her liaison with you. Did you meet him to fix a time to exchange money for the letter? Or did you make the exchange then?"

"I do not need to answer you. You are not a magistrate or a judge."

"Damn you, but you are obstinate. I am trying to prove you did not kill Turner. If you'd already made the exchange for the letter, then you'd have no reason to kill him. Your dealing with him would be over."

"It is none of your business what I did in that room," he said stiffly.

"Very well. Perhaps they will let you weave the rope for your inevitable hanging, because that is what you are doing."

"That is preposterous."

"No more preposterous than you taking Turner aside and driving a knife into his heart."

Brandon looked away.

I grew impatient. "Mrs. Harper believes you killed him, and you believe Mrs. Harper killed him. You are a fine pair. You might be pleased to know she did not kill him when she found him. A witness saw all she did in that room. While it was true she searched Turner's coat for the letter—which she did not find—she did not murder him."

He started. I saw it dawn on him he might be mistaken, that he might be in Newgate for no reason at all.

Then he rearranged his expression. "None of this is your business, Lacey. Leave it alone."

"I truly believe you did go to the anteroom at eleven to make the exchange," I said. "Turner probably did not trust you enough to meet you somewhere too privately. You are a man of uneven temper after all. Mrs. Harper, he might have handled, but you were a different matter. If he meets you in the ante-room, and you try to obtain the letter by violence, he can cry out. People nearby would come to see what was the matter."

"If that is true, then why did he not call out when he was stabbed?"

"I have thought of that. I believe he trusted the person who stabbed him. Or did not believe they had the strength to hurt him. He was not expecting it."

"A woman, then," Brandon said.

"Perhaps. Or a male lover. I have learned Turner preferred men to women. That fact might make any of the gentlemen present at the ball a candidate."

Brandon made a face. "Such a thing is too disgusting to even contemplate."

The unimaginative Colonel Brandon would never understand or condone such goings-on. I'd felt much the same until I'd become acquainted with two officers during the war, who'd always spent the night before battle with each other. We all, except Brandon, had known but said nothing, and the two in question fought the more fiercely for each other the next day. When one was finally killed, the other had sunk into so much grief he'd retired his commission and returned to England. Those officers had loved as strongly as any devoted husband and wife, or any man and his longtime mistress.

I said none of this to Brandon, however.

"That lover might be your savior, sir. But let us return to your meeting with Turner. How much money did he want?"

"Five hundred guineas."

My jaw dropped. "Good God." A gentleman could live for a year on five hundred guineas. Many gentlemen, indeed, entire families, lived on far less. "That is a princely sum. You paid it?"

"It is what he asked," Brandon said.

Brandon was wealthy enough to have come up with the money. I would query his man of business, make him tell me if Brandon actually did liquidate five hundred guineas.

"You did not have five hundred guineas in your pocket when you were arrested," I said. "Pomeroy would have mentioned that. So you must have given it to Turner. In return, he gave you the letter."

"So you say," Brandon replied, too calm. "I did not have a letter in my pocket, did I?"

"I know." I stood up and faced him. "So what did you do with it?"

He met my gaze, his eyes so cold he froze me through. "I have told you, Lacey, leave it be."

"That letter could save your life."

"You have called me foolish," he said softly. "But you are the biggest fool of all."

"Help me, God damn you."

"I told you, I do not want your help." Brandon's jaw tightened. "Now go, before I call the turnkey to throw you out."

"It would serve you right if I let you rot," I said savagely. I wanted very much to throttle him, could feel the satisfaction of my hands closing on his neck. "But I care too much for Louisa to do that."

"I know you care for her. I am sure you will now go to her and comfort her."

I backed away to prevent myself from striking him. "You do not understand what you have. You never did."

His eyes narrowed, chill and hard. "Get out."

I left him.

I felt unclean as I made my way, angry and shaking, back through Ludgate Hill and Fleet Street toward Covent Garden.

Brandon hated me so much. I'd given up my entire life for him, had tried to be the man he wanted to make, and I'd failed. I'd tried to please him just as I'd tried to please my father, and got nothing for my pains either time.

Louisa had once told me that what Brandon could not forgive was that I'd taken her side when things had gone wrong between them. I'd stood behind Louisa, and he'd hated me since that day.

I had not tried very hard to heal the breach. I'd been too wounded by him, both physically and inside my heart.

Now Brandon needed me, and he knew it. Why he was being so bloody obtuse, I did not understand. I could not believe even Brandon would take himself to the gallows to spite me.

As I rolled along in the hackney, I tried to calm myself and look at things logically. I went over the conversation I'd just had with Brandon, pulling out the facts I'd learned.

If Brandon *had* made the exchange with Turner at eleven o'clock—the letter for the five hundred guineas—several of my assumptions had to change. Imogene Harper would not have been searching Turner's rooms for the letter if she knew

Brandon already had it. She'd let me believe that had been her purpose in looking through Turner's coat when she'd found him dead and had not corrected me.

When Pomeroy had searched Turner's body, he never would have missed something so obvious as a bank draft for five hundred guineas. Therefore, if Brandon had given Turner the money, then Imogene Harper had removed the cheque or the cash when she'd delved the dead Turner's pockets.

What then, my mind prodded me, *did she come to Turner's rooms to find?*

Brandon had done *something* with the letter he'd purchased from Turner. He'd left the anteroom just after eleven and stepped into a private alcove with Mrs. Harper. She was the most logical person to whom he would have passed the letter.

Perhaps Brandon had decided to trust no one but himself and had refused to give Mrs. Harper the paper. Or perhaps Turner had promised to bring him the letter at a later date, and Brandon had paid him the money anyway like an idiot.

I rubbed my temples in frustration. If I could trace the letter and the money, I would be happy, indeed.

Putting my hands on the murderer would make me even happier.

By the time I arrived home, I had calmed somewhat and turned back to my plans. Tonight at the theatre, I would meet and interview Mr. Bennington and Mr. Stokes. If nothing else, they might be able to give me more ideas about what had happened the night of the ball.

I let Bartholomew draw a bath for me, then he helped me dress in my dark blue regimentals. As I attached the last of the silver cords across my chest, someone knocked on the outer door. Bartholomew darted into the front room to answer and returned quickly.

"Mrs. Brandon, sir," he said.

CHAPTER 10

*L*ouisa was staring mutely into the fire when I emerged. She wore a drab, long-sleeved, high-waisted gown and a woolen shawl that hung limply from her shoulders. A bonnet trimmed in green silk ribbon lay on the table.

My usual course in greeting her would be to take her hands and kiss her cheek, but when Louisa turned to me, her white face and haunted eyes made me stop.

"I thought Lady Aline was preparing to take you to Dorset," I said.

Louisa reached for my hands. "She is. But I could not remain in the house any longer. The walls seemed to press on me. Aline is a dear friend and my servants are loyal, but I believe they mean to keep me prisoner in my rooms." She heaved a sigh. "Why I ever thought yellow a cheerful color, I have no idea. It glares at me—laughs at me. Bloody horrible color for a sitting room."

I took her elbow and guided her to a chair. "Well, there is nothing cheerful here, so that should not worry you. You are in sore need of refreshment, and if I know Bartholomew, he's already run off to obtain it."

Louisa sank into my armchair. "I am sorry, but I simply could not stay home. I legged it, as my maid would say. Aline will be frantic, and I know it is childish of me, but at the moment, I truly do not care."

"I think I understand."

"Thank you. I somehow knew you would enter the conspiracy with me instead of scolding me and taking me home."

I smiled. "That, I will do later."

Bartholomew banged back in at that moment, carrying a tray of steaming things. He set down the tray and poured out a mug of coffee. "You get that into you, ma'am," he said, handing it to her. "And a few of these sausages. You'll be right as rain."

Louisa fell upon them hungrily. "My maids believe thin slices of bread and weak tea are all my constitution will abide," she said as she ate. "Aline simply keeps plying the brandy. I shall be in a sad state before long."

"I will send instructions to fatten you up," I said. "Is that why you fled? In search of food?"

Louisa dabbed her mouth with a handkerchief when she finished, and Bartholomew removed the empty plate and the tray. "The magistrate questioned me. Sir Nathaniel from Bow Street, I mean, along with your Sir Montague Harris."

"In the Bow Street House? I hope not." I thought of the smell of unwashed bodies in the lower rooms, the dirty, callused palms thrust out for coins.

"No, they came to me. They asked me all sorts of awful questions. Had I known my husband was having an affair with Mrs. Harper? What had he told me about Mr. Turner? Did Aloysius behave in a peculiar fashion that night? How did he not remember bringing the knife with him? Did I know beforehand if he would kill Turner? And other nonsense."

"I will speak to Sir Montague," I said, my temper rising. "They should not have harangued you."

"No, no, do not grow angry with him. The pair of them

obviously did not think me an accessory. They see me as the poor, betrayed wife, deceived by her husband." She gave me a bitter look. "Which is what I am."

I took her hand. "Louisa, I will do everything in my power to restore him to you."

Louisa's fingers briefly tightened on mine then flowed away. "I have been lying awake these last few nights thinking of you trying to save him. And sometimes, in the small hours of the morning, when I am most alone, I am not certain I still want you to."

I gazed pensively at her, unsure of what to say.

She went on, "Oh, I do not mean I wish for him to be hanged. Of course not. But I believe I do not want him to come home."

"Louisa . . ."

"I know now what you felt when Carlotta left you. I felt sorry for you at the time, but I see that then I did not truly understand. To live your whole life for someone, to stand by them and to care for them, no matter what happens, and then to have them betray you, throwing your devotion back in your face, is the hardest thing a person can bear. You feel foolish for having spent so much time on such an unworthy person. You feel as though you've given everything but been found wanting." She broke off, her eyes filling. "And I am so bloody tired of weeping. If you pat my hand, Gabriel, I shall never forgive you."

I took a handkerchief from my pocket and handed it to her in silence.

I knew Brandon *had* found Louisa wanting. He'd told her so once, and not tried very hard to hide his disappointment in her inability to have children. Louisa had been forced to stand by a few nights ago while Brandon was arrested, and look into the face of the woman Brandon admitted was his mistress. I thought she was holding up well, considering.

"What you do with him after his trial will be your choice," I said. "Leave him, obtain a legal separation—that is for you to decide. I will help you as much as I can, use my few connections to bring about a happy ending for you."

Louisa lifted her head. "Gabriel, take me to France."

I started. "To France?"

"Yes." She crumpled my handkerchief in her hand. "You told me you wanted to go to France to find Carlotta. I offered to accompany you. Let us go, and leave London and all of this behind."

Her eyes blazed fire in her pale face. Despite her anguish, she looked beautiful, resolute and glittering, like a diamond.

"Louisa, if you hie off to France with me while your husband endures a murder trial, you will never live it down."

"What does it matter? We are ruined. I am ruined. Even if Aloysius is found innocent, we shall always be known for it—the colonel who was tried for murder, arrested in front of his mistress and his wife. It will follow us all our lives."

"I know," I said.

She sprang to her feet and began pacing. "I want no part of it. Take me to France. I am certain Paris will be slightly more exciting than a country village in Dorset."

"Suggest a journey to Paris to Lady Aline. I will persuade her to accompany you."

Louisa stopped and faced me, two dark red spots on her cheeks. "I do not wish to go with Aline. I wish to go with you."

I studied her flushed face, her brittle eyes, her bosom as it rose with her agitated breath. If she had offered me this in 1814—after Napoleon had been temporarily defeated, when France was open again—I would have gone with her in a flash.

I would have taken her to Paris and bought her frocks and drunk wine with her while the English delegation decided what to do with France and the restored Bourbon king. I would have abandoned honor and everything else to be with her, to take her hand and explore the world with her, to never to return to England again.

I would have done it. I would have done it in 1815, after Waterloo, when my life was nothing and the Continent was free and open once again. I would have fled with her to begin anew.

But not now. Now, I'd begun to build something from the wreck of my life. I'd laid a foundation with my friendship with Grenville, discovered an interest in investigating crime with Pomeroy and Sir Montague Harris. I had made friends with the Derwents and Lady Aline Carrington, Mr. Thompson of the Thames River patrol, and my landlady, Mrs. Beltan.

And I had met Lady Breckenridge.

I thought that in Lady Breckenridge I'd found a friend who understood me, one who could keep me from making too great an idiot of myself. I remembered her lips on mine the day before I'd journeyed to Epsom, and how much I'd liked that feeling.

I had forged tenuous things that were new and needed to be explored. I now had something to lose.

I cared for Louisa more than I'd ever cared for myself. But I no longer wanted to give up my entire life for her.

She saw that in my eyes as I gazed at her. Her expression became one of defeat, and her shoulders drooped.

"I am sorry," I said, as though it would make any difference.

She shook her head. "I ought to have known that in the end, you would abandon me, too."

I got to my feet. "No, never abandon you. Never that." I took her hands. "I will never leave you to face anything alone. You have my word. But if we did dash away together to France, or Italy, or any number of places, you would soon grow ashamed. You would dislike yourself, and you would grow angry at me for not stopping you. You would begin to dislike me, and that I could not bear."

Tears stood in her eyes. "Gabriel."

"In any case, I am horrible to live with. Ask Bartholomew."

She did not smile. Louisa stood looking at me for a moment longer, then she lowered her gaze and walked away from me. She moved to the window and stood looking out at the gray drizzle that had begun.

I did not know what else to say to her. I felt numb.

"I should not have asked you," Louisa said. "Forgive me."

Her back was slim, but straight and strong. She might not believe she could weather this problem, but I knew she could. Louisa had a core of strength that the stoutest general would envy. Her strength had taken her through the hellish living on the Iberian peninsula, and through the grief that both Brandon and I had put her through.

"Louisa," I said gently. "I swear to you that I will get his charges dismissed. I will bring Aloysius Brandon home. Because as much as I despise him for what he has done to you, I do not believe he committed murder."

"Why not? The rest of the world does."

"What did Sir Montague and Sir Nathaniel tell you?"

She turned around. "They said Aloysius had reason to kill Mr. Turner. He had been seen growing angry with him, they had gone off alone together where Aloysius claims he called the man out. Aloysius named Mr. Turner a coward when he refused, and the knife was his."

"The knife." I paused. "Was the knife truly Brandon's, without question?"

"I do not know. I did not know all of his private possessions. And in any case, he admitted the knife was his."

"But he does not remember carrying it into the party. Or at least, so he says."

Louisa made an exasperated noise. "The two magistrates asked me that as well. As though I go through my husband's pockets before we leave the house. I'm not the sort of wife who dresses her husband. He has a valet for that."

"So if anyone would know about the knife, it would be the valet."

"Yes, they asked Robbins. Interviewed him quite closely. Robbins agreed the knife belonged to Brandon and said he placed the knife in the pocket of Aloysius's frock coat. Aloysius did not ask for it, but he liked to have the knife with him. Aloysius insisted he did not notice if the knife was in his pocket."

"Therefore," I said, "the knife is Brandon's in all likelihood. What we must discover is how it got from Brandon's pocket into the wound."

"Most people think he put it there," Louisa said.

"Well, I am one person who does not. But it would not be difficult to steal the knife from him. Someone could easily dip into his pocket. The most likely person to have taken the knife is, of course, Mrs. Harper."

"You believe she is a murderess, not simply a Jezebel?"

"I do not know yet what I believe. She lied to me, that is certain. Brandon is lying too. Once I clear out the lies of these two, I believe the solution will present itself."

Louisa sagged. "I no longer know what to believe."

I went to her and put my hands on her shoulders. "Please trust me. I will do whatever I can to make your world better for you. I love you that much."

The tears that had been threatening to fall now spilled down her cheeks. "I love you too, Gabriel. I always have."

I kissed her forehead. Her curls were like silk beneath my lips.

It was difficult not to embrace her, not to whisper that the world could go to hell, that we could leave England together.

But I resisted. I stepped back from her and let her go.

In silence, Louisa gathered her shawl and her bonnet. She would not look at me as she tied the green silk ribbon under her chin. "For some reason," she said, trying to keep her voice light, "I feel as though I should be wearing black."

"Have you seen your husband since he has gone to Newgate?"

"No. How could I?"

"Go and see him," I said. "Have Sir Montague take you."

Louisa looked at me in anger but she said nothing. She finished tying the ribbon then she gathered her shawl and walked to the door. "Goodbye, Gabriel," she said.

And she was gone.

~

MUCH DIVIDED IN MIND, I SET OFF FOR COVENT GARDEN Theatre.

The arched piazza leading to the theatre stretched along the northwest side of Bow Street, its soaring columns sheltering theatregoers, game girls, pickpockets, and servants from the April rain and wind. I walked among ladies and gentlemen dressed in the finest style as well as girls in tawdry gowns picked from secondhand stores or parish charities.

A lord descending from a carriage marked with a coat of arms was instantly surrounded by beggars with hands outstretched. The lord scattered a few pennies among them before he lifted his head and swept past them. His footman swatted at the group, telling them to clear off, then hopped back onto the coach and rattled away to no doubt drink and dice with the coachman.

I stopped to bow to a gentleman I recognized and then his wife, a large woman with feathers balancing atop a mass of gray curls. I had met the man through Grenville, and the three of us exchanged polite pleasantries. Just as the gentleman drew his wife on toward the doors of the theatre, someone hissed at me from the shadow of a pillar.

"Lacey!"

I waited until the gentleman and his lady had entered the theatre, then I peered into the darkness under the piazza.

"Marianne," I said. "What are you doing?"

She stepped from the shadow. She wore blue velvet trimmed with gold and silver tissue, and a bonnet with a long blue feather. She ruined this semblance of respectability by lurking behind the column like a street courtesan.

"Is *he* here?" she asked.

"I am to meet Grenville in his box, yes."

Her tone grew bitter. "He has come to see Mrs. Bennington. He suggested a gathering afterward with her to his friends. I heard him as he arrived."

"Did you hide here and spy on him?"

"Well, if I did not spy on him, I would never know where he was, would I?" she said heatedly. "He has not come to see me for days. He does not even write me, and his servants are useless for information."

"He and I spent the last two days in Epsom. At a funeral, if you must know. It was not a frivolous outing."

"He might have been plowing a field, for all he told me. And now, he arrives, sweet as you please, to ogle Mrs. Bennington in yet another performance."

I remembered Grenville's evasiveness about Mrs. Bennington. I did not want to lie to reassure Marianne, but she was becoming most obsessed about the subject.

"Grenville invited me tonight so I'd have a chance to speak to more of the guests from the Gillises' ball," I said.

Marianne stepped closer to me. "If you'd like to know something interesting, *he* seemed quite keen to go to that ball. Kept saying there was something he had to do there."

My interest perked. "Did he? He seems to have spoken to you a little about it, in any case."

"Mrs. Bennington was also there. I can imagine what he had in mind."

"Well, I cannot." I became aware of people glancing our way as they passed, of their raised brows and disdainful looks. "I must go in, Marianne. Go home and cease lurking under pillars. Someone might mistake your intentions."

"I believe I will stay," she retorted. "I will be interested to see what direction he takes when he leaves—and with whom."

"You'll catch cold. Go and wait in my rooms if you cannot bring yourself to go home. I know you have a key. Bartholomew has the fire hot. If he is there, you can interrogate him about Grenville's motives, if you wish, though I imagine he knows not much more than I do."

Marianne scowled. "Gentlemen so enjoy giving orders."

"I know better than to expect you to obey. Use my rooms if you want to keep warm; if not, wait out here in the rain, and follow him as you please."

Her expression darkened. Marianne stepped back into the shadow of the column, but she leaned there and did not walk away.

I left her and entered the theatre.

Grenville's box was located almost directly above the stage, where the viewers could look down on the drama below as well as see who waited in the wings. Comfortable mahogany chairs stood in two rows with tables between them for lorgnettes or gloves or glasses of claret and brandy.

The box was filled with gentlemen tonight, not a lady in sight, which made it, in my opinion, rather dreary. But I was interested enough in the gentlemen present to tolerate the absence of female company.

An empty chair waited next to Grenville, I assumed for me. Grenville introduced me all around, beginning with Basil Stokes.

Mr. Stokes was tall and white haired. As usual in a man of his age, he had a large belly from years of consuming at least a bottle a day of port, but he did not have the usual gout. He had a booming voice, and, when he greeted me, heads throughout the theatre turned in our direction.

Stokes was from Hampshire, which, he assured me, afforded excellent hunting and fishing if I ever wanted to take the trouble. He laughed loudly and made a comment about the large bosom of an actress who had just entered the stage.

The actress, indeed a buxom young lady, heard him. She simpered, and the audience guffawed.

Mr. Bennington was a complete contrast to Stokes. He was about my age, an inch or two shorter than I was, and very lean, as though he ate sparingly and drank little. He had a long face and a longer expression, a man devoted to sardonic observation. His handshake was rather limp.

"Pleased to meet you, my dear Captain Lacey. Have you come to watch my wife stun the masses of London again?" He said it with no pride, only a drawl of resignation.

"I have seen her perform," I said. "She is a lady of great talent."

"Oh, yes, indeed," Mr. Bennington said. "Her reputation is well deserved."

I thought I heard a slight emphasis on the word *reputation,* but I could not be certain.

The other gentlemen in the box were club fodder, gentlemen I'd met in passing while visiting Grenville or going with him to Tattersall's or Gentleman Jackson's boxing rooms. They greeted me with varying degrees of enthusiasm, some warm, some indifferent, each making a polite comment or two.

We settled down to watch the performance, which was already well into the first act. As usual, the restless audience talked amongst themselves, shouted to the actors, drank and ate.

In our box, the conversation turned to sport, namely pugilism and the best exhibition fighters. I leaned to Grenville and apologized under my breath for being late.

"Not at all," he said. "I take it some new twist in the investigation?"

"No. Marianne Simmons."

Grenville started. "I beg your pardon?"

"She accosted me under the piazza outside," I said.

Grenville's mouth hardened. "Why the devil is she under the piazza outside?"

"She must be gone by now. I told her to go to my rooms and get warm."

Grenville's body stiffened and his gaze became fixed. He brought one closed fist to his mouth. "Damnation."

Below us, the audience began to applaud, then to stamp, then to cheer, as the lovely Mrs. Bennington glided onto the stage. She waited, poised and gracious, while London adored her.

Grenville rose from his chair and woodenly made for the door of the box. In alarm, I followed him, excusing myself to the other gentlemen. I heard murmurs below as people noticed Grenville's abrupt exit.

Outside the box, the halls were deserted. Grenville swiftly walked away from me. By the time I reached the stairs, he'd already gone down, flinging himself out of the theatre without stopping for his hat and coat.

I went in pursuit, leaving the relative warmth of the theatre for the cold wind and rain of the night.

Marianne had not gone. Just as I entered the piazza, Grenville yanked her out from behind a pillar. I heard him begin, "What the devil?"

I quickly stepped to them. "Do not begin an altercation in front of the theatre, I beg you," I said to Grenville. "It will be all over England by morning if you do. Take Marianne and have things out in my rooms. They are a short walk from here."

Grenville swung to me, his eyes narrowing in anger.

"Marianne has the key. Go, Grenville. You cannot be such a fool as to have a falling-out with your mistress in front of Covent Garden Theatre while Mrs. Bennington plays inside."

Grenville drew himself up, but the sense of my words penetrated his anger. He seized Marianne's hand. "Come along."

She tried to resist. "Go," I told her. "Shout all you want to once you get there. Mrs. Beltan has gone home. The house is quite empty."

Without waiting for them to depart, I turned on my heel and stalked back into the theatre.

By the time I entered the box, Mrs. Bennington had finished her scene and left the stage. The audience was talking loudly, laughing and gesturing, some, I saw to my alarm, at Grenville's box. They completely ignored the new scene and the actors desperately trying to say their lines over the noise.

"How strange," Mr. Bennington drawled as I resumed my seat. "I have never before observed anyone *leave* a theatre once my wife has taken the stage. And Mr. Grenville, no less. The event will be the talk of the town."

CHAPTER 11

*B*ennington looked amused, not angry. Basil Stokes boomed, "Yes, what happened? Did the fellow take ill?"

"He was not feeling his best," I said. "I am not certain he will return."

"Ah, well," said a gentleman I'd met at White's. "We must endeavor to endure the finest claret and best seats in the theatre without him."

Several men chuckled.

The play dragged on, a lackluster affair. I found little trouble turning the conversation with Mr. Bennington next to me to the events at the Gillises' ball. "Did you know Mr. Turner well?" I asked him.

"No," Bennington said, rolling his claret glass between long fingers. "I do not have much acquaintance in London, after living so long on the Continent. He was rather a rude fellow, and I had little interest in him."

"Did you see him enter the anteroom that night? Just before he was killed, I mean?"

"Oh, yes. He went in about a quarter to the hour. I told the Runner. The Runner is a friend of yours, I believe. He mentioned you."

"He was one of my sergeants in the army," I said. "So you saw Turner enter, but no one else?"

"Not really paying attention, I am afraid. I know you wish to get your colonel off, and I commend your loyalty, but I would not be surprised if Brandon really did peg the fellow. He was red-faced and angry with Turner the entire night."

I silently cursed Colonel Brandon, as I had many times since this business began, for being so obvious. "Any man might be angry with another, but murder is a bit extreme, do you not think?"

"Not in this case." Bennington took a sip of his claret and assumed a philosophical expression. "Turner was a boor. It was long past time someone stuck a knife into him. I truly believe a man should be hung for having appalling manners. They are as criminal in my opinion as a pickpocket. More so. Pickpockets can be pleasant fellows. So charming that you do not realize your handkerchief or purse has been lifted until too late."

"You believe Turner was murdered because he was rude?"

"He ought to have been. I believe our Mr. Turner died because he was obnoxious to a lady. Mrs. Harper, I mean. The colonel defended her. He should not be hanged for that."

As he said his last words, the audience began their cheering and stamping again as Mrs. Bennington returned for her next scene.

Interested, I turned to watch her. As before, she waited until the applause died down, and then she began her speeches.

I could not help but be entranced. Mrs. Bennington was young, with golden hair and a round, pretty face. But her girlish looks belied her voice, which was strong and rich. She spoke her lines with conviction, as if the soul of the person written on the page suddenly filled her. She was still Mrs.

Bennington, and yet she flowed into her character at the same time. She had a voice of sublime sweetness and a delivery that made the listener's troubles fade and fall away.

Mr. Bennington poked me with his elbow. "I will procure an introduction if you like."

He was smirking. I knew he needled me, but at the same time, I did want the introduction. "Please," I said.

When Mrs. Bennington finished her scene and left the stage, the magic faded. Apparently, that was to be her last appearance, because the audience began to drift away, uninterested in the rest of the play.

Mr. Bennington rose. "Shall we greet her backstage and tell her how splendid she was?"

I had wanted to stay and become better acquainted with Basil Stokes, but Bennington seemed ready to fly to his wife's side. Before I could say anything, Stokes broke in.

"I hear you are all agog for pugilism, Lacey," he bellowed in my ear. "Come to Gentleman Jackson's tomorrow, and I'll show you some boxing." He grinned and winked.

I accepted. I had, with Grenville, attended Gentleman Jackson's on occasion and had even gone a few practice rounds in my shirtsleeves, but to tell the truth, I could take or leave the sport. However, the prospect of questioning Stokes was not to be missed.

I agreed then let Mr. Bennington escort me out.

"He is so terribly hearty, is he not?" Bennington asked. He had to raise his voice over the other theatregoers who poured out of boxes. "So appallingly English. So John Bull. He is what I went to Italy to escape."

He rolled his eyes, oblivious of the disapproving stares he received from the John Bulls around us.

As we walked, I wondered why, if Bennington had gone to Italy to escape utterly English Englishmen, had he returned?

I followed Bennington down a flight of stairs into the

bowels of the theatre, then through a short corridor to the green room. Mrs. Bennington was there, surrounded by flowers and young dandies.

The gentlemen present could have been cast from the same mold as Henry Turner. They wore intricately tied cravats, high-pointed collars, long-tailed frock coats, black trousers or pantaloons, and polished slippers. They varied only in the type of cravat pin they sported—diamond, emerald, gold—and in the color of their hair. Brown, black, golden, or very fair hair was curled and draped in similar fashion from head to head.

I did not miss the flash of annoyance in Mrs. Bennington's eyes as she beheld her husband. She obviously wanted to bask in the attention of these lads who brought her bouquets and kissed her hand. Bennington ruined the mood.

From the twitch of Bennington's lips, he knew precisely what he'd done.

"My dear," he said, drawing out the words as he took her hands. "You were too wonderful this evening. Mr. Grenville was so overset with emotion he had to flee. He left Captain Lacey behind as his emissary. Captain, may I present my wife, Claire Bennington. Claire, Captain Lacey, a very dear friend of Lucius Grenville."

Mrs. Bennington had been looking at me in a rather vacant fashion, but at the announcement that I was Grenville's friend, her expression changed to one of trepidation.

She had hazel eyes, an indeterminate shade between brown and green. Her lips were full and red, and they parted slightly while she gazed at me. As I bowed over her hand, I realized what Louisa and Lady Aline had meant when they said she was an empty vessel. Except for that flash of trepidation, she seemed a rather vacuous creature.

Her hand was soft and not strong, the flesh yielding to the press of my fingers. Her hair was artificially curled; close to, it looked frizzled from too many times with a crimping iron, the color dulled with dye.

"Greet the good captain, my dear," Mr. Bennington prodded.

Mrs. Bennington jerked, as though she were an automaton needing a push to begin its trick. "How do you do?" she said. Her voice, too, was rather breathy, holding none of the quality she'd had on stage. "Grady," she said to an older woman who was tidying the room, seemingly the only person with anything to do. "Bring the captain some port."

"None for your husband, eh?" Bennington said. He gave his wife a deprecating look and strolled away.

Mrs. Bennington had not let go of my hand. Now she pressed it tighter, her nails sinking into my skin. "Captain, I am glad you have come. I must speak with you."

"I am all attentive, madam," I said.

Mrs. Bennington shot a furtive glance at the dandies, who were eyeing me with jealous dislike. "Not here. Later. Alone. In my rooms. Grady will tell you." She released me abruptly as her maid approached with a glass of port carefully balanced on a tray. Grady stopped in front of me, and Mrs. Bennington turned away and seized the arm of the nearest dandy.

The young man gave me a triumphant look and led her off. Grady, who had far less vacant eyes than her mistress, handed me the port. As I drank, she gave me instructions. I was to appear at number 23, Cavendish Square, at half-past three and be admitted to her mistress. I was to come alone, no followers, excepting, if I wanted, a servant.

Grady marched away, leaving me with the port and nothing to do but watch the dandies fall all over Mrs. Bennington. Mr. Bennington joined the throng and made cutting remarks to his wife's face, looking amused when she did not notice.

I realized, listening to him, that Bennington severely disliked his wife. It was clear in his drawling comments, in the looks he shot her when her attention was elsewhere. He viewed her as contemptible, and he despised her.

Why then had he married the woman? He might have

stayed on the Continent, happily avoiding hearty Englishmen as long as he liked. But he had married Claire Bennington and then returned to England with her. It was a puzzle among the other puzzles I needed to solve.

I stayed in the room until I could politely take my leave. When I told Mrs. Bennington good night, she shot me a meaningful look that was plain for all to see. Her husband saw it. He gave me a beatific smile and shook my hand.

"I hope I have made your visit to the theatre worthwhile," he said, his teeth gleaming.

I responded with some polite phrase and departed.

As I walked home through the rain, I let the vivid picture of Bennington killing Henry Turner fill my mind. Bennington had made no bones about the fact that he thought Turner had deserved to be murdered. The look Bennington had given me as I'd departed his wife's dressing room had been filled of self-deprecating amusement, but also of anger. He knew bloody well that later I'd be visiting Mrs. Bennington and that he would be expected to keep out of the way.

I longed to tell Bennington that I had no intention of making him a cuckold, but I didn't think he'd believe me. I would have refused Mrs. Bennington's invitation altogether, but she intrigued me with the worry in her eyes, and also, she'd been at the Gillises' ball.

As I turned to Russel Street, making my way to Grimpen Lane, a few game girls called to me from the shadows. They laughed when I merely tipped my hat and did not respond.

They knew by now I treated street girls with kindness and did not turn them over to the watch or to the reformers. But they saw no reason not to capitalize on that kindness.

"Come, now, Captain," one called. "I'll only ask a shilling. No better bargain in London."

"Tuppence," another girl insisted. Her voice was hoarse, her throat raw from coughing. "Only tuppence fer you. 'Cause it wouldn't be work for me."

The girls bantered with me often, but I was never tempted by them. The poor things were always wracked with some illness or other, a few of them with syphilis. It was not simply pity and caution of disease that kept me from them, however. Most of them were younger than my daughter, and all were accomplished thieves. Their flats, as they called the gentlemen who hired them, never paid enough, and the girls saw no reason why they should not lift the handkerchief of anyone passing to sell for an extra bob or two.

A year or so ago, I'd helped one of their number, Black Nancy, by taking her to Louisa Brandon. Louisa, used to taking in strays, had found the girl a place as a maid at an inn near Islington.

I distributed a shilling to each of them and told them to go get themselves warm.

"A fine gentleman yer are," one said. She reached out to stroke my arm, and I backed quickly out of reach. I wanted to keep the contents of my pockets. They laughed, and I tipped my hat again and walked away.

When I entered Grimpen Lane, I half expected to hear the altercation between Marianne and Grenville filling the street. All was quiet, however, even when I opened the door that led up to my rooms.

In the past, the staircase had been painted with a mural of shepherds and shepherdesses frolicking across green fields. Now the paint had mostly faded except for the occasional shepherdess peering out of the gloom. Mrs. Beltan didn't bother painting the staircase because it would be an extra expense, and no one saw it but her boarders.

I climbed the stairs slowly, my knee stiff from the weather. At the top of the stairs, my door, once ivory and gold, now gray, stood ajar.

I eyed it in irritation. If Marianne and Grenville had departed for more comfortable surroundings, they might have at least closed the door and kept out the cold.

I heard a quiet step on the stairs above me. I looked up to see Bartholomew descending from the attics, his tread surprisingly soft for so large a young man. When I opened my mouth to speak, he thrust a finger over his lips, urging me to silence.

I peered through the half-open door and saw Marianne and Grenville close together in the middle of the room. Marianne's arms hung at her sides, but she looked up at Grenville as he cradled her face in his hands. As I watched, he leaned to kiss her.

I shot Bartholomew a surprised glance. He shrugged. I signaled for him to follow me, and he tiptoed down the stairs and past the doorway to me, then we both descended quietly to the street.

"The argument seems to be over," I said.

"I hope so, sir. They shouted for the longest time."

"Well, let us hope they have come to some accordance. Are you hungry?"

"Famished, sir."

I suggested the Rearing Pony, a tavern in Maiden Lane, and Bartholomew readily agreed. We walked through Covent Garden square to Southampton Street and so to Maiden Lane, where we ate beefsteak and drank ale like every good John Bull.

It was there James Denis found me.

Denis was still a relatively young man, being all of thirty. But his dark blue eyes were cold and held the shrewdness of a born trader or dictator. If Emperor Bonaparte had met James Denis over a negotiating table, Bonaparte would have ceded everything and fled, and considered himself lucky to get away so easily.

I was surprised to see Denis in such a lowly place as a tavern. He kept a wardrobe as costly and fashionable as Grenville's and lived in a fine house in Curzon Street. He did not often venture out to see others; he had others brought to him.

Two burly gentlemen flanked him to the right and left, former pugilists he employed to keep him safe. He studied me for a moment or two, his eyes as enigmatic as ever, then he gestured to the seat next to me.

"May I?" Denis wasn't asking my permission. He simply said the polite words for benefit of those around us.

"Of course," I said, also for benefit of those around us.

Bartholomew moved off the bench, swiping up his ale as he went. He sauntered across the room, where he smiled at the barmaid, Anne Tolliver, who gave him a large-hearted smile in return.

James Denis seated himself. His men took up places on nearby benches, which magically cleared of patrons. Anne approached with tankards of ale. The lackeys gladly took them, but Denis waved his away. He laid his hat on the table and folded his gloved hands over his walking stick.

"I've come about your Frenchman," he said.

I had assumed so, although, with Denis, one should never assume anything.

"I have not much more to tell you about him than what I wrote in my message," I said.

He lifted one perfectly groomed brow. "No need for more of a description. I have already found him."

"Truly? I only wrote you of it this morning."

"I heard of the incident before you journeyed to Epsom," he said. "One of my men saw the Frenchman fleeing your rooms. My man followed him across the river, but lost him in Lambeth. That at least gave me a place to begin. We found him tonight, and he is waiting at my house. He is from Paris and answers to the name of Colonel Naveau."

I had never heard of him. But my idea that he'd had a military bearing seemed to be correct.

"You could have written this information to me," I said. "And fixed an appointment for me to meet him."

"I thought you might be anxious to interview him," Denis

answered without expression. "I began to call at your rooms, but my man said he'd seen you walking toward Maiden Lane."

And he'd know I liked to come to the tavern here. I wished I could meet this "man" of his, who watched all my movements and reported them to his master.

"I have an appointment tonight," I said. "As much as I wish to interview Colonel Naveau, I will have to leave it until morning."

"I will accompany you to your appointment."

I wondered why the devil Denis was so anxious for me to see this colonel right away. "It is with a lady," I said.

His eyes flickered in surprise, then slight distaste, as though speaking with a lady should never come between a man and his business. I had never bothered to wonder why there was no *Mrs.* Denis. James Denis was cold all the way through.

"Very well, then," he said, his expression still neutral. "We will fix an appointment for breakfast tomorrow. Nine o'clock. I will tell Colonel Naveau he is welcome to spend the night with me."

I was certain Colonel Naveau would not like that arrangement one bit. I was equally certain Denis would give him no choice.

I took a casual sip of ale, as though his turning up at one of my haunts did not unnerve me. "You could not tell me, while you are here, who murdered Henry Turner?"

The corners of his mouth moved in what might be an expression of amusement in a more feeling man. "I am afraid not, Captain. I had not anticipated your colonel would get himself into trouble at a society ball, or I should have had a man in place to prevent it."

I was not sure whether he jested or not. Denis's countenance was as blank as ever as he rose to his feet. He did not shake my hand, but he bowed and took up his hat. "Until morning, then, Captain."

I nodded stiffly in return. Denis made for the door and exited, placing his hat on his head in the precise moment before he stepped outside. His lackeys fell in behind him like trained dogs.

Bartholomew drifted back to the table. "Well, that was what I call interesting," he said.

"Yes." I watched the dark doorway that Denis had exited. "I will know more what he wants tomorrow. Tonight, we will take a hackney coach to Cavendish Square and pay a call." I drank the last of my ale and thumped the tankard to the table. "No doubt Denis's man will follow and tell him exactly who we visited and why."

Bartholomew grinned, a little shakily, and then we left the tavern. The married Anne Tolliver smiled at us both as we went.

THE HOUSE IN CAVENDISH SQUARE WAS NO DIFFERENT FROM its fellows, being tall and narrow with tall, narrow windows and a tall, narrow front door with a polished knocker.

I arrived at half-past three precisely, and the maid, Grady, answered the door. She seemed used to dealing with visitors at all hours, because she calmly took my hat and ushered me upstairs to a sitting room.

The room was rather anonymous, with fashionable uphol-stered Sheraton chairs in a salmon-colored stripe and studded wood, salmon-colored swags on the windows, and cream silk on the walls. Nothing personal marred the room, as though the house's inhabitants had ordered the furnishing to be as elegant yet innocuous as possible.

I expected Mr. Bennington to pop up at any moment, drawling sarcasm about his wife receiving male visitors in the small hours of the morning. Grady must have noticed me looking for him, because she said, "Mr. Bennington is staying at his hotel tonight," and departed to fetch her mistress.

Again, I wondered at the strangeness of the Benningtons' relationship. They'd married for convenience, that was certain, but what convenience? Would a husband truly vacate the house so his wife could receive a gentleman caller?

I paced the room while I mulled this over. The room was cool despite the fire on the hearth, its anonymity shutting me out.

I turned when the door opened behind me. Claire Bennington paused on the threshold just as she'd paused on the stage earlier tonight, waiting for the adulation to die down before she spoke her lines. She was dressed in a peignoir, similar to the one Lady Breckenridge had worn when she'd received me two days ago.

The difference was that Lady Breckenridge wore her peignoir with an awareness of how it enhanced her body. I, as a man, had not been unmoved by the garment. Mrs. Bennington looked like a child in clothes too old for her.

Mrs. Bennington glided to the center of the room. She had no rehearsed lines, and she obviously found it difficult to begin. She wet her lips, but said nothing.

I was struck anew with how young she was. I'd read in newspaper articles that she was in her twenties, but she could not be far into them. She might be comely, and she might have lived in the harsh world of theatre, but she seemed far less conscious of her enticements than had the game girls to whom I'd given shillings earlier tonight.

"Mrs. Bennington," I said after the silence had stretched. "Why did you ask to see me?"

She wet her lips again and touched the lapel of my coat, her fingers light as a ghost's. "Captain Lacey," she said. "I am so very much afraid."

She let the words roll dramatically from her tongue. But I

realized that as much as she embellished her delivery, her eyes held real fear.

"Of what?" I gentled my voice. "It is all right. You may tell me."

She studied me with round eyes, then drew a breath and said, "I am afraid of Mr. Grenville."

CHAPTER 12

The statement was so unexpected that I started. "Of Grenville? Good Lord, why?"

Mrs. Bennington shuddered, her fingers trembling on my chest. "Please tell him to stay away."

"You needn't worry about Mr. Grenville," I said, trying to sound reassuring. "He might not show it at times, but he has a good and kind heart. There is no need to be afraid of him."

I felt as though I were stilling the fears of a child. Mrs. Bennington swung away from me. "Yes, there is need. He comes here, and to my rooms at the theatre, and remonstrates with me. He scolds me, grows angry when I speak to young men. Why should I not speak to young men? There is no harm in it. Mr. Bennington sees nothing wrong in my speaking with gentlemen. But Mr. Grenville will have none of it. He shouts at me." Her hazel eyes filled with tears. "He is so jealous he frightens me."

"Jealous?" I had never seen Grenville behave like a jealous lover. With the exception of his obsession with Marianne, he'd always conducted his affairs coolly, never voicing any disapprobation of the lady, no matter how she behaved.

When he ended the liaison, he departed from the lady just as coolly.

Only Marianne had ever angered him, and that was not jealousy, but frustration. Marianne could drive anyone distracted.

The idea that Grenville drove off Mrs. Bennington's suitors and took her to task for speaking to them was beyond belief.

"It is true," Mrs. Bennington said fiercely. "Ask Grady if you do not believe me. The last time he came to see me, he was in a horrible temper. He saw Mr. Carew try to kiss my hand. Mr. Grenville threw his walking stick across the room and threatened to give the poor Mr. Carew a thrashing if he ever came near me again."

Grenville had? These actions sounded more like me in a temper, not those of the man whose sangfroid London gentlemen tried to imitate.

"Forgive me, Mrs. Bennington, but I find this difficult to credit. Was this Carew behaving badly to you?"

"Indeed, no. Mr. Carew was quite the gentleman. But Mr. Grenville did not like it." Mrs. Bennington clasped her hands in a pleading gesture. "You must believe me, Captain. I am not lying. I do not know how to invent things. Mr. Bennington says it is because I have no imagination."

"Mr. Bennington should not be so rude to you."

She shrugged, as though her husband's jibes slid easily from her. "Mr. Grenville said so too. He also said I should try to obtain a divorce from Mr. Bennington. Or an annulment. I have grounds, he says, because Mr. Bennington cannot father children." She mentioned this impotency without a blush. "But I did not marry him for children. I do not want children. I could not go on the stage if I were increasing. Mr. Bennington said he would allow me to continue acting, which is the only thing I like to do. I was very popular in Italy and Milan, but I had run into a bit of difficulty with debts, you see."

"And he offered to pay them if you married him?"

"Mr. Bennington has ever so much money, from a legacy, from the Scottish branch of his family, he says. He paid my notes as though they were nothing." She toyed with the frills on her bosom. "His name is not really Bennington, you know. That's my name. He said I ought to keep it because I'm already well known by it, but I'm not supposed to tell anyone that."

I wondered how many other people she'd babbled this to, and if Bennington knew she was the kind of woman who could not keep a thing quiet.

"What is his real name?" I asked.

"Do you know, I no longer remember. It has been five years since we married. *I will be called Mr. Bennington,* he said to me. *And you are Mrs. Bennington. And none need to know any other.*" She did a fair imitation of Bennington's drawling voice, which might have amused me any other time.

I wondered. Perhaps the reason Bennington had lived in Italy was that he dared not return to England under his own name. Trouble with creditors? Or over a woman? Or some more sinister crime?

Perhaps those long-fingered hands had held a knife before, knew how to thrust it with uncanny accuracy into a heart to stop it beating.

Bennington, or whatever his true name had been, had promised to take care of Claire's debts and let her stay on the stage she loved. So that he might return to England under a new name? His wife so eclipsed him that most people thought of him, when they bothered to, as "Mrs. Bennington's husband." A good hiding place. But hiding from what?

This young woman seemed to find the arrangement perfectly acceptable, at any rate. She had what she wanted — freedom to remain on the stage and security from creditors. And she provided a blind for a husband for whom she cared nothing. Her seeming vacant-headedness when she said she no longer remembered his true name sounded sincere, but then, she was an actress.

"I am beginning to agree with Grenville," I said, half to myself.

Her eyes widened. "Please do not say you will take his side. He has me very frightened. His jealousy will be the death of me, I think." Her voice rose to a fevered pitch.

"I will speak to him," I promised.

She sighed, putting every ounce of her stage presence into the throaty little moan. "Thank you, Captain Lacey. I knew you would not fail me."

She flung herself away from me, the skirts of her peignoir swirling. Then, rather anticlimactically, she stopped and rang for her maid.

"You attended the ball at the Gillises' the night Henry Turner died," I said, trying to bend to my true purpose for visiting.

Mrs. Bennington's dramatic expression faded, and she made a face, much like a girl who has been given porridge when she expected thick ham. "Yes, that was quite horrible."

"It was. Did you know Henry Turner?"

"No. I'd never heard of him until he got himself killed." She sounded sublimely uninterested.

I asked a few more questions about Turner and whether Mrs. Bennington had seen him or Colonel Brandon enter the anteroom, but it soon became clear she had noticed nothing. Mrs. Bennington noticed only the people who noticed her.

Grady entered the room in answer to the summons and frowned at me.

"Grady," Mrs. Bennington said. "Tell Captain Lacey how Mr. Grenville behaved the other night."

Grady looked me up and down, like a guard dog eyeing an intruder. "He did rail at her, sir, that is a fact. I was afraid I'd have to call for the watch."

"And he threw his walking stick?" I asked, still surprised.

"Yes, sir. Look." Grady marched to the wall and put her hand on the cream silk. "Just there. It's left a mark."

Below her work-worn hand was a faint black mark and a tear in the fabric. "The footman couldn't quite get it to come clean. Have to do the whole wall over, like as not."

I straightened up, very much wondering. "I will speak to him," I said.

Grady gave me a severe look. So had my father's housekeeper looked at me when I was a small boy and came home plastered from head to foot with mud. "See that you do," she said.

I would have smiled at the memory if the situation had not been so bizarre. I thanked Mrs. Bennington for her time, promised again I would look into the matter of Grenville's strange tempers, and departed.

GRENVILLE AND MARIANNE HAD GONE FROM MY ROOMS BY the time Bartholomew and I returned to Grimpen Lane.

I felt I could hardly look up Grenville that night to make him explain what he meant by terrorizing the feeble-witted Mrs. Bennington, so I went to bed, conscious that not much later, I would be breakfasting with James Denis and my Frenchman.

In the morning, I dressed with cold fingers and rode across London in a gentle rain to number 45 Curzon Street. The façade of this house was unadorned, and the interior was elegant and understated, in a chill way. Mrs. Bennington's sitting room had reminded me a bit of this house—cool and distant.

Denis's butler let me in and took me to the dining room. I'd been in this room before, but not for a meal. Two people now sat at the table, Denis and the Frenchman who'd attacked me in my rooms. A third setting had been placed at one end of the table, for me, I assumed.

James Denis sat in an armchair at the head of the table,

elegant in dress as usual, betraying no sign he'd stayed up very late last night and had risen relatively early this morning.

As I sat, I reflected that I had never seen James Denis do anything so human as eat. I'd always imagined he must exist on water alone. However, he had a plate of real food before him—eggs and beef, a half-loaf of bread, and a crock of butter.

The Frenchman's plate held thick slices of ham, which he was shoveling into his mouth. He shot me a look of defiance over his fork.

"Captain Lacey," Denis said in his cool voice. "May I introduce Colonel Naveau."

Colonel Naveau nodded once, his eyes filled with dislike. His close-cropped hair was a mix of gray and brown, and his eyes were dark. He wore a suit tailored to his lean body, a fact that spoke of expense. His emperor might have lost the war, but this colonel still had his fortune.

"Colonel Naveau is quite the pugilist," I remarked, as a footman slid a plate of steaming sausages in front of me. "Gentleman Jackson might be interested in some of his moves. Were you cavalry?"

Naveau watched me a moment, then inclined his head. "A hussar."

I had guessed he was light cavalry because of his lean muscles, which spoke of hours in a saddle. French hussars had been known for their not-always-prudent courage. They'd been fond of throwing away their lives in some act of bravery that usually cost the English dearly.

"They fought hard at Talavera," I said. "I was there. In the Thirty-Fifth Light Dragoons."

Naveau grunted. "The Thirty-Fifth Light did well at Waterloo." He barely moved his lips when he spoke.

"So I hear." I lifted my fork and cut a bite of sausage. "I had retired before then. I'd been injured."

Denis broke in. "Captain Lacey's commander was Colonel

Aloysius Brandon. The one who now awaits trial for the murder of Henry Turner."

"I read of Monsieur Turner's death in the London newspapers." Naveau's tone was clipped.

"You knew I had searched Turner's rooms," I said. "And you thought I'd found the letter with which Turner had been blackmailing Colonel Brandon and Mrs. Harper. You followed me home and waylaid me in my own lodgings in an attempt to find it."

"I did." He seemed in no way ashamed.

"I have puzzled and puzzled why on earth you would want a letter between Brandon and Mrs. Harper," I said. "Was Mrs. Harper your mistress? Your wife, perhaps?"

Naveau's brows drew together. "I have no wife. And what is this letter you speak of? I was not looking for a letter; I was seeking a document. A very important document. Mr. Denis says you will know where to find it."

I looked from him to Denis. "What is this about?"

"Mr. Turner stayed for a time in Paris, as a guest of Colonel Naveau," Denis said. "After Mr. Turner had departed for London, Colonel Naveau discovered a document missing from his house. He searched and concluded Turner had absconded with it. Naveau came to London as soon as he could and learned of Turner's death after he arrived."

So Henry Turner had stolen a document from Naveau. "What has this to do with Colonel Brandon?" I asked.

"Because your colonel knows where it is," Denis said. "Or at least, where it last was."

The footman came forward to pour more hot coffee into my cup. "Why should Colonel Brandon know anything about a French document?" I asked.

Naveau made a noise of exasperation. "Because Monsieur Turner was blackmailing your colonel for the document. I know this."

"Turner was blackmailing Brandon over a love letter to or

from Imogene Harper." A letter that would make their affair embarrassingly public. But as I sat there I realized I'd been thinking about this all wrong.

"No, no, Captain," Naveau said. "Not a love letter. A letter he and Mrs. Harper wrote while we were in Spain. A letter to me."

"To you?"

"Yes." Naveau seemed annoyed at my disbelief.

"What is this document?"

"Nothing of concern to you," Naveau snapped back. "It is in French."

"I read French."

"Still you would not understand it."

"And Colonel Brandon would?" I asked.

"Mrs. Harper would."

"Why Mrs. Harper?"

Naveau looked at Denis. "You told me he would help without question."

"No," Denis replied. "I said he would find the document, but Captain Lacey must always ask questions. It is his nature."

"It is an inconvenient nature."

I ignored Naveau. "Why did you promise him I would find it?" I asked Denis.

Denis laid his knife and three-tined fork carefully across his plate. "The matter is simple. Colonel Naveau needs this document. He has entered a bargain with me to restore it to him. You are close to your colonel and can persuade him to tell you where it is. If it has not turned up among Turner's things, that means Henry Turner either destroyed it or passed it to someone. Most likely, to Colonel Brandon."

"Colonel Naveau has paid you," I said, my eyes narrowing.

"Yes," Denis said.

"In that case, you should have told him one of your own men would find the document for him."

Denis looked at me. Nothing existed behind his cold expression but more coldness. "I did."

Damn him. From the first, James Denis had informed me he wanted me to work for him, and that I would, in the end. I refused, because Denis was a criminal, no matter how well he lived or what help he'd given me. Any deed he'd done for me had been to suit his own purposes and to make me beholden to him. I would pay him back, he'd said, in his own coin.

He knew I wanted to find the document in order to clear Colonel Brandon. He was holding my feet to the fire.

"I do not work for you," I said.

"But you need this paper. Colonel Naveau will remain here as my guest, and you will bring it to him."

My temper stirred. "I want the paper only to help prove Brandon's innocence."

Denis lifted his slim shoulders. "If you wish, but you will bring it to me and not give it to the magistrates."

His gaze, if anything, had become colder. I remembered what had happened to a young coachman who'd once disobeyed Denis. Denis never discussed the matter, but I knew one of Denis's lackeys had murdered the young man.

"I searched Turner's rooms thoroughly," I said. "I also paid a visit to his father in Surrey and looked over his rooms there. I found nothing. No documents, no letters of any sort. What makes you believe I can find it?"

"Because you have an uncanny knack for turning up things that need to be found. You will do this."

I promised nothing. Denis watched me steadily, but damned if I'd bow my head and obey.

I pushed away my now-cold sausages and rose to my feet. The butler appeared in an instant, understanding that I was going.

"I have no doubt the man you have following me will report my every action to you," I said.

Denis's face was expressionless. "Yes."

"Then I need make no vows to you that I will find and return the paper. You will know what I do."

Denis inclined his head. He had no need to answer.

Colonel Naveau looked blustery, but I ignored him. I departed the room without taking leave or saying goodbye, and followed the butler down the stairs again to the street.

STILL SEETHING, I WALKED THE LENGTH OF CURZON STREET through Clarges Street to Piccadilly. As I walked, I again went over the extraordinary conversation I'd just had. A document, written by Brandon *and* Mrs. Harper to Colonel Naveau, in French.

My temper began to cool as worry took over. James Denis had been strangely insistent I pursue this. Why? So he could make me do a job for him? Or for some other reason?

And why the devil should Brandon care about the document? What was he trying so hard to keep from me? The only thing certain was that there was more to this than any party let on. Denis had not asked me to find the paper to please Colonel Naveau, no matter how much the man had promised to pay. Denis did things for his own reasons, and not all his reasons involved money.

I wiped rain from my face. I had searched Turner's rooms and found nothing. But I might as well do so again. I must have overlooked *something*.

As I passed through Clarges Street, I wondered whether Grenville was in his house there with Marianne. I deliberately turned my gaze away from the windows, as though to give Grenville his privacy, even from the street.

Grenville was another person I was not happy with. Why had he gone to Mrs. Bennington and berated her so? I might be able to accuse Mrs. Bennington of exaggerating his behavior, overdramatizing it, but then her plain and very sensible maid had said the same thing.

My friends, I reflected, were busily driving me mad.

I turned onto Piccadilly, making my way past Berkeley Street, Dover Street, Albemarle Street, and Old Bond Street. I passed Burlington House, a huge edifice that had dominated Piccadilly since the reign of Charles II. Owned now by Lord George Cavendish, the interior was lavish, I'd been told, with no expense spared on decoration. Grenville had pronounced it excessive.

Turner's landlord looked puzzled when I said I wanted to see Turner's rooms again, but he led me upstairs. The sitting room was a mess. Open crates stood about half-filled. The furniture had been lined up along one wall, apparently waiting for men to load it into a wagon and drive it to Epsom.

In the bedroom, I found similar disarray, along with Hazleton, Turner's valet. The man lay across Turner's bed, fully clothed, snoring loudly. Two empty bottles, which had likely held more of Turner's claret, stood on the night table.

I approached the bed and shook Hazleton's booted foot.

The man snorted. He fumbled his hand to his face and rubbed one eye. "Wha— ? Devil take it, man."

"Hazleton," I said, shaking the foot more firmly.

Hazleton blinked, trying to focus on me at the foot of the bed. He sat up, then groaned and pressed his hand to his forehead.

"What a head I have," he mumbled.

"Emptying bottles of claret by yourself will do that." I dragged a chair from a corner and sat down. "While you are recovering, I want you to tell me everything you know about a Colonel Naveau, and Turner's last visit to Paris."

"Ah. You know about that, do you?"

"Not as much as I'd like. I have met Naveau. These bruises on my face are courtesy of him. You would have saved me much trouble if you'd told me about him from the start."

Hazleton gave me a belligerent look. "Well, you didn't ask, did you?"

"Did he come here the same day I did, looking for something?"

"That he did. Not two minutes after you departed."

"And you helpfully told him I had already been here, and anything the colonel needed to find, I no doubt had?"

"Yes," Hazleton said defiantly. "I didn't know he would crack your face. I couldn't, could I?"

"What was he looking for?"

Hazleton looked surprised. "Well, now, you'd know about that."

"No. I looked, and I found nothing. Naveau has found nothing. I know the document is a paper written in French, but I do not know what it is."

He shrugged. "I don't know either. I can't read Frog-speak."

"Tell me why Turner went to Paris, what he did there, and why he came home."

"Persistent, aren't you, Captain?" Hazelton pressed his hand to his head again and climbed down from the bed. "I'll need a bit of something to settle my head. So I can remember."

I watched impatiently as he opened the armoire and drew out another bottle. He uncorked it and poured ruby liquid into a glass. "Have some, Captain?"

I declined. I craved coffee, not claret, and I would reward myself with some after I finished with Hazleton.

Hazleton drank then let out a satisfied sigh. "That's good, that is. I'm knackered from straightening out my master's affairs. And then, once I'm finished, that is the end for old Bill Hazleton. Mr. Turner—senior, that is—said he'd look after me, but a man needs only one valet. So what is to become of old Bill?"

"Perhaps Colonel Naveau can avail himself of your services," I said, wanting him to get on with it.

Hazleton took another long gulp and sat on the bed. "Oh, no, never him. That man frightens me, and not just because he's a Frenchie. And anyway, he was a spy. You did know that, didn't you? That he was an exploring officer during the war? For the Frogs?"

CHAPTER 13

*N*o, I had not known. Both Denis and Colonel Naveau had omitted that interesting detail.

Exploring officers had been those men sent off in the night to do covert missions for Wellington or for Bonaparte's generals. They'd crept across lands held by the enemy and spied out troop movements, intercepted papers, or infiltrated the enemy camp itself. Men who could speak fluent French were prized by the English; likewise those fluent in English were prized by the French. So many Englishmen and Frenchmen had mixed blood, mothers from London and fathers from Paris, that it was difficult to decide sometimes who fought for whom.

Exploring officers had done a dangerous job, I knew, but they'd been more or less despised. Instead of standing and fighting in the open, they skulked about in darkness and lied and cheated their way into defeating the enemy. Commanders prized their exploring officers and found them distasteful at the same time.

Naveau had a fairly thick accent, so I doubted he'd ever infiltrated English lines, but he might have been a receiver of information.

My heart grew cold. The fact that Brandon and Mrs.
Harper had written to Naveau during the Peninsular War
filled me with foreboding. Why the devil should they have?
That Colonel Brandon, a high stickler for loyalty, would send a
document to a French exploring officer for any reason seemed
ludicrous.

Something was wrong here, very, very wrong.

"Tell me about your master's visit to Paris," I said. "Now."

Hazleton rubbed his face and took another fortifying drink.
"Well now, we went out to the Continent about a year ago. Mr.
Turner likes to travel. Don't know why. The food is rotten, and
I can't understand a word no one says, even excepting some of
the ladies in Milan and Paris are sweet as honey. Not that they
wash as much as I'd like, but they're friendly. Mr. Turner met
this fellow Naveau in Milan. After that, he tells me we're
packing up to go with Colonel Naveau to his home in Paris."

"What was the purpose of the visit to Naveau?" I asked.
"Business?"

Hazleton barked a laugh. "Naw, Captain. It was sordid
lust. My master was bent the wrong way, you know. Started
when he was a lad, and he never gave it up. So long as he
wasn't bent for me, I said, I didn't care what he did. He starts a
fascination for this colonel, and there's nothing for it but we
must go to Paris with him."

"They were lovers, then."

Hazleton gave me a glassy stare. "Never went that far. My
master was keen for the colonel, but I do not think it went
the other way. My master threw himself at him for nothing.
The Frenchies, you know, they don't care when a fellow is
bent. They just pass on by. But here now, you go to the
stocks quick enough. But my master never got what he
wanted from the colonel. The two of them argued much,
never could agree about anything. One night, my master
wakes me up and says we're going back to England. 'Why?' I
asks. 'Tired of plying your charms?' He boxed my ears for

impertinence, but I got up and packed his duds, and we fled back to England." He drained his glass and upended the bottle for more.

"What was Naveau like? Did you speak to him much?"

"Not I. Didn't have much to say to him, did I? But his own man, name of Jacot, had no complaints about him. Told me about the colonel being an exploring officer and what they did in the war. Naveau was decorated for services to the French army, he said. Very intelligent man, Jacot claimed. Good at soldiering. A bit at a loss in civilian life."

Such a thing had happened to many, including me. "Napoleon was deposed and the French king restored. Did Naveau remain a good republican?"

"Jacot said it seemed like he was glad all the fighting was over, no matter who was at the helm. I heard Naveau himself say war was bad for France, that so many men had died for so little. But Mr. Turner didn't like to hear about the war and the colonel's career. Every time Colonel Naveau started going on about life in the army, Mr. Turner would change the subject."

I thought of Turner, young and fresh-faced with his soft curls of brown hair. I imagined listening to stories of an old war horse had wearied him.

"About this paper Naveau was looking for," I began.

Hazleton shrugged. "Don't know much about it. Naveau came bursting in here and started going on about Mr. Turner being a thief and ruining him. He demanded I return a paper what Mr. Turner stole. I said I didn't know nothing about it, but that you had been up here for a time by yourself, so maybe you'd taken it. Then he ran off after you." Hazleton glanced at my fading bruises again. "Didn't know he'd pummel you."

"I would like to know why that document was worth pummeling me for."

"No idea, Captain. No idea at all. At any rate, it's not here."

"It seems it is not. You never saw it?"

Hazleton burped. "If I did, I wouldn't have paid it much

mind, if it were in Frenchie talk, 'cause I don't know it, as I said."

"Then how did you communicate with your ladies in Paris?"

"Oh, I know enough for *that*." He grinned. "You don't need much language to tell a lady you fancy her, now do you?"

"No, I suppose you do not."

I asked him a few more questions, but it was clear Hazleton did not know what the document was or where it could be found. I left him to finish imbibing the last of his master's claret.

Outside, I bought a bit of bread from one vendor and coffee from another. I chewed through my repast and thought about what to do.

The likeliest person to have that document, if it had not been destroyed, was Mrs. Harper. If Brandon had told me the truth, if he'd met with Turner at eleven o'clock and made the exchange—a bank draft for the document—and left the room again with Turner still alive, then he must have rid himself of the document between eleven o'clock and about one, when Pomeroy's patroller took him to Bow Street and made him turn out his pockets.

After meeting with Turner, Brandon had taken Imogene Harper aside in one of the alcoves in the ballroom. Had he passed her the paper and told her to hide or destroy it? Or had he strolled to a nearby fireplace and burned it himself?

It would have taken some time to push it into a fireplace and watch until it burned to ash. Brandon would have had to ensure the paper actually did burn and didn't fall behind a log or into the ash grate. I could not fathom no one would notice him doing this.

No, he must have passed it to Imogene Harper. But then, if Mrs. Harper had it, why had she come to search Turner's rooms? Either she did not have it, or she'd been looking for something else.

I ground my teeth in frustration. Nothing made sense.

Piccadilly ran before me, misty in the rain, skirting St. James's, the abode of clubs and hotels, as well as gaming hells where fortunes were lost on a single throw of dice. As I walked again in the direction of Green Park, I reflected on Mr. Turner's propensity for wagers and his keen luck.

Leland had told me Turner would wager on whether a cat would walk a certain direction or whether a maid would be sick or well. Arbitrary events. I wondered if his machinations with the document were part of a wager—can Mr. Turner procure a document from a French colonel and blackmail an English colonel with it?

I found this farfetched, but I wondered how Turner knew the document would be important to Colonel Brandon and Imogene Harper.

It was only ten o'clock, and few of the *haut ton* were up and about. The streets were busy with servants and working people scurrying about to make ready for when their masters rose that afternoon. I strolled into Green Park, observing nannies with children who'd been brought to London with fathers and mothers for the Season.

Seeing them made me think about my own daughter running about the army camps with little regard for danger, and her frantic mother railing at me to stop her. Carlotta had been raised by a nanny and a governess and had expected her daughter to be looked after in the same manner. I had hired a wet nurse, naturally, but after that, Carlotta was dismayed to find she'd have to take care of the baby herself.

I had not minded looking after Gabriella and had not understood my wife's distress. Louisa, too, had lavished attention on the child. But Carlotta had been miserable, and I had not been patient with her.

I wanted to see Gabriella again. I could taste the wanting in my mouth. I wanted to see Carlotta as well. I wanted to end things cleanly with divorce or annulment or whatever solicitors could cook up in their canny brains. I wanted to be free so I could turn to the rest of my life.

Lady Breckenridge had told me any victory she would have with me would be hollow. I did not want that to be true. I was an impetuous man and liked to rush into affairs of the heart, but this time, I wanted to ensure that what I had with Donata Breckenridge was real.

She'd thought the reason for my hesitation was that my heart was engaged elsewhere. The truth was I wanted to go to her a free man, so if I offered her my heart, it would come with no impediments.

The surprising thing was that Lady Breckenridge seemed not to mind that I had nothing to offer her. She asked nothing from me but myself, and I knew better than to sneer at such an offer.

I stood watching the nannies herd the children for a while longer, then turned my steps toward a hackney stand. I needed to consult Pomeroy, discover where Mrs. Harper lived, and then pay her a visit.

WHEN I LEFT BOW STREET AFTER SPEAKING TO POMEROY, a lad in the street tried to pick my pocket. My hand closed around a bone-thin wrist, and the small, dirty-faced boy attached to it cursed at me.

I released him and gave him a thump on the shoulder. "Clear off and go home."

He jumped and fled as fast as he could, no doubt thinking me stupid for not marching him off to the magistrate on the spot. He must have been desperate—or else highly confident— to try to rob me just outside the Bow Street office.

Mrs. Harper, I'd learned from Pomeroy's clerk, had lodgings in a small court north of Oxford Street, near Portman Square. I decided to take care of another errand on the way, and took a hackney back to Mayfair and South Audley Street. At one o'clock, I was knocking on the door of Lady Breckenridge's townhouse. Barnstable opened the door to me.

"Has her ladyship arisen yet?" I asked.

"She has indeed, sir." He looked critically at my face. "Healing nicely, sir. Always swear by my herbal bath. If you'll come this way, sir."

He led me upstairs to Lady Breckenridge's sitting room and left me there while he ascended to her rooms to inform her I'd called. I steeled myself for Lady Breckenridge to send me away, but before long, I heard her light footsteps approach.

I turned as Lady Breckenridge entered the room. She looked awake and alert, but she did not smile at me. Today she wore a light green morning gown and lace shawl and had pinned her hair under a white lace cap.

"I apologize for visiting you at such an appalling hour," I said.

She lifted her brows. "I would have called it a beastly hour myself, but never mind. My cook informs me she has prepared tea for me. I can offer that and cakes if you like."

"I am full of bread and coffee, thank you. I have been wandering about London eating from vendors' trays."

She gave a slight shrug as though she did not care one way or the other. "I assume you had some reason for this call."

"I did." I hesitated. I'd thought it a good idea to come when I'd made the decision, but Lady Breckenridge did not seem happy to see me. After the manner in which we had parted the last time, I could hardly blame her.

"I came to ask if you might give me an introduction to Lady Gillis," I said. "I would like to speak to her about the night Turner died, and I would like to look over the ballroom again."

Lady Breckenridge folded her arms, and the lace shawl slid down her shoulders. "I see." Her voice was cool, her stance, unwelcoming.

"I have presumed," I said quickly. "I beg your pardon. I did not mean to take advantage of you."

"You do presume." She gave me a quiet look. "But I am happy you did."

Something inside me relaxed. "The last thing I want is to take advantage of you."

She gave me a humorless laugh. "The last thing? I do not believe you, you know. There must be plenty of other things you do not want more than that. But very well, I will take you to visit Lady Gillis so you may once more look at the scene of the crime. Give me a day or two to speak to her. From what I've been told, Lady Gillis is most distraught about the murder, and has refused to leave her bed."

"I am sorry to hear that. I do not wish to distress her, but I truly need to see the anteroom and the ballroom again."

"You will," Lady Breckenridge said, tone confident. She trailed her long-fingered hands down her arms. "I will give you a bit of advice, however. If you wish to speak to courtesans by the pillars at Covent Garden Theatre, you should not speak so loudly or so obviously."

Her face was very white, and I saw something flicker in her eyes. Hurt, I thought, and anger.

"Damn it all," I said feelingly.

I had hoped my conversation with Marianne would go unnoticed, but I ought to have known better. My face warmed. "As I have observed before, you are a very well-informed lady."

"Good heavens, Gabriel, it is all over Mayfair. I could not stir a step last night without someone taking me aside and asking me whether I knew my Captain Lacey had been pursuing a bit of muslin under the piazza."

"They should not have spoken to you of such a thing at all," I said indignantly.

"Yes, well, my acquaintances are a bit more blunt than

necessary. They seemed to believe I would find this *on dit* interesting."

"They ought to have better things to talk about."

"I agree. I did tell them quite clearly to mind their own business." She was rigid, her eyes glittering.

"Gossip is misinformed, in this case," I said. "She was not a bit of muslin. She was Marianne Simmons."

Her brows arched. "And what, pray tell, is a Marianne Simmons?"

"Hmm," I said as I thought about how to explain Marianne. "Miss Simmons is an actress. She occupied rooms above mine for a time, and made the habit of stealing my candles, my coal, my snuff, and my breakfast whenever she felt the need. I let her; she never had enough money. She is shrewish and irritating, intelligent and bad-tempered, and has fallen quite in love with Lucius Grenville, although I must swear you to silence on that last point. She has a habit of accosting me whenever she perceives something wrong between herself and Grenville, which, unfortunately, is often."

As I spoke, Lady Breckenridge relaxed, and by the end of my tale she even looked amused. "So you have become the peacemaker."

"To my dismay. I do not know how effective a peacemaker I am. I generally want to shake the pair of them. I can hope the storm has died down for now, but I know better."

Lady Breckenridge strolled to me. "Poor Gabriel. Besieged on all sides. Your colonel and his wife; Grenville and his ladybird."

"True. They resent my intrusion, but they also expect me to have answers for them."

"That must be difficult for you." She spoke as though she believed it.

"It is difficult. And my own fault. If I minded my own affairs, I would not get myself into half the predicaments I do."

"No, you would sit at a club and play cards until numbers

danced before your eyes. It is your nature to interfere, and you have done some good because of it." Lady Breckenridge laid her hand on my arm. "Besides, if you did not poke your nose into other people's business, you would not have journeyed down to Kent last summer."

She did not smile, but her eyes held a sparkle of good humor. Last summer, I had gone to Kent to investigate a crime and had met Lady Breckenridge in a sunny billiards room, where she'd blown cigarillo smoke in my face and told me I was a fool.

I lifted her hand to my lips and kissed her fingers. Her eyes darkened.

"Here is where things grew complicated on your last visit," she said.

I kissed her fingers again. "And I very much wish everything to be simple."

She grew quiet. Slowly, I slid my arm about her waist. The lace cap smelled clean with an overlay of cinnamon. She always smelled a little of spice, this lady.

I truly wished things were simple, that I could come here, as though I had a right to, and sit in her parlor and hold her hand. I wanted more than that, of course. I wanted to love her with my body and drowse with her in the comfortable dark. I wanted things to be at ease between us—no secrets, no jealousies, no fear. I leaned down and gently kissed her lips.

She allowed the kiss then smiled at me as we drew apart.

"You must continue prying into other people's business until you put everything aright, Gabriel," she said, touching my chest. "It is your way."

"I wish I could put it aright. But this affair is a tangle."

"You will persist." Lady Breckenridge stepped from my embrace, but slid her hand to mind. "Who are you off to see this afternoon?"

"Mrs. Harper. I must discover what happened to that piece of paper she and Brandon were willing to pay Turner for."

"How exhausting for you. Go in my coach. No need to take a horrid hackney."

"I had decided to walk."

She gave me a deprecating smile. "Your stay in the country has made you terribly hearty, has it? There is a dreadful damp. Take the carriage."

I gave her a mocking bow. "As you wish, my lady."

She lifted her brows again, then she laughed. "Oh, do go away, Gabriel. I will send word when I have smoothed the way with Lady Gillis. And remember not to speak to your Miss Simmons under the piazza again, or tongues will continue to wag."

She mocked me as only she could, but as I departed, I thought only on how much I liked to hear her laugh.

LADY BRECKENRIDGE HAD APPARENTLY GIVEN ORDERS TO Barnstable to prepare her coach before she'd even offered it to me, because I found the carriage waiting for me outside the front door. Barnstable helped me inside, and Lady Breckenridge's coachman drove me straight to Mrs. Harper's lodgings.

However, when I reached the fashionable house near Portman Square in which Mrs. Harper resided, the lady was not at home. "You may leave your card, sir," said a flat-faced maid, holding out her hand. I put one of my cards into it, and she backed inside and closed the door. That, for now, was that.

I found myself at a standstill in my investigation, so I took care of more personal business on Oxford Street, such as paying some debts and purchasing a new pair of serviceable gloves. Lady Breckenridge's coachman obliged me in this too, saying it was her ladyship's orders to drive me about. I tried to call on Grenville, but he, too, was not at home. Matthias told me Grenville had sent word he would be staying at the Clarges Street house. He winked knowingly.

I hoped the news meant a closing of the breach between himself and Marianne, although I was disappointed I could not speak to Grenville himself.

I told Lady Breckenridge's coachman to leave me there, seeing no reason for him to transport me across the metropolis to my appointment with Sir Montague Harris, and took a hackney to Whitechapel.

After Lady Breckenridge's cozy rooms and the luxury of her carriage, the room in the Whitechapel public office was a cold and austere place. The fire smoked and burned fitfully, and the wine Sir Montague offered me was sour.

I told him all I'd discovered since I'd last written, from Turner's funeral to my interview with Hazleton this morning.

"What you say about Bennington interests me," Sir Montague said. He shifted his bulk in his chair, which had grown to fit him. "If he is so clever, why does he tell his featherheaded wife to keep secret he's changed his name to hers?"

"I cannot say. Either he is not as clever as he pretends to be, or he counted on Mrs. Bennington spreading around that secret, for his own purposes. Although what that is, I cannot imagine."

"Why change his name at all?" Sir Montague asked.

"Fleeing from creditors?"

"Or the law. I will focus my eye on this Mr. Bennington. Dig into his past, find people who knew him in Italy, and so forth. I will enjoy it."

I had no doubt he would. Sir Montague was shrewd and intelligent and little got past him.

He turned that shrewd eye on me. "Anything else you wish to tell me, Captain?"

I had avoided talking about Colonel Naveau and the paper he wanted me to find. I was not yet certain what it meant for Brandon, and I somehow did not want Sir Montague examining the matter too closely.

"No," I said.

His eyes twinkled, as usual. "This is where I, as a common magistrate, have the advantage over you, Captain Lacey."

I tried to look puzzled. "What do you mean?"

"I mean that when I investigate crime, I am purely outside it. I can look at the facts without worry, without knowing a suspect is a dear friend."

I barked a laugh. "I hardly call Brandon a dear friend these days."

"But you are close to him. His life and yours are tied in many ways. You feel the need to protect him, for various and perhaps conflicting reasons." He spread his hands. "I, on the other hand, see only the facts."

I could not argue that he viewed things more clearly than I did where Colonel Brandon was concerned. "And what do the facts tell you?"

Sir Montague gave me a serious look. "That Brandon was mixed up in something he should not have been. That the death of Turner was an aid to him. That Mrs. Harper knows more than she lets on. That you are afraid to trust yourself."

The last was certainly true. I had some ideas about Brandon's involvement I did not like. I had admired Colonel Brandon once, and some part of that admiration lingered. He'd disappointed me—as much as I'd disappointed him—but I still wanted my hero of old to exist.

"What do I do?" I asked, half to myself.

"Discover the truth. The entire truth, not just what you want to know. Did Saint John not say, *The truth shall make you free?*"

I looked at him. "Will it?"

"It will." Sir Montague nodded wisely. "It always does."

MORE UNCERTAIN THAN EVER, I LEFT SIR MONTAGUE AND returned home. I thought about all I had learned that day over the beef Bartholomew brought me, and then tried to distract myself with a book on Egypt I'd borrowed from Grenville.

That evening, I put on a thoroughly brushed frock coat and traveled to Gentleman Jackson's boxing rooms in Bond Street to meet Basil Stokes.

When I entered the rooms at number 13, I saw the unmistakable form of Lucius Grenville. He detached himself from the gentlemen he'd been speaking to, came to me, seized my hand, and shook it warmly.

"Well met, Lacey," he said. "And thank you."

CHAPTER 14

$\mathcal{B}$asil Stokes came up behind Grenville and eyed us curiously. "You seem damned grateful, Grenville. Has the good captain given you a tip on the races?"

"More or less." Grenville released my hand and turned away, his dark eyes sparkling.

"Perhaps I'll have more tips for you tonight," Stokes said jovially. "What shall you do, Captain? Box? Or just observe?"

"Observe, I think. The damp is making me long for a soft chair and a warm fire."

"Too much of that renders a man weak, Captain. You stride around well enough even with your lameness, but better take care." He laughed loudly.

I decided Basil Stokes was the sort of man who said whatever he liked then laughed afterward to soften the blow. He wore his white hair in an old-fashioned queue and dressed in breeches and shoes rather than the newer fashion of trousers or pantaloons.

He was an old Whig, much like my father had been, probably a crony of the late Charles James Fox, the famous statesman, and vehemently opposed to the now conservative Prince Regent and his followers. I suspected my father had embraced Whigishness not only because it was traditional for the Lacey family to do so, but because most of the men to whom he owed money were Tories.

Stokes led us across the room and introduced me to several gentlemen of his acquaintance. They already knew Grenville, of course. We talked of the usual things: sport, politics, horses. Then Gentleman Jackson entered and attention turned to the lessons he gave in the middle of the room.

"Gentleman" Jackson had been a famous pugilist until his retirement, when he'd decided to open a school for gentlemen who wanted to learn the art of boxing. These gentlemen, the cream of the *ton*, would never fight a match in truth, but we all enjoyed learning the moves that made pugilists prized. Grenville made a decent boxer; he was wiry and strong and could move quickly. I was more ham-handed in my moves, but I could hold my own.

Tonight, I sat on a bench next to Stokes and watched while two younger fellows stripped to shirt sleeves and took up positions in the center of the room, fists raised.

"A quiet wager?" Stokes said into my ear. He might have said "quiet," but I am certain everyone in the room heard him. "Ten guineas on Mr. Knighton."

"Done," Grenville said before I could speak. Stokes beamed at him and nodded.

"Captain?"

"I do not know these gentlemen," I answered. "Let me study their form before I throw away my money."

Stokes chortled. "I like a careful man. I do not know their form myself. That is why it is called gambling." He sat back, laughing, but did not prod me to wager.

The gentlemen commenced fighting. They had apparently taken many lessons with Gentleman Jackson and boxed in tight form, keeping arms bent and close to their bodies. After a time, Jackson moved in and gave them pointers. Several of the observing gentlemen tried to imitate what he told them to do.

"Well, then, Captain, what did you want to ask me about the night poor Turner died?" Stokes said loudly into my ear.

I glanced about, but the others, except Grenville, were fixed on Gentleman Jackson and his instructions. "I want only a report from another witness," I said. "No one seems to have noticed much."

Stokes gave me a shrewd look. I sensed, for all his tactlessness, that he was an intelligent man. "The truth on it, sir, was no one saw much, because all the gentlemen were vying for the attention of the beautiful Mrs. Bennington. Many a man would be glad to escort her home for an evening."

Grenville's smile died, and his eyes began to sparkle.

"Is that what you did?" I asked, ignoring Grenville. "Vied for Mrs. Bennington's attention?"

"Not me, sir. Oh, I'd love to give the woman a tumble, but at my age, a warm glass of port is more to my taste on a cold night than a lass who'd not look twice at me. That is what I was searching for at the fatal hour of midnight—drink. Gillis did not lay in near enough. I had to walk the house looking for more. Your colonel was doing the same."

"Was he? You spoke to him?"

"He was growling about lack of servants. Where were they all? he wanted to know. I told him the house had been built so servants walked in passages behind the walls. That's why we couldn't find a footman when we needed one. The colonel said it was bloody inconvenient and walked away, toward the back stairs. I assume he was about to descend to the kitchens, but I don't know, because I went back to the ballroom, still wanting drink. When I reached it, Mrs. Harper began her screaming. She stabbed him, Lacey, mark my words. Women are easily excitable. Lord knows my wife was, God rest her."

What he said interested me. "Would you be willing to swear to this in court?" I asked. "If you saw Brandon making for the back stairs at the time the body was discovered, perhaps I can prove he didn't have time to kill Turner."

"Oh, he might have had the time," Stokes said cheerfully. "I did not see the colonel until a minute or so before the screaming commenced. He might have done it before that." Stokes chuckled at my expression. "But truth to tell, Captain, I do not believe he did. If Colonel Brandon wished to kill a man, he'd call him out and face him in a duel, not quietly shove a knife into him. A question of honor, don't you know."

Honor, yes. I agreed with him. But I thought of the missing document Colonel Naveau wanted. Something dangerous was going on here that might make a man throw honor to the wind.

"Of course," Stokes went on, "I might have done it. Oh, good form," he shouted at Knighton as the man began punching his opponent.

"You might have," I said. "But why would you?"

"Because I owed Mr. Turner a ruinous amount of money." Stokes kept his gaze on the boxers. "Should have learned my lesson when I lost to him at the races, but I wagered on the outcome of a cockfight, and lost heavily. Not my fault. I could not have foreseen that the champion bird would expire of apoplexy so soon into the match. The lad had a nose for wagering. Saved my pocket when he died. But I didn't kill the chap. I'd have paid up. I always do."

Stokes was just ingenuous enough for me to believe him. He seemed a straightforward, no-nonsense sort of gentleman, one who might be persuaded to bet on a ridiculous outcome but turn over his money amiably when he lost.

Then again, Turner was dead.

"So," Stokes said, "if I didn't murder the chap, and Brandon didn't murder him, who did?"

"That is the question." I returned my attention to the boxers. The gentleman called Knighton had just landed another good facer on his opponent. I felt relieved I had not bet against him. "And at this moment, I have no bloody idea who."

GRENVILLE INVITED ME BACK TO GROSVENOR STREET FOR brandy and hot coffee to chase away the chill of the evening after we left Gentleman Jackson's. I readily accepted.

The Knighton fellow had done well. I'd bet on him in a round against a tall, muscular boxer, and won a few guineas. I resisted the temptation to let it all go again and, flushed with success, accompanied Grenville home.

Now in his upstairs sitting room, the one that housed curios from his travels, Grenville reclined in a Turkish chair, clad in slippers and a suit meant for relaxing in his own house. He fingered a small golden beetle he called a scarab and let out a wistful sigh.

"Egypt is a magical place, Lacey," he said. "All the wonders of a lost world buried in the sand, waiting to be discovered. The Turks don't care about it one way or another. I have followed the career of that Italian fellow, Belzoni, out there looking for treasure. He used to do a strongman act at Tunbridge Wells. Would carry seven men on his back. Amazing fellow."

"And you wish to travel to Egypt to help him?"

"Not help, watch and learn. I doubt I would do much good chucking blocks of stone about. I long to go back. It is a beautiful place."

"You speak of it much."

"I told you before, we could go together. I believe you'd enjoy it."

I poured my brandy into my coffee and sipped the spicy, warm mixture. "What would Marianne say?"

"I believe she would be furious with me. That is the trouble with falling under a woman's enchantment. A man becomes reluctant to leave her side."

"Are you reluctant to leave her side?" I asked.

Grenville gave me a self-deprecating look. "I am, as you have guessed. That young lady has gotten under my skin." He took a drink of brandy. "Well, you warned me about her. Perhaps I should flee to Egypt so I might come to my senses."

"She would never forgive you, I think."

"She might be happy to see the back of me. Especially if I left her with a great deal of money. Yes, I believe that is my solution."

"I believe you wrong her," I said.

"Do I?" he asked in vast disbelief.

"You stayed last night with her, did you not?"

His smile was cynical. "A night with a lady does not mean a softening of that lady's heart. You are a romantic."

"Perhaps. What about Mrs. Bennington?"

His brandy glass stopped halfway to his mouth. "Mrs. Bennington?"

"I visited her after her performance last night. Her husband introduced me. She asked me to speak to you."

Any friendliness vanished. "Did she?"

"I found it rather incredible what she told me, that you shouted at her over a gentleman called Carew and threw your walking stick across the room. I was shown the mark you left in the wallpaper. I must wonder why you did so."

Grenville sat stiffly, his eyes glittering with anger. "Lacey, I often am amused by your curiosity, but this time, I am not. Please cease to ask me questions."

"You frightened her."

"Good. She ought not to let young fellows make up to her, nor should she have married that God-awful Bennington. The man is a mountebank."

"She told me his name was not Bennington. Who is he then?"

"The devil if I know."

"You seem extraordinarily angry. Do you know Mrs. Bennington well? I never heard you speak of her before she came to London."

"I told you, Lacey," Grenville said in a hard voice. "Cease asking me questions about Mrs. Bennington."

"I admit, her story seemed incredible. I thought it likely you'd have a reasonable explanation for the entire matter, even if I had to thrash you for frightening a rather pathetic young lady."

Grenville stared at me in outrage, then he began to laugh. "Good God, you have audacity."

"I know. That is why I anger so many people."

"I admire it, you know—even when it makes you a bloody nuisance."

I noted his backhanded compliment let him nicely avoid the question. "Will you not tell me the explanation?"

He stopped laughing. "No. I will not. This incident with Mrs. Bennington is none of your damned business. That is all I will say on the matter."

I inclined my head. My curiosity was not satisfied, but I saw I would get no further with him tonight. "Very well, but I must ask you to cease frightening her. If she tells me again you have thrown your walking stick or shouted in her face, I will consider the thrashing."

He gazed at me, lips parting. "You truly do have audacity, Lacey."

"Yes."

I knew I jeopardized my friendship with him by being high-handed, but Mrs. Bennington had been truly frightened, and Grenville had not denied her accusations. Mrs. Bennington was not the most apt young lady in the world, but that was no reason for a gentleman to threaten her or terrify her. That Grenville, who prided himself on impeccable manners, had done so, was astonishing.

Grenville drank his brandy in silence for a moment then said, tight-lipped, "I suppose we should turn the conversation to other things. What do you think of what Stokes told you?"

"It is the first time I have been able to verify the truth of Brandon's story that he was wandering the house just before the body was discovered. But there are other things going on I do not understand."

I told him of my meeting with Denis and Colonel Naveau, and the request to find the document Turner had stolen from Naveau. Grenville listened, his animosity fading as his interest rose.

"I agree with you that Brandon most likely gave the paper to Imogene Harper," he said. "However, she must have been looking for it when you caught her entering Turner's rooms, which tells me she does not have it."

"This is what I have concluded. I plan to ask Mrs. Harper when I visit her and try to force her to tell me the truth. But if she does not have it . . ." I trailed off, taking a sip of coffee. "That means Brandon got rid of it somehow. I cannot imagine him passing it to any other person, except perhaps Louisa. But she has given no indication she knew anything about a letter, nor do I think he'd had time to give it to her."

"Then what is your theory?"

I clicked my cup to its saucer. "That Brandon hid it some-where. That he found a place to put it in the Gillises' house where even their servants would not find it. He hid the docu-ment before Pomeroy arrived, knowing he might be questioned about Turner's murder. An awkward thing to have on him if Pomeroy simply arrested people right and left and let magis-trate sort it out in the morning. He probably meant to return to retrieve the letter or to send Mrs. Harper for it. But Pomeroy whisked him to Bow Street so quickly he did not have the chance to pass on the message. Mrs. Harper has not visited him, nor has Louisa. And he does not want me to find the damned thing."

"Hmm." Grenville tapped his fingertips together. "How could he be certain the servants would not find it?"

"He must have thought the hiding place a good one." I studied the shelf beside me, which was filled with oriental ivory. "If a Gillis servant did find it, would they be able to read it? It was in French, and not all servants can read even English. They might think it a stray bit of paper and destroy it."

"Or wrap fish in it or polish furniture with it," Grenville said. "My footmen use my old newspapers to polish the silver. So they tell me."

"Perhaps Bartholomew and Matthias can infiltrate the Gillises' servants' hall again and find out. I am not certain how I will explain to Lord Gillis I want to search his house from top to bottom for a stray piece of paper, but I will try."

"I can speak to Gillis at my club."

"Lady Breckenridge has promised she will gain me entry through Lady Gillis."

His brows climbed. "I see. Lady Breckenridge has been quite helpful to you of late, I've observed."

I poured more coffee into my cup from the pot on the tray. I felt Grenville's keen gaze resting upon me, but I chose to ignore it. "Some things are none of my business," I said, keeping my voice light. "Some things are none of yours."

He looked pleased. "You will never have a moment's boredom with Donata Breckenridge, Lacey. She is decidedly unconventional."

"She is intelligent," I said. "And does not waste time on frivolous conversation."

"Exactly."

He wore a faint, superior smile. I said, "Her marriage to Breckenridge I know was unhappy. She loathed him. I gather it was an arranged match?"

Grenville nodded, always ready to delve into the affairs of his fellow man, or woman. "It was a good match on the basis of pedigree and financial benefit. Her father, Earl Pembroke, was great friends with Breckenridge's uncle. Both men had large and prosperous estates, and Pembroke wanted his daughter and grandchildren provided for. Breckenridge's uncle was a man of sterling worth, but Breckenridge grew up spoiled, hard-nosed, and selfish. As you noticed." Grenville turned his glass in his hands. "Interesting thing. I met Lady Breckenridge at her come-out, when she was Lady Donata. She was quiet and well mannered, never spoke a word out of place. A regal young lady. Not until after she married Breckenridge did she blossom into what she is now."

I contrasted Grenville's picture of the quiet ingénue to the frank, acerbic lady with the barbed sense of humor I'd come to know.

I said, "Breckenridge must have infuriated her until she grew fed up and dropped her polite veneer in self-defense."

Grenville shot me a look. "Breckenridge was horrible, Lacey. You knew him only a couple of days. Very few people could stick him. He paraded his mistresses about in front of his wife; I hear he even took a few home and forced her to share her dining room with them, took them to his bedchamber under her nose. I admire Lady Breckenridge for not running mad or shooting him outright. She must have the strength of ten to live through what he did to her."

"She does have strength," I said in a soft voice. "She can stand up to me and tell me to go to the devil."

He chuckled. "So very few men would prize that in a lady."

And yet, I did. My wife Carlotta had been a fragile, tender creature. I'd needed a wife who could bash crockery over my head and tell me not to run roughshod over them. Carlotta had said nothing and let me become more and more heavy-handed. I doubt I'd ever be able to be heavy-handed with Donata Breckenridge.

"Lady Breckenridge is a lovely woman," I said.

Grenville grinned. "That does not hurt, either." He lifted his glass. "To comely ladies with sharp tongues. Bless them."

I lifted my cup and joined him in a toast.

THE NEXT AFTERNOON, I RETURNED TO THE COURT NEAR Portman Square to attempt another visit to Imogene Harper. This time, I found her at home.

She received me in a tidy parlor whose windows overlooked the foggy lane. This was a quiet court, rather like the one I lived in on the other side of the city, though a bit more prosperous. The house was respectable, the sort a well-to-do widow might hire.

Mrs. Harper looked the part of the respectable, well-to-do widow. Again, I was struck by what a comfortable-seeming woman she was—not a beauty, but not displeasing, either. The disheveled look she'd had when I'd encountered her in Turner's rooms was gone. Her yellow-brown hair had been combed back into a simple knot, and she wore brown again, a high-waisted gown trimmed with black.

Once the requisite politeness had finished and a maid had settled us with the requisite tea, I told her, "I have met Colonel Naveau."

Mrs. Harper's eyes widened, and she set down the teacup she'd just lifted. "Oh."

"He has commissioned me to find a letter stolen from him in Paris by Mr. Turner. I believe that same letter was sold to Colonel Brandon for five hundred guineas in the anteroom of Lord Gillis's Berkeley Square townhouse."

Mrs. Harper bowed her head, but a flush spread across her cheeks.

"Am I correct?" I asked.

"You believe so," she answered, her voice hard. "What does it matter what I think?"

"It matters a great deal, Mrs. Harper. I need to find that
document. I want to find it. Will you tell me where it is?"

CHAPTER 15

*M*rs. Harper lifted her head. "And if I tell you I have no idea where the bloody letter is, will you believe me?"

"I will, actually."

She looked surprised then skeptical. "You will? Why?"

"Because I know Colonel Brandon better than you do."

She stared at me a moment then sagged back into her chair. "Oh, what does it matter? No, Captain, I do not have the letter. I begged and begged Aloysius to give it to me, but he would not."

"But you do have the draft for the five hundred guineas Brandon gave Mr. Turner, do you not?"

"Yes, I found it in the pocket of Mr. Turner's coat. I took it and put it into my reticule."

"You searched his dead body for it. I admire your coolness."

"I was anything but cool! Believe me, Captain, when I screamed, I did so from the heart. Mr. Turner was still warm when I searched his pockets. It was ghastly. But I knew I had to take the money away before someone else found it. When I saw I'd gotten his blood on my glove, it sent me into a horrified panic. I do not know much of what happened after that."

"Grenville sat you down and gave you brandy. He also took your glove away."

"Yes, he did." Mrs. Harper drew a long breath. "When I could no longer see the blood, I calmed somewhat. Even so, my maids had to take me home. It was awful."

"You made the Bow Street magistrate feel sorry for you. He did not want to summon you there for questioning."

"No." Her lips thinned. "Sir Nathaniel came here, instead."

"And what did you tell him?"

"That I'd danced and talked and done things one does at a ball. Yes, I stepped away with Colonel Brandon to speak to him privately, and why should I not? I went to the anteroom later to snatch a quiet moment and found Mr. Turner."

"This is the story you told the magistrates?"

"Yes."

I took a sip of tea, which was weak and too sweet. "You and Colonel Brandon tell slightly different stories. He admitted to Sir Nathaniel that he spent most of his time with you and that you were upset by Mr. Turner's insolence more than once. So much so that Brandon had to stalk out of the ballroom to find you a glass of sherry at the moment Turner was being murdered."

She flushed. "I never wanted to find Mr. Turner dead in the anteroom. My sole purpose in attending the ball was to obtain the letter and destroy it."

"So his death and Brandon's arrest inconvenience you greatly."

"Inconvenience?" Mrs. Harper sprang to her feet. "It has been hell, Captain Lacey. I do not know where the letter is. Colonel Brandon might be hanged for murder. Now you tell me Colonel Naveau has come from France to ruin us all."

I came to my feet with her. "How can he ruin you? What is this letter?"

She stopped, her eyes steady. "What do you believe it is?"

"I first thought it a love letter between you and Brandon, but I only assumed that. You never corrected me, and neither did he. I have since learned it is a document Colonel Naveau very much wants returned. You and Brandon have each told me that the pair of you had an affair, but is that true?"

Mrs. Harper nodded. "We did. At Vitoria, just after my husband's death."

"You were grieving," I said, "and alone, and he was helpful."

"I was not simply grieving. I was devastated. I loved my husband desperately. I was so angry he'd been taken from me, and I was also in a good deal of trouble. Colonel Brandon was there. He was strong and helped me, and he was . . . I cannot explain what he was to me. I should not have surrendered to him; I felt the betrayal of my husband, but I could not help myself. I admired Aloysius, and I was so grateful."

She broke off. But I understood. Brandon could be a compelling leader when he chose. He needed followers and needed to be admired, and Aloysius Brandon had the confidence and the strength to make men follow him. I had felt the same pull when I'd first met him, the compulsion to do anything for him.

"Why were you in a great deal of trouble?" I asked.

"Because of my husband, Major Harper. He'd done a terrible thing. And I was afraid, so afraid he'd be disgraced, even in death, stripped of his rank, branded a traitor. And I would be branded a traitor's wife. I did not understand the horror until I went through my husband's things in preparation to return to England. I did not know where to turn. Brandon, unbelievably, said he'd help me."

"I am supposing your husband had dealings with this Colonel Naveau?"

The look she sent me was filled with appeal. Though she

did not have the beauty of Lady Breckenridge or Louisa, I was touched by the need in her eyes.

"Mrs. Harper," I said. "My purpose today is to prove Colonel Brandon did not murder Henry Turner. I am not here to condemn your husband for what he might have done in the past, or you for helping him. The war is over. What happened then no longer matters to me."

"It ought to matter," she said savagely. "What my husband did could have cost lives, the lives of your men. Perhaps your own life, if you'd been unlucky."

"Naveau was an exploring officer," I said. "Did your husband pass him information?"

"That is what I discovered when I went through his things. My husband had been taking money from Colonel Naveau in exchange for dispatches."

I let out a breath. Spying could be a lucrative game but a deadly one. If her husband had been caught sending information to the French, he would have been tried for treason. Shot at best, drawn and quartered at worst. Major Harper had been fortunate to die in battle.

I did not tell the entire truth when I said I no longer cared what had happened on the Peninsula. Men who sold secrets were the worst of humanity. A dispatch sent to the enemy could destroy battle plans and slaughter thousands of soldiers, for nothing.

"What did you do?" I asked quietly.

"I destroyed all his papers." Mrs. Harper quirked a brow at me. "What would you have me do, Captain, run at once to his colonel and confess he'd been selling secrets to the French? My first loyalty was to my husband, who had been good to me. I destroyed every last scrap of evidence he'd done anything wrong. But then, only a few days after my husband's death, Colonel Naveau sent a message. It was sheerest good luck I found it before my husband's batman did. The message was odd, but I understood Naveau was waiting for something. I did not know what to do. So I confessed to Aloysius and swore him to secrecy."

"And he agreed?" I was baffled. Brandon was a stickler for proper behavior in a soldier, in an officer, in a gentleman.

"Aloysius agreed to say nothing. My husband was dead— he'd died honorably, saving other men. And Aloysius did not want dishonor or punishment to fall on me. He suggested we send a message to Colonel Naveau explaining Major Harper was dead and to leave me alone."

Bloody hell. "That was unwise and not even necessary. Naveau was a professional exploring officer. If he received no more word from your husband, he would conclude his source had dried up, and he'd turn elsewhere. Likely he would have heard of your husband's death on his own, in time."

"But Naveau's message frightened me. He did not know when he wrote it that my husband was dead. He was angry and threatened to reveal to Wellington what my husband had been doing. Colonel Brandon wrote a letter to Naveau, in French, and somehow got it delivered to him; I have no idea how he managed it. As a peace offering, he included a dispatch Naveau had been asking for."

"Good God."

"Yes, he risked much for me."

I had been angry at Aloysius Brandon in the past, but my rage rose to new heights today. "He did risk much. He risked ignominious death and ruin for himself and his family. And for what? Your pretty eyes? Did he ask you to elope with him?"

Mrs. Harper looked perplexed. "He asked me to marry him, yes. How did you know?"

"Because I was at the other end of the matter. Did you know he planned to leave his wife for you? You must be a remarkable woman to lure him from Louisa Brandon, who I assure you is quite remarkable herself."

She flushed a dull red. "I refused him. He was very excited after we'd delivered the message and begged me to marry him once he obtained the annulment of his marriage. But I could not. I'd loved my husband dearly. I did not want to rush to another man as though my husband had meant nothing to me. So I turned Aloysius away."

"Yet you admit you had an affair with him," I said.

"A very brief one. I was afraid and alone, as you said, and needed comfort. Then I told him to go."

Which he'd done. Brandon had returned to his wife to discover Louisa had run to me in her distress. He'd been furious and would not believe she and I had not had a liaison. But if Brandon had been indulging himself in another woman's bed, small wonder he'd instantly believed I'd indulged his wife in mine.

"And you returned to England?" I asked.

"To Scotland, actually. My sister had married a man from Edinburgh, and they invited me to live in their house. She has two small children, and they welcomed me as part of the family. It was a peaceful existence."

"Until this spring?"

Mrs. Harper moved back to a chair and sank into it. "I received a letter from Henry Turner in February. He said he had the very letter Aloysius had written to Colonel Naveau. How he came by it and how he found me, I do not know. Mr. Turner instructed me to come to London and to pay him the sum of five hundred guineas, or else he would take the letter to the Horse Guards and proclaim my husband and I and Colonel Brandon had been traitors together."

Now I understood Brandon's outrage at Turner. I felt it myself.

She went on. "I hurried to London and wrote to Aloysius. I was petrified. And he . . ." Her eyes sparkled with anger. "At first Aloysius wanted nothing to do with me. He said bluntly that our affair was long ago, that he and his wife were happy, that I should cease to pester him. I was furious with him. He had as much to lose as I did."

"I read the letters you wrote back to him. You declared both your names would be revealed. I took it to mean your love affair would be made public."

"Aloysius finally agreed to help, though he was not best pleased about it. Turner wanted to meet us at the Gillises' ball, knowing Colonel Brandon and his wife had been invited. So we made the appointment and brought him the money."

"And then Brandon made a mare's nest of it." I shook my head. "I do not know why anyone would suppose Colonel Brandon could do anything covert. He got himself talked about, upset his wife, and was arrested for murder."

To my surprise, Mrs. Harper smiled. "I do not think he anticipated being arrested for murder, Captain. As for Aloysius being ham-handed, the result was that people only talked of us having an indiscreet affair. They did not guess the worst of it. Even you did not."

She made a good point. "I admit I was sorely misdirected."

Mrs. Harper studied her hands in her lap. "I regret hurting Mrs. Brandon. She does not deserve this."

"No, she does not." I resumed my seat. "Tell me exactly what happened at the ball. You might still believe Colonel Brandon killed Turner to keep him quiet, but I do not. If he successfully obtained the letter from Turner, there was no need to murder him. Unless Turner had something more on you?"

Mrs. Harper shook her head. "There was nothing else. Just that letter. And Aloysius said he'd made the exchange."

"Tell me again what happened."

"I want so much to forget what happened, and everyone wants me to remember." She rubbed her forehead. "It is true Aloysius called too much attention to me—to us. But I feared Mr. Turner, and I did not want Aloysius to leave my side. Aloysius was angry at Mr. Turner, but also at me. Mr. Turner did offer to dance with me several times, but I knew he simply wanted to talk alone with me. Aloysius chased him away."

Lady Aline's version of events confirmed this. "The meeting was set for eleven o'clock? In the anteroom?"

"Eleven, yes. Aloysius told me I was not to go, although I wanted to see the letter for myself. But he was adamant, and I obeyed. He and Turner went into the anteroom together. No one followed. Not five minutes later, Aloysius emerged, rather red in the face, and Mr. Turner came out behind him. Aloysius took me to an alcove and told me the deed was done."

"Colonel Brandon provided the payment as well?"

"He insisted. I did not protest too much. While I am of comfortable means, I cannot part with five hundred guineas with impunity. Aloysius spoke of the sum as almost trivial."

"Brandon has a large income. When he spoke to you in the alcove, did he show you the paper?"

"He refused. He told me he had it, and I was not to worry."

"If it was in his handwriting, he'd be anxious to keep it," I reflected. "But Brandon did not have the letter when he was arrested. Do you have any idea what he did with it?"

"None. I was agitated, not surprisingly so. Aloysius told me he would find me some sherry, and left me. I stayed in the alcove, trying to catch my breath. Then, when he was a long time coming, I decided to emerge. Others would wonder what I did there so long. I tried to behave normally and have a conversation with Lady Gillis, but I was too agitated. I decided to sit alone in the anteroom. But when I entered, I found Mr. Turner."

"Dead."

She shuddered. "I thought him merely foxed, and I was angry at him, celebrating at our expense. But he sat too still, and then I realized he was not breathing."

"And you decided to search him for the bank draft."

"Yes."

"Why? To save Brandon a bit of blunt?"

"That was not all I thought. I did not think the draft should

be found on a dead man. I did not want it to point to a connection between Mr. Turner and Aloysius."

"It was a good thought, but Brandon's behavior did that for
him. Well, I am back to not knowing what became of the
paper. Brandon is most reticent to tell me."

"He is ashamed."

I snorted a laugh. "He is afraid I will use the knowledge
against him. Well, Mrs. Harper, instead of clearing Brandon, I
now have information that gives him still more of a motive. He
killed Turner not to cover up an affair with you but to keep
himself from being arrested for treason. Damn."

Mrs. Harper looked at me limply. "I am sorry."

"Brandon is an idiot, which is not your fault. He never
should have written that letter."

"I know."

"The only way I can save him is to discover who truly did
murder Turner. Did you see anything that can help me?"

She shook her head. "I was in the alcove. By the time I
made my way to the anteroom, Turner was already dead."

"You said his body was warm, so he could not have been
dead long. Are you certain you saw no one leave the room
before you entered it?"

"I did not."

I imagined the small gilded room with its simple furnishing
and scarlet walls. I remembered the opulent staircase hall and
Basil Stokes complaining that one never saw the servants
because they walked through back passages behind the walls.

Anyone who knew how to get into those passages could
have slipped into the anteroom—if indeed, a door from the
anteroom led to the passages. They need not have been seen in
the ballroom at all. Brandon had been observed striding
toward the back of the house, ostensibly in search of sherry.

Damn, and damn, and damn.

I rose to my feet. "Mrs. Harper, I thank you for being frank
with me. I am going to find that blasted paper if I have to tear

apart London to do it. And I will clear Brandon, too. Please, if you remember anything else, any small detail that might be helpful, send me word."

She promised to, but her face was wan, her eyes tired.

I left her with my card and my direction penned on it. Mrs. Harper said goodbye, her eyes quiet in defeat.

I knew she believed that if I had to betray her to save Brandon, I would. And, I thought as I left the house for the spring fog, she might not be wrong.

LADY BRECKENRIDGE HAD SENT ME A NOTE VIA A SERVANT that morning, telling me she'd procured an appointment for me with Lady Gillis. She'd instructed me to call at the South Audley Street house at three o'clock.

I had just enough time now to journey from Portman Square to South Audley Street, and I arrived on Lady Breckenridge's doorstep at three o'clock precisely.

Lady Breckenridge greeted me in a swirl of silk and cashmere and pressed a cool kiss to my cheek. "You are amazingly punctual, Gabriel. Shall we go?"

I was pleased—first, that she had done this favor for me, and second, that she felt comfortable enough with me for a kiss as greeting, without awkwardness. I was pleased, too, to sit next to her in her carriage, and have her shoulder brush my arm with the carriage's movement.

I suddenly was sorry Lord Breckenridge was dead, because I longed to shoot the man myself. I had, however, thoroughly bruised his face in an impromptu boxing match, and that would have to satisfy me.

Lady Breckenridge's small hand lay loosely in her lap, and I reached down and closed it in mine. "You told me once I resembled the late Lord Breckenridge," I said.

She gave me a startled look. "You and he had a similar

build, true. And hair the same color. But you are a completely different man, thank God."

"I share the sentiment. I promise you, Donata, I will never subject you to the humiliations he did. Ever."

Lady Breckenridge gave me a half-smile. "I know. You have too much damned honor."

"Not only honor," I corrected her. "Affection."

She stared at me. I do not know whom I surprised more with the word, Lady Breckenridge or myself. She looked at me for a long moment, then she laid her head on my shoulder and kept it there for the rest of our short journey.

The carriage stopped before the entrance to the Gillises' home in Berkeley Square. A double door flanked with tall columns led us into the rotunda of the front hall. Maids took our coats and hats, and a butler led us to a drawing room somewhere in the vast interior.

There, I met Lady Gillis for the first time. When she entered, I was struck by how much younger she was than Lord Gillis. Grenville had mentioned Lord Gillis was older than his wife, but Lady Gillis looked little more than a girl. I put her age as barely into her twenties, the same as Mrs. Bennington.

"Violet." Lady Breckenridge greeted Lady Gillis with kisses to her cheeks, French fashion. "Captain Lacey wishes to poke about your house. Shall you allow him?"

CHAPTER 16

*L*ady Gillis did allow it, although she was flustered. "It is not a nice thing to have a murder in your home," she said. "We have been at sixes and sevens since the ball."

"I am sorry it had to happen," I said.

"It was dreadful. Absolutely dreadful. I have been abed for days."

"Did you know Mr. Turner?"

Lady Gillis started, then flushed. "No. Not well. He was an acquaintance of a friend, who suggested I invite him. Lord Gillis did not like Mr. Turner and told me vehemently not to let him come, but I owed my friend a favor. I'm sorry now I did not listen to my husband."

Before I could ask further questions about this friend and why Lord Gillis did not like Turner, Lady Gillis suddenly said she felt unwell and declared she'd retire to her rooms.

Lady Breckenridge offered to accompany her upstairs, but Lady Gillis said quickly that she would be fine in care of her maid. I rather think Lady Gillis wanted Lady Breckenridge to keep an eye on me.

The ballroom in daylight was a very different place from what it had been in the middle of the night. The arched windows at the end of the room let in gray light, and the chandeliers hung empty, devoid of candles.

A footman obligingly lit sconces for us then disappeared on noiseless feet.

"Lady Gillis's servants are well trained," I observed as the tall man glided out, leaving us alone. "They seem to take in stride even a sordid murder."

"Lady Gillis is a duke's daughter," Lady Breckenridge said. "She brought many of her mother's servants with her after her marriage. They are an efficient lot, but rather cold."

I thought of Lady Breckenridge's butler, Barnstable, ready with a pleasant smile and a cheerful inquiry into my health. I, too, would prefer a human being to a silent automaton.

"I am surprised they allowed the murder to occur," I remarked.

Lady Breckenridge shrugged. "Well, if their master will allow in the rabble . . ."

I smiled with her then moved off to examine the ballroom.

The longest wall held arched openings that led to the small alcoves. Each alcove housed a chair or two, and some included small tables. Dark green velvet curtains draped the openings.

I loosened a tied-back drape and let it fall. Both curtains would easily cover the alcove, rendering the inside a private, if rather stuffy, compartment.

"Do you remember to which Colonel Brandon took Mrs. Harper?" I asked Lady Breckenridge. "After Colonel Brandon left Mr. Turner in the anteroom?"

Lady Breckenridge studied the alcoves a moment. "That one," she announced, pointing to the opening just to the left of me.

I entered it and seated myself on one of the chairs. Wainscoting covered the wall from the baseboard to a chair rail about three feet above the floor. I ran my hands around the chair rail, looking for openings into which a folded piece of paper could have been wedged behind the wainscoting. I did the same with the baseboards, then turned over the little table and both chairs to examine the undersides and upholstery.

I found no rents or gouges into which a paper had been pushed. I examined the chair's and table's legs in case one proved hollow — I did everything short of taking the furniture completely apart.

Lady Breckenridge watched me curiously. "They say women ask too many questions, but I must know what you are doing."

"Looking for Colonel Brandon's letter."

I had not told her the story Mrs. Harper had given me today. I could not. Brandon needed my silence. Let Lady Breckenridge continue to believe the problem was a love letter about a simple affair.

I righted a chair and sat on it. "Brandon led Mrs. Harper here after he paid Turner in the anteroom. Then he left Mrs. Harper to search for sherry. Where would he likely have gone?"

Lady Breckenridge beckoned me to follow her. She glided across the ballroom as silently as any of Lady Gillis's servants and led me out a double door to a wide hall.

Several rooms opened off this hall, dedicated to the comforts of guests or for displaying the Gillises' artwork. "He might have come into any of these chambers," Lady Breckenridge said. "There would be decanters and so forth in them."

"Brandon said he could not find any sherry." I walked into one of the rooms and looked about at its gilded furniture and paneled walls.

Lady Breckenridge shrugged, following me. "Shall I ring for a footman and ask him in which room they'd put it that night?"

"Not just yet." I crossed the hall and entered another sitting chamber. This one had similar paneling, but everything was gilded in silver rather than gold. "Lord Gillis's servants do not seem the sort to leave guests thirsty. So was Brandon's search for sherry a sham? And why?"

I hated this. Every bit of evidence I went over pointed more and more to Brandon having committed the crime. He'd been wandering this hall while Turner was being murdered, but none had seen Brandon except Basil Stokes, who'd only caught sight of him just before Mrs. Harper screamed.

Brandon had to have known, when Turner was found dead with Brandon's knife in his chest, that he might be arrested for murder. In the confusion between the discovery of Turner's body and the arrival of Pomeroy, Brandon would have striven to rid himself of the incriminating document.

He might have handed the paper to Mrs. Harper, but she'd claimed he did not, and I believed her. He might have given it to Louisa, but according to witnesses, Brandon had not gone much near Louisa until Pomeroy started taking him to task, and she'd come to stand by him. Or he might have hidden it in a place he'd spotted when he'd been roaming these rooms looking for sherry for Mrs. Harper.

I turned in a circle, taking in the room. Lord Gillis's servants would be certain to clean these chambers thoroughly every day. They were correct, well trained, and aloof, probably some of the most experienced in their class. Where could Brandon hide something where they would not find it?

Then again, this was Colonel Brandon. He had not made it through the ranks to colonel for nothing. He was a good and inspiring commander, and sometimes, uncannily perceptive. Only where his personal life was concerned was he lacking in wisdom.

The place he would hide his letter was in plain sight.

My gaze went to the books in the glass-doored bookcase, and my heart beat faster.

I saw in my mind, clear as day, Colonel Brandon striding into one of these rooms, snatching a book from a shelf, sliding the letter between pages, jamming the book back among its fellows, then striding out again before anyone in the ballroom wondered where he'd gone. By the time Pomeroy arrived to begin his questioning, the letter had been well hidden.

I crossed the room, pulled open a bookcase door, and began examining the books.

Most of the leather spines were uncreased and unbroken. The pages on the few I pulled out likewise were uncut. When a man bought a book, the pages were still folded into sixteen-page signatures; many signatures made up a book. One used a paper knife to cut each folded bundle open so the book could be read. Some men purchased libraries for the look of them rather than for intellectual pursuit; often pages of entire collections remained uncut.

In one of these books, unread by the inhabitants of the house, must lay the secret Brandon was willing to go to the gallows to protect.

"Help me," I said. I began pulling out books and opening them.

Lady Breckenridge's cinnamon and spice perfume touched me as she came to assist me. I was close—so close. Her slender hands touched mine as she pulled out books and copied my movements.

The books in the silver-gilded room yielded no secrets. Anxiously, I shoved the last book back into the shelf and hobbled back to the gold-leafed room. Only a dozen books decorated a bookcase here—I searched those and found nothing.

There were four more rooms along this corridor. Lady Breckenridge and I looked through every book in each of them. By the time I'd slit open the last book, I'd found nothing. My leg was hurting, and I wondered if my suppositions were wrong. But they felt right—seemed right. My vision of Brandon's actions had been so vivid.

I sank down on one of the chairs, in too much pain now to stand.

Lady Breckenridge stopped before me and smoothed a strand of my always unruly hair. "Are you well?"

"No, I am disgusted," I said. "The bloody thing must be here. I know Brandon. He would have hidden it. He would not have risked Pomeroy finding it."

Lady Breckenridge's cool fingers felt good. She rested herself on my lap and continued to stroke my hair.

I did not want to push her away. My head ached from speculating, and her presence, her touch, soothed me. I closed my eyes.

"I am not a man of complex thought," I said. "In the army I solved problems as they came to me. I did not sit in a chair and contemplate them."

"You were a soldier," she said, her voice low. "Not a general."

"What the generals decided after sitting back and contemplating was often foolhardy. They could not solve problems that were right in front of them." I opened my eyes. "Neither can I, it seems."

"You are working your way through lies."

"I know. The only person who has not lied to me is you."

Lady Breckenridge smiled a little, her red lips curving. "Are you certain?"

"You never hide your opinions."

"That is true. I was brought up to be demure, which I was until I married my foul husband. Then I realized a demure and timid lady won nothing. But I did lie to you, Gabriel."

"About what?"

She reddened. "About why I helped Louisa Brandon the night of the murder. I told you I did it because she was your friend. That was not entirely true."

I fixed my full attention on her. "No?"

"I helped her because I wanted to observe her. To learn what sort of woman had won your adoration."

I studied Lady Breckenridge in silence. Her eyes held a defiant light, but behind that defiance lay—worry?

"It is not adoration," I said.

"Is it not?"

She challenged me. She wanted truth. I was not certain what truths I could give her, because I was confused about truth these days myself.

One thing I knew was she was warm, and her touch delighted me in ways I had not known for a long time.

"No," I answered. "It is not. Admiration, certainly. And friendship."

"And love," Lady Breckenridge said.

"Love." I touched her face. "But not love that is covetous. I would see Louisa happy, but I do not need to possess her."

She looked unconvinced. "Gentlemen often express admiration, when in truth they mean desire."

"Your husband might have done so. My desire lies along another path." I drew my finger across her lips.

Her eyes still held caution. "I can never be this paragon you admire. No matter how I try."

"I do not want you to be. I want you to be witty and acerbic and blow smoke in my face when I am stupid and soothe me when I am hurting. You have proved excellent at all these things."

She dropped her gaze. "From the beginning I have made a complete cake of myself for you. That you do not despise me amazes me."

I regarded her in surprise. Lady Breckenridge had always seemed a woman who did exactly as she pleased for reasons of her own.

"You make me long to be tender," I said.

She looked up at me. In that moment, when her eyes met mine, I knew I'd never in my life met a woman like her.

"We do not have time to be tender," she reminded me. "We must find your colonel's letter so you may save him from the noose."

Thus, Colonel Brandon, even imprisoned, reached out to make my life difficult.

"Yes," I said. "But damned if I know how I will do it."

Lady Breckenridge slid from my lap and pressed a kiss to the crown of my head. "You will find a way, Gabriel."

I gave her an ironic look. "I am pleased at your faith in me."

She took my hand and helped me to my feet. "If Colonel Brandon did not leave the letter in a book, then we must look elsewhere."

"He did," I said with conviction. "I know he did."

I thought glumly that in truth, a servant must have found it, had not realized what it was, and destroyed it.

As I studied the room again, I noted the paneling in one corner did not fit quite right. Closer scrutiny showed a door had been cut into it, probably one that opened into the servants' passage behind the walls. No attempt had been made to completely hide the door, but the paneling had been fashioned to make it unobtrusive. Few would pay attention to it until the servant came through with tea or to lay the fire or whatever his or her particular duty might be.

I ran my fingers down the edges of the paneling until I found a piece of gilded molding that moved. The designer had cleverly used the molding to conceal the door's latch. I pressed the latch, and the door swung smoothly toward me.

I looked inside at a narrow passage with plastered walls lit with sconces. A footman, hurrying through on some errand or other, saw me and started, his eyes going wide.

"I beg your pardon," I said to him.

The footman regained his composure, changing from human being to well-trained servant in the space of a moment. "Sir?" he said coolly. "May I assist you?"

"Yes." I motioned with my stick. "Where does this passage lead?"

"To the ballroom, sir. And in the other direction, to the stairs to the kitchens."

"Do all the rooms have access to this passage?"

"Yes, sir." I heard the *Of course they do,* in his voice.

"May I look?"

His brows climbed. "It is no place for a gentleman, sir. Or a lady."

"Even so. Please show us."

The footman gave me the same look a put-upon colonel had when wives new to the regiment requested a tour of the army camp. Lady Breckenridge and I did not belong there, the look said. This passage was the servants' territory, and ladies and gentlemen were not welcome. However, the footman gave me a nod and led us inside.

The passage was dim and stuffy, but I could see it would be handy for moving about the house quickly, not to mention unseen. The walls were plastered but not painted, and the doors were rough wood, very unlike their elegantly disguised counterparts on the other side.

The doors also looked alike. "How do you know which leads where?" I asked. "For instance, which would lead to the anteroom in which Mr. Turner was killed?"

The footman led us to the door second from the end on the left. "This one, sir."

"But how do you know?"

He gave me his look of faint disdain. "We know."

"You are thinking the murderer came this way," Lady Breckenridge said. "How would *he* have known which door it was?"

"He might live in the house himself," I said. "Or, someone in the house told him, or he scouted beforehand." I turned to the footman, who remained stiffly disapproving. "Did you or any of the other servants observe anyone back here who should not have been the night of Mr. Turner's murder? Or anything unusual at all?"

"I did not, sir. But I will ask Mr. Hawes. He is butler, sir."

"One more question. Did you or any maid or footman remove a paper from any of the books in these rooms? Say the day after the murder? While they were cleaning? Perhaps they found something sticking from a book and pulled it out?"

"I clean these rooms myself, sir. And I did not find anything unusual among the books. But I will ask Mr. Hawes, sir."

Hawes seemed to be the font of all wisdom. "Please do," I said. "We will wait in the anteroom."

The footman opened the door, and I ushered Lady Breckenridge through to the anteroom.

I examined the passage side of the door before the footman closed it but could find nothing to differentiate it from the other doors in the servants' corridor. Inside the anteroom, the door fitted well into the scarlet and gold wall, although the line was visible if one knew where to look for it. The door was not a secret.

The footman disappeared, obviously relieved to see us back on our side of the walls. I studied the gilded molding and red silk above the wainscoting. The scheme was bright and a bit overwhelming, as I remembered, but I saw nothing to indicate someone could have marked the door from this side—nothing shoved through the crack or any such thing.

"So the murderer entered through the servants' door," Lady Breckenridge said. "Which is why no one noticed him enter from the ballroom. Guests roamed in and out of the ballroom and all over the downstairs rooms all night. I do not think anyone would notice who was in or out at a given time. Even so, the murder must have been very quick."

"It likely was." I left my examination of the door and laid my walking stick across the writing table. "The murderer has made up his mind to kill Turner. He makes the appointment, leaves the ballroom, and enters the servants' passage through

one of the other rooms. He comes here, meets Turner. He has
Colonel Brandon's knife, which Brandon must have left about
somewhere, or he'd previously stolen it from Brandon's pocket." I turned to Lady Breckenridge. "He approached Turner.
Turner knew him—or her—and did not fear. There was plenty
of noise in the ballroom, the orchestra, the dancing, the conversation. Before Turner knows what is happening, the killer steps
to him, possibly covers Turner's mouth so he won't cry out, and
drives the blade home."

I saw it in my mind. Without realizing what I was doing, I
covered Lady Breckenridge's mouth with my hand and pressed
my fist against her chest, right where the killer would have
plunged the knife.

It would have been fast and quiet. Turner would have
grunted if he'd made any noise at all, then fallen limp. The
killer had caught him, lowered him into the chair, and arranged
him to look as though he were drunk or asleep. The murderer
then left the way he'd come.

Lady Breckenridge's eyes glittered above my hand. "Very
exact," she said, stepping away.

I came back to the present. "I beg your pardon."

"Not at all. It was an apt demonstration. You do know, do
you not, that you are only succeeding in making the case
against Colonel Brandon tighter? He was in a room with a
door to the passage. He admitted it. Basil Stokes saw him."

"And likewise, Brandon saw Basil Stokes. Stokes said they
exchanged a few words, then Brandon made for the back of
the house. Why Brandon says he saw no one back there, I
don't know, unless Stokes is lying about the entire encounter.
Stokes claims he went back to the ballroom and then heard
Mrs. Harper scream, but we have only his word on it."

"But why should Basil Stokes kill Henry Turner? Mr.
Stokes is rather irritating, but he hardly seems the sort to kill
in such a clandestine fashion. He'd challenge Turner to a fight
if he truly wanted to harm him. Loudly."

"I agree with you, in part," I said. "But Stokes, by his own admission, owed Turner a huge debt. And he expressed relief Turner was dead and he no longer had to pay it."

Lady Breckenridge shivered. "It is all so horrible."

"Murder is horrible. Death while fighting is one thing—a deliberate and underhanded murder is another."

"It is good of you to help your colonel," she said. "No matter what I think of your motives."

"I need to," I said. "Not simply because of Louisa. Colonel Brandon aided me when I needed it most. He took me, a callow young man with no future, and made me into something. No matter what else is between us, he gave me that."

Lady Breckenridge did not answer. She did not need to. She slid her arms around my waist and rested her head on my chest.

At this inauspicious moment, the butler, the all-knowing Hawes, entered the room.

Lady Breckenridge stepped away from me, looking in no way embarrassed.

Hawes, like a good butler, pretended not to notice. "Sir," he said. "My lady." He turned to me, his butler hauteur in place. "John told me you wish to know if anything unusual was seen in the passage the night of the ball, or any person not meant to be there."

I nodded. "That would be helpful."

"I am afraid none of the staff saw any person untoward at the time in question. I have inquired. Most of the footmen were circulating champagne in the ballroom or cleaning up the supper rooms. The passages would have been empty for a time, so someone might slip through without us noticing. However, one of the maids did mention she noticed a scrap of lace caught near one of the doors."

I came alert. "A scrap of lace?"

"Yes, sir. As might come from a lady's gown."

"Near which door?"

"The door to this room, sir. I will show you."

He glided across the room and unlatched the panel that led to the servants' corridor. He pointed to a small nail that stuck out a little from the wooden doorframe. "Just there, sir. The silly girl left it there, and when she reported it to me, I ordered her to return and take it away. But she claimed that when she returned, the lace had gone. Possibly another footman saw it and disposed of it."

Or possibly, I thought, excitement rising, the killer had taken it from the door and put it into Turner's pocket, where Mrs. Harper found it when she examined the dead man's coat.

"Will there be anything else, sir?" Hawes asked.

I distinctly felt his wish for us to leave. We were intruding on his and his staff's routine.

"That will be all, thank you. You have been quite helpful."

Hawes bowed again. "Her ladyship has retired to bed. She asked me to bid you good afternoon when you take your leave."

I inclined my head. "Tell her ladyship we wish her good health."

Lady Breckenridge added her wishes and the message she would visit again when Lady Gillis was feeling better. Hawes saw us upstairs and the footmen brought our wraps.

Before we departed, Hawes handed me a folded piece of paper, written over in fine printing. The words were English and the message seemed to be about cakes, so I dismissed the idea that Hawes was handing me the document Colonel Naveau and I sought.

"Begging your pardon, sir," Hawes said. "The cook asked leave to give you this receipt for cakes Mrs. Brandon admired."

"Mrs. Brandon?" I asked in surprise.

"Yes, sir. She expressed a liking for Cook's lemon cakes when she visited, and asked for the directions, so her own cook might prepare them for her."

"I see." I took the paper. "I am certain Mrs. Brandon will thank her."

"Not at all, sir." He saw us out the door, and then Lady Breckenridge's footmen took us in hand. I tucked the paper into my coat and climbed into the carriage, trying to stem my excitement.

Lady Breckenridge saw through me. "What is it, Gabriel? You look positively triumphant."

I settled back and stretched my leg toward the box of hot coals while she watched me. "I now know what became of the letter."

Her eyes widened. "Do you? Shall you retrieve it at once, then? What direction shall I give my coachman?"

"It will keep. First, I would like to return to Bow Street and look at the scrap of lace that Pomeroy took from the dead man's pocket."

Without waiting for explanation, Lady Breckenridge told her coachman to drive to Bow Street. Then she sat back and looked at me. "You are very interested in this lace. Do you think a woman did this murder?"

"Not necessarily," I answered.

"But the lace was caught outside the door. Perhaps a woman slipped through the passage and tore her gown on the protruding nail."

"No, if I am correct, the lace was used to mark the door to the anteroom. So that when the killer hastened down the rather dark servants' passage, with the doors that look all alike, he would know which to go through."

"Then that dismisses the idea that one of the Gillis servants had anything to do with it," Lady Breckenridge said. "They would have no need to mark the door."

I hadn't thought any of Lord Gillis's staff had done this, thinking they'd be wise enough not to kill Turner inside the house, where servants were well supervised and anything out of the ordinary quickly noticed. Though when Leland had first revealed Turner's proclivities, I'd briefly pictured Turner making advances to one of the robust footmen, and said footman taking exception, with Brandon's knife somehow convenient.

But then, if a hearty footman had grown angry at me and picked up a knife, I'd certainly try to fight him off, shout, or run away. No, Turner had not been expecting the blow, which meant it was a person he thought entirely harmless.

"You seem to be sanguine suddenly about the whereabouts of Colonel Brandon's letter," Lady Breckenridge said. "This after your near despair when we could not find it in the house."

"If it is not where I think it is, then it has been destroyed."

"You believe Louisa Brandon has it," Lady Breckenridge said with sharp perception. "You believe she came to retrieve it on her husband's orders. Perhaps she raved over the cakes and demanded the recipe in order to slip down to the ballroom and find the paper."

"I imagine she truly liked the cakes. Louisa is fond of lemon."

She gave me a steady gaze. "Mrs. Brandon must love her husband very much."

"She does."

Lady Breckenridge laid her hand on my arm and did not speak further.

We rattled through the streets of London against a breeze that held the promising warmth of spring. Still it was chilly enough that I was grateful for the warm interior of the coach. When we reached Bow Street, I told Lady Breckenridge to stay inside the carriage. The rooms of the magistrate's house were no place for a lady.

Pomeroy, luckily, was in. I asked him what he had done with the things he took from Turner's coat. For a moment, as he paused in thought, I feared he had rid himself of them, or perhaps sent them to Turner's father.

"I still have 'em," he said, to my relief. "Upstairs. Was

saving them for the trial, in case they could tell us anything about how Mr. Turner got himself stuck."

He took me to a small room on the second floor and removed a wooden box from a cupboard. Pomeroy emptied the contents onto the table and separated what he said were Henry Turner's belongings. They consisted of a snuffbox, a few silver coins, and the scrap of lace Mrs. Harper had mentioned.

I picked up the lace. As I'd suspected, the ends were blunt, not raveled. It had been cut. The lace was stiff, because, I saw when I examined it, strands of real gold had been woven through the silk thread.

I closed my hand around it. I knew which lady at the ball had worn this lace, because I had seen her in the gown after the ball was over. "May I take this?" I asked Pomeroy.

"It ain't much use to me," he said. "Mr. Turner didn't pull it off the coat or dress of his killer. It was tucked, nice and safe, inside his waistcoat pocket. Can't imagine what for."

"Thank you."

"The trial is in four days, Captain," Pomeroy said. His usually jovial face was grim.

"I know. But Brandon did not murder Mr. Turner. He is only guilty of misplaced honor."

"Best you come up with a way to prove it, sir, or the colonel will swing."

"I am proving it now, Sergeant. Good afternoon."

I descended through the house and outside to the carriage. "Did you find it?" Lady Breckenridge asked, her eyes animated with interest.

I climbed in next to her, took her gloved hand, and laid the scrap of lace into it.

She stared at it. "Good Lord." Her face lost color. "You said *this* was found in Mr. Turner's pocket? How on earth did it get there?"

"I hoped you would tell me," I said. "This lace is from the ball gown you wore to the Gillises' last week, is it not? I remember seeing you in it that night when I arrived at Mrs. Brandon's."

CHAPTER 17

*L*ady Breckenridge looked up at me, bewildered. "Yes, this is from my gown. But I never gave this lace to Henry Turner. I confess to be amazed."

"I would be less surprised if it looked to be torn," I said. "Anyone might have found a bit of lace that had fallen from your gown while you danced. But this was deliberately cut—"

"I know," Lady Breckenridge broke in impatiently. "I cut it myself. For Mrs. Bennington."

It was my turn to be amazed. "Mrs. Bennington?"

"Yes. We were in a withdrawing room—my maid was helping me into my dancing slippers, and Mrs. Bennington expressed rather gushing admiration for my gown, especially the lace. She asked me for a snippet so she might have her dressmaker find some like it. So I cut a little bit off where it would not show and gave it to her."

I took the lace back from Lady Breckenridge and laid it on my glove. The innocent scrap glittered with wires of gold against my glove's cheap leather. It was feminine and pretty, yet strong, like Lady Breckenridge herself.

"This killer is of ruthless and nasty mind," I said. "He does

not mind using another man's dagger to do the deed, nor
stealing from an innocent woman to assist him. Every clue left
behind will point to a different person, each completely
removed from the crime. The killer planned this with deftness
and care then sat back and laughed while we scrambled about
to solve it."

Lady Breckenridge watched me with intelligent eyes.
"What will you do?"

I thrust the lace into my pocket. "Speak to Mrs. Bennington. I wish to ask her why she wanted a piece of your lace and
what she did with it after you gave it to her."

"She is performing tonight."

"I will make an appointment to see her after the play. She
invited me once before; she might be persuaded to invite
me again."

"She will."

"You seem confident," I said.

Lady Breckenridge smiled. "My dear Gabriel, you are
handsome, polite, and unattached. She will see you."

"But penniless," I reminded her.

"Some ladies do not mind this. Sit in my box tonight, and
we will visit her afterward. We are in Russel Street now. Shall
I have my coachman set you down here?"

I agreed, and she ordered her coachman to stop.

"Until this evening, then," she said as I descended. "And
tell your Miss Simmons not to accost you under the piazza."
She chuckled as the footman closed the door behind me, and
then the carriage pulled away.

I smiled to myself and tapped my way down Grimpen Lane
to my rooms.

Bartholomew greeted me with hot coffee, and I reflected,
as I often did, what a luxury it was to have a valet in
training.

I found a letter from Sir Montague Harris waiting for me.
As I read it, I mused that I envied his network of resources.

He'd managed to find, through inquiries, a man who'd known Mr. Bennington on the Continent.

Said gentleman, a solicitor by trade, had moved from Italy to London shortly after Bennington had. Bennington, the man had told Sir Montague, had come to Italy from the north of England. That interested me, because Bennington certainly did not have a north country accent.

The next statement interested me further. This man who'd known Bennington said Bennington had been known as Mr. Worth, but at his marriage five years ago had changed his name to his wife's family name, Bennington. Why he'd wanted to, the man did not know, but then, Bennington—or Worth— had always been whimsical.

Armed with this knowledge, Sir Montague had found the man of business of this Bennington-Worth and visited him.

Yes, Mr. Worth had spent years in Italy, said the man of business, and arranged to have his name changed on his marriage. Mr. Worth did have a legacy; he'd inherited a fortune about ten years ago when a Scottish gentleman, Mr. Worth's fourth cousin, had died. Mr. Worth drew a large sum —how much, the man of business refused to specify—every quarter, a substantial living.

The man of business had of course asked Mr. Worth why he wanted to change his name. Mr. Worth had explained his wife was already so famous, it would avoid confusion if she were to continue to be known as Mrs. Bennington, and her husband as Mr. Bennington. The man of business had been skeptical but had not pursued it further. No, Mr. Worth was not heavily in debt. He paid his bills regularly and so was not hiding from creditors or moneylenders.

Mr. Worth seemed to have a stellar reputation. And yet, the drawling, sardonic man had married a woman he despised and insisted on taking her name.

Make of that what you will, Sir Montague had finished his letter. *I am certain you will come to some interesting conclusions.*

For some reason, I imagined Sir Montague had already formed his own conclusions and was waiting for me to catch up. I could see him smiling as he wrote.

I read the letter again, shook my head, then sat down to pen a note to Mrs. Bennington, asking to see her again that night.

LATER, I LOUNGED IN LADY BRECKENRIDGE'S BOX WITH Lady Aline and a few other ladies and gentlemen of the *ton* with whom I'd become nodding acquaintances. Mrs. Bennington had granted me leave to visit her an hour after the performance, at her house in Cavendish Square. Grady would admit me, the note delivered to me in the box said, even if Mrs. Bennington were running late.

The play seemed to take a long time tonight. As usual, the audience talked to each other while the drama dragged on; they paid attention to the stage only when Mrs. Bennington stepped upon it. She was particularly brilliant tonight, her voice clear and ringing, the character coming to life through her.

Grenville's box remained dark and unused. I heard people speculate on where Grenville was hiding this evening. I ventured the opinion, when asked, that he'd chosen to have a quiet night at home, but no one believed me. Because I had no idea where he was myself, I could not elaborate.

After the performance, Lady Breckenridge offered her carriage to take me to Mrs. Bennington's in Cavendish Square. She accompanying me, of course. I accepted. I knew Lady Breckenridge was as curious as I, and she deserved to hear the explanation of how her lace got into the pocket of Mr. Turner.

I wanted also to bring Grenville. Something was in the wind between Grenville and Mrs. Bennington, and I did not want to chance it had nothing to do with Turner's murder.

Grenville would not thank me, but in the choice between saving Colonel Brandon and not offending Grenville, I had to choose Colonel Brandon's life.

Lady Breckenridge acquiesced and told her coachman to drive first to Grosvenor Street. Grenville, however, was not at home. Matthias, who answered the door, informed me Mr. Grenville again was spending the evening in his house on Clarges Street.

I spent a few moments debating whether I should intrude upon Grenville's privacy, then I decided to intrude. I told Lady Breckenridge's coachman to drive us to Clarges Street, and in ten minutes' time, we stopped before the house.

"I will have to ask you to remain here while I go inside," I said to Lady Breckenridge. "There are reasons."

She laughed. "My dear Lacey, it would hardly do for a lady of the *ton* to enter a house in which a gentleman keeps his mistress."

"You know far too many things for comfort, Donata."

"Gossip is popular entertainment. After you told me about Grenville's little actress, I put two and two together. There is little I do *not* know."

The thought unnerved me a bit. I descended from the carriage into the rain and plied the doorknocker. The haughty maid, Alicia, opened the door and looked me up and down.

Lucius Grenville employed the best-trained servants in London, even more so than Lady Gillis's elegant horde. Alicia stolidly refused to admit me. I had to talk long and hard to convince her the matter was of utmost urgency.

She at last let me in but forbade me to move past the front hall. She sent the footman Dickon upstairs with a message for Grenville, then Alicia hovered nearby, as though not trusting me not to dash up the stairs the instant her back was turned.

After an appallingly long wait, a door opened above, and I heard Grenville's footsteps on the stairs.

In the year or so I'd known Grenville, I had never seen him

in dishabille. Even now he was in only relative dishabille. He wore pantaloons and a lawn shirt covered with a silk dressing gown, and his hair was a bit mussed. His expression was wary and not a little annoyed.

"Lacey," he said in his cool man-about-town voice. "I respect and admire you, but this is hardly the best time for a visit."

"I realize that," I answered. "But I was on my way to see Mrs. Bennington, and I hoped you would come with me."

Grenville stopped his descent. "Mrs. Bennington? Why?"

"Because I believe she is the key to this murder. I thought you might want to be present."

Grenville came alert, all thoughts of privacy forgotten. "Yes. Yes I do. I must dress. Wait here."

"Be quick, please. I do not want Mrs. Bennington's dragon of a maid to refuse to admit me because I am late for the appointment."

Without answering, Grenville turned and dashed back up the stairs. The sound of a door banging followed.

I waited while the clock ticked steadily in the corner. I wished Grenville could be the sort of gentleman to simply snatch up a greatcoat and dash out the door, but no. He'd once told me that if he were seen on the streets of London without waistcoat and cravat and the proper footwear, the newspapers would be filled with stories that he'd run mad. Not even to catch a murderer would Grenville take chances with his reputation.

When the door banged again, I looked up in anticipation, but the voice that sailed down to me was not Grenville's.

"Lacey, what the devil do you think you're doing?"

Marianne Simmons, in true dishabille in a loose peignoir, her hair floating free, raced down the stairs to me.

"Trying to discover a murderer," I said.

"You came here to snatch him away to visit *Mrs. Bennington,* of all people! Why, I'd like to know? Let me come with you. I will claw her eyes out."

"No," I said firmly.

"Dear God, Lacey, why must you torment me?"

"I want to question Mrs. Bennington about the murder. I want Grenville there as well."

"And I suppose you will not tell me why?"

"No."

Marianne looked as though she might fly at me on the moment, claws raised, but she stopped, her face taking on a canny expression. "Did Mrs. Bennington do the murder? That would suit me."

I looked past her at Grenville, who was at last coming down the stairs. He had heard her. "Mrs. Bennington had nothing to do with Turner's death," he said in a sharp voice. "I am accompanying Lacey to prove it."

Marianne sent him a look of fury, but I saw the hurt in her eyes. She dropped her gaze and turned away before Grenville could spot it. "Alicia," she called to the prim maid. "Come upstairs and dress me. I am going out."

Grenville's face set. Saying nothing, he strode past Marianne and out of the house.

So great was Grenville's anger he'd climbed into the carriage before he realized it belonged to Lady Breckenridge, and she was waiting inside.

He flushed. "Good evening, my lady."

"Mr. Grenville," Lady Breckenridge said. Her eyes glinted with humor.

Grenville sent me an accusing stare. He was angry, and he was embarrassed, but I could not wait upon the nicety of his feelings.

As the carriage wound through the streets to Cavendish Square, I showed Grenville the scrap of lace and explained about the servants' passage at the Berkeley Square house and my thoughts about it. As I talked, Grenville's expression changed from frustrated anger to one that was worried and grim.

"If this is true, Lacey," he began. He broke off, as though unable to complete the thought. "I never believed . . ."

Grenville trailed off again, closed his mouth, and looked away in uncomfortable silence.

The Bennington house in Cavendish Square was quiet. We were admitted by a maid I'd not seen before, who curtseyed to us and led us to a reception room to wait. Grenville paced, moody and quiet, while Lady Breckenridge looked about her with interest.

Mrs. Bennington's maid, Grady, entered the room not long later and sent the three of us a look of disapproval.

"My lady has decided she is not receiving tonight," Grady said.

I had feared as much. "I do not wish to disturb her for long." I took the scrap of lace from my pocket. "Please give her this, and tell her Captain Lacey wishes to ask her about it."

Grady frowned but when she saw what I held out to her, paled. "She will know nothing about that."

"Take it to her, please."

Grady pressed her mouth closed. She snatched the lace from my hand and marched swiftly from the room.

Grenville shot me a dark look. "Lacey, you cannot mean Claire Bennington committed this crime, can you? I simply will not believe it."

"I do not know whether she committed it. That is why I want to ask her questions."

Grenville paced again, his distress evident. "She could not have killed Turner. She is not strong enough. She's only a girl."

He seemed inordinately upset, more so than a gentleman with simple concern for a young woman. Before I could speak further, Grady returned. She did not look pleased but said we could go up.

Grady led us to the sitting room in which Mrs. Bennington

had received me on my last visit. This time the salmon-striped sofa and chairs were strewn with gowns, bonnets, and shawls. I was reminded of Turner's rooms when the valet, Hazleton, had emptied the cupboards in preparation for sending Turner's things back to his father.

Grenville looked at the jumble in surprise. "You are leaving London?"

Mrs. Bennington flinched and avoided his gaze. "Grady, why did you let Mr. Grenville come here? I wanted only Captain Lacey."

"I came to help you," Grenville said, anger in his tone.

"We don't want your help," Grady retorted.

Mrs. Bennington sank to a chair and put her hand to her forehead. "I have such a headache. I do not want these people. Send them away; I feel unwell."

"You see?" Grady said to Grenville. "You have upset her again."

"I have done nothing of the sort. Claire, Captain Lacey has come to ask you about the murder of Henry Turner. I know you had nothing to do with it, and if you answer honestly, I can make him take his questioning elsewhere."

I stared at Grenville in amazement. His face was red, his gaze uncomfortable.

Mrs. Bennington's eyes swam with tears. "My head. Grady, I need my draught."

Grady rushed to the cupboard and pulled out a glass bottle full of dark liquid.

Lady Breckenridge, who had lifted a silk shawl to admire it, suddenly laughed. "Good heavens, how dramatic we are." She folded the shawl and replaced it on the chair. "We are not on the stage, Mrs. Bennington. Captain Lacey only wishes to know what became of that bit of lace you asked of me."

"Oh." Mrs. Bennington sat up, looking relieved. "From your ballgown? You ought to have said. I gave it to my husband."

"Your husband?" I asked. "What on earth for?"

"Because he asked me to."

She seemed to think this a fine enough reason. "Did it not occur to you to wonder why?" I asked.

"Not really."

"I think you do know why," I said. "I believe you know more than any of us about this matter."

She looked bewildered. "How could I?"

"You play the dupe well, Mrs. Bennington," I said. "But I believe you are not one."

Mrs. Bennington gazed at me, stunned, then the eyes that bewitched London audiences each night filled with tears.

"Leave her be, Lacey," Grenville said.

"I cannot. She is key to this. I want Colonel Brandon released, and I will do what I must to bring it about."

"Including browbeating a young woman?"

I stared at him. Grady had accused Grenville of shouting at Mrs. Bennington and throwing his walking stick, but now he bristled at me like a guard dog.

"Mrs. Bennington," I said, gentling my tone. "Why did your husband ask you to obtain a piece of lace from Lady Breckenridge?"

"I don't know. It was a game of some sort."

"A wager?" I supplied.

Her brow cleared. "Yes, that was it. He wagered I could not obtain a piece of lace from a highborn lady. Because I am so lowborn, you see."

"He said that?" Grenville asked, face thunderous. "What the devil made you marry that lout? Do not tell me you could not have the pick of gentlemen on the Continent."

"He was good to me," Mrs. Bennington said. "I had debts —he paid them. He must be kind to do that."

Or he'd wanted something. Claire Bennington, absorbed in herself and her life on stage, would not have realized that.

"Is he kind to you?" I asked.

"I suppose he is." Mrs. Bennington pressed delicate fingers to her temples. "Really, Captain, my head does ache."

Grady, her face set, poured a thick liquid into a small glass and pushed it at Mrs. Bennington.

Lady Breckenridge, still looking interested, sat down amid a pile of velvet gowns. "So you handed over the scrap of lace to your husband. When was that?"

"Oh, good heavens, I hardly remember." Mrs. Bennington took the draught from Grady and drank it down. She sighed in contentment when she handed the glass back, as though her headache already had started to fade. "Before supper, certainly. My husband escorted Lady Aline to the supper room. He'd told me to obtain the scrap of lace from *her*, but I'd only had opportunity to speak to Lady Breckenridge. Mr. Bennington was annoyed, I remember, that I had not approached Lady Aline."

Who was large and strong and could have driven a knife into Turner's heart were she cruel enough to do so.

"Do you love your husband, Mrs. Bennington?" I asked abruptly.

Her eyes widened. "Why ask that?"

"Because he is a murderer," I said. "And I wondered if you would help me or be loyal to him."

CHAPTER 18

*L*ady Breckenridge looked at me in complete astonishment. "Mr. Bennington?" She grew thoughtful. "Yes, I see."

Mrs. Bennington lowered her gaze. "I should be loyal. He is my husband."

Grady broke in fiercely, "She's nothing to do with it. I'll not see her in the dock for this."

"Nor will I," I said.

I tried to sound reassuring, but Grady moved between me and her mistress. "She is innocent. She can't help what that fiend of a husband does."

"I know," I said. "I imagine Mr. Bennington used her from the moment he met her. He knew as the husband of a celebrated actress, he would be eclipsed by her, and he was correct."

Grenville did not look terribly surprised by my assessment, but he was not happy.

Lady Breckenridge's eyes sparkled with interest. She was possibly the only person in the room not charged with emotion.

"I can work out how he must have done it," she said. "He

challenged Mrs. Bennington to obtain a bit of lace from a lady. Which she did—from me. Mr. Bennington goes into the anteroom at some time before supper, opens the door to the servants' passage, and affixes the lace to the nail to mark the door he needed. He does not want to use something of his own or his wife's in case it is found.

"He makes an appointment to meet Turner in the anteroom at midnight. Just before midnight, he slips out of the ballroom and into one of the sitting rooms along the hall. He waits until the servants' passage is empty, enters it, finds the door he marked, and enters the anteroom, taking the bit of lace in with him. He stabs Mr. Turner, eases him into the chair, and places the lace in the pocket. He leaves Colonel Brandon's knife in the wound and exits through the back passage just before Mrs. Harper enters." She stopped and drew a breath. "Yes, I believe that explains everything neatly."

"Though not how he obtained Brandon's knife," I said.

"Nor why Mr. Bennington should want to murder Mr. Turner at all," Lady Breckenridge added, looking only at me.

"I've made some guesses about that," I said. "Both Turner and Bennington were on the Continent at the same time and both recently returned to London. Perhaps Turner knew things Bennington did not want others to know. Turner seems to have been good at finding guilty secrets. Perhaps he knew the things that led Mr. Bennington to change his name." I fixed my gaze on Grady. "Do you know?"

Grady glanced at her mistress, who kept her gaze fixed on her lap. Grady wet her thin lips and said, "Bennington is a bad sort. But my lady, she was deep in debt—she *will* wager recklessly. That was not the first time she'd been in deep."

"You should be more careful," Grenville said to Mrs. Bennington. She flushed but did not look up.

"Aye, that's what I tell her," Grady said. "One of her creditors, he was threatening her with arrest. And us being in Italy, what would happen if she was taken by foreign police? Then this Mr. Worth, he comes backstage one night and says he'll pay the debts, all of them, free and clear, if only she'll marry him, in name alone."

"That must have seemed an answer from heaven," I said.

Mrs. Bennington raised her head. "I was so relieved, I could not refuse him. I saw no reason *to* refuse him. He said I could do what I pleased, and he would keep me out of trouble with the creditors. Why should I not marry him?"

"Because he is a blackguard," Grenville said. "Did you not sense that?"

"But he offered to help me. I wanted to go to London to perform, and he enabled me to do so. He has heaps of money. He was left a grand inheritance."

"He was," I said. "From a relative in Scotland."

"Yes," Mrs. Bennington answered.

"Did your husband know Mr. Turner on the Continent?"

Mrs. Bennington looked blank. "I have no idea."

"Aye, he knew him," Grady said, her face grim.

I started to ask why the devil she hadn't mentioned this on my previous visit, but I remembered Grady had not been in the room when I'd discussed Turner with Mrs. Bennington. When I'd spoken to Grady, she'd only wanted to talk about Grenville's anger at her mistress.

"You saw him?" I asked Grady. "In Italy?"

"Yes," Grady said. "Mr. Turner came to visit Mr. Bennington when we were in Milan. Talked to him like he wasn't a stranger, like they'd met before, but Mr. Bennington wasn't best pleased to see him. Then Mr. Turner went away, and I forgot all about it."

"A magistrate would be interested in knowing this," I said. "Why have you said nothing?"

"I didn't think it mattered, and I didn't want my lady bothered by Bow Street. That's the truth. That Runner, the one who came to the ball, was a great bully. And my lady had nothing to do with Turner getting himself killed. Besides, if her husband's convicted of murder, my lady loses his money. What's to become of her then?"

Grady looked anguished, but Mrs. Bennington seemed more resigned. "I have my money from the stage," she said. "And I have been poor before."

"You will not be again," Grenville said. "I will see to it."

Both Lady Breckenridge and I looked at him in surprise. Grenville's face was flushed. "I will take care of you, Claire," he said. "I offered to before, remember?"

Mrs. Bennington turned to him, eyes wide. "You frightened me. You said I must divorce my husband. I did not know what to think."

Neither did I. Grenville and Mrs. Bennington looked at each other, and the pair of them seemed to forget the rest of us were in the room.

"When you are free of Bennington, I will take care of you," Grenville said. "I told you this, and I promise it. I should have done so long ago."

I exchanged a glance with Lady Breckenridge. She raised her brows, and I shook my head slightly to indicate I too did not know what to make of the conversation.

Lady Breckenridge broke in. "Mr. Turner is dead now. So who can know what he wanted with Bennington? To blackmail him, presumably, over the fact that Bennington was not Mr. Bennington. Did Bennington want to leave Italy because of Turner, or because others also had got wind of his deception? And why did it matter so much?"

"I plan to ask him," I said. "Where is Mr. Bennington at present?"

Mrs. Bennington shrugged. "I never notice where he goes."

"He likes the Majestic Hotel in Piccadilly," Grady said. "He doesn't have a club like a proper gentleman."

I took up my walking stick, my usual restlessness getting the better of me. "If I can get a confession out of Bennington and have him arrested, that will solve many problems."

Lady Breckenridge looked alarmed. "He is a murderer, Gabriel. He killed one man who knew his secrets; why would he not kill you?"

"Because I have one advantage Turner did not—a very large and loud former sergeant who is now a Bow Street Runner."

"I will come with you," Grenville said. "If Bennington is guilty, I want to put my hands on him." He looked angry and dangerous.

"Then shall we adjourn to Piccadilly?" Lady Breckenridge asked. "In my carriage. I will accompany you, gentlemen."

"No, you will not," I said immediately. "We will return you home, and I will go from there."

She gave me a scornful look. "I am not a fainting flower, Captain. I do not intend to enter a gentlemen's hotel, but I certainly will not sit home and wait for you to remember to call on me and tell me what happened, if you bother to at all."

Grenville seemed uninterested in our disagreement. "Let us away, Lacey. I am ready to arrest a murderer."

"I want Pomeroy," I said.

"Very well. We'll fetch him." He swept out of the room without taking leave of Mrs. Bennington. I bowed to Mrs. Bennington, but she gazed after Grenville with a mixed expression of fear and wonder.

Lady Breckenridge and I descended the stairs together. Grenville paced in the foyer, waiting for us. I held him back as Lady Breckenridge went out the door to the carriage.

"Do you love her?" I asked in a low voice. "Mrs. Bennington?"

"What? Of course I do." Grenville's scowl softened suddenly. "Forgive me, Lacey, I ought to have told you. But it caught me a resounding blow when I found out, and I have not yet recovered." He lowered his voice and said, with a little smile, "Hadn't you guessed? Claire is my daughter."

WE FOUND MR. BENNINGTON IN THE SITTING ROOM OF THE Majestic Hotel in Piccadilly. The hotel itself was not far from the house where Henry Turner had kept his rooms.

Mr. Bennington sat in an armchair reading the *Times,* his immaculate suit attesting to the exactness of his valet. He crossed his legs and held the newspaper in carefully manicured hands.

He glanced up when I walked into the room alone but betrayed no surprise. "I will be with you in a moment, Captain," he said. "I am reading a fascinating story about a gentleman's journey through the wilds of Prussia. I must ask, if he complains of not having the comforts of London in the middle of Germany, why did he leave England in the first place?"

"I could not say," I said.

He hummed a little tune in his throat as he read on, then he finally laid the paper aside. "Sit down, Captain. We might as well be civilized. You have found me out, have you? I wondered how long it would take you. People talk about your cleverness, but I believe you are not as clever as your reputation paints you."

I did take a seat, but one out of his reach. We were the only ones in the sitting room, and the windows were muffled with drapes against the night. The room was quiet and genteel, with a gilded clock ticking on the mantelpiece and decanters of wine and brandy resting on tables for the guests' convenience.

Grenville and Pomeroy waited in the next room for me to call them in. I wished I could have had time to speak to Grenville a bit more after he made his astounding statement about Mrs. Bennington, but we'd had no moments of privacy. His revelation, however, explained some of his odd behavior — he was a worried father, not a jealous lover.

"In this instance, I was distracted by Colonel Brandon," I

said to Bennington. "The knife pointed too much to him, and he did not help by being stubbornly vague with both me and the magistrate."

"He is a stubborn gentleman," Bennington said with a smile. "I was pleased, quite pleased, actually, to discover I was not the only person that horrible young man tried to blackmail. I did Colonel Brandon a favor."

"By landing him in Newgate?" I asked, my temper rising.

"That was unfortunate, I agree. But I saved him from whatever dire revelation with which Turner threatened him."

"You do not know what that dire revelation was?"

"No, nor did I care. My dear Lacey, I cared only that Turner knew I should not have enjoyed my glorious inheritance over the years."

"No?" I asked, speculations coming together. "An inheritance from a fourth cousin, probably one you would rarely, if ever, meet, especially when he lived in Scotland and you stayed on the Continent. His family and friends might not have seen the man's heir for decades, if they'd ever seen him at all. Which means they might not realize you weren't his fourth cousin after all."

"Excellent, Captain." Bennington applauded me softly. "A man can steal an inheritance, you know, if he is very clever and very lucky. And I was both. Mr. Worth, the true heir, had moved to the German states as a lad of ten and hadn't returned to England in forty years. He'd never met his so-wealthy distant cousin from Scotland. I convinced the Scottish solicitors and Worth's London man of business that *I* was Mr. Worth—made easier because I knew my friend Worth was dead. Fell down a mountain in Bavaria, poor fellow. He was all alone, with no one to know but me."

"Then you stayed in Italy," I finished for him, "far from people who'd known the true Mr. Worth—or knew you well, for that matter. But then, Henry Turner discovered your secret."

Bennington watched me with an amused expression. "Ah, Captain, I'd grown used to my comfortable means. I could do whatever I pleased, and living on the Continent suited me fine. Why the devil should I lose it all because Henry Turner could not mind his own business?"

"How did he know you were not the true Mr. Worth?" I asked.

"My bad luck. Mr. Turner apparently had met someone who'd known Worth in Germany, and then he met me. I'd never kept it entirely secret that I'd changed my name when I'd married Claire—a blind is better when you pretend it is of no importance. But Turner was too shrewd for his own good, and he realized after a time the George Worth his acquaintance had spoken of was an entirely different man from me. I suppose then Henry decided to dig around and find out what he could about me. He was a careful gambler—was good at doing his research so he'd more likely win. He took me aside and explained this to me one day while I was strolling about Milan for my health, Turner smiling in a rather nasty way. He liked money, so it was quite easy to press a bank draft into his hand and make him leave me alone."

"But he returned?"

"Oh, yes. I made a mistake believing that giving him money would see the end of it. I'd never dealt with a blackmailer before, you see, and I thought I had been so careful to cover my tracks."

"But Turner persisted."

"Yes, he was quite obnoxious. He told me he planned to settle on the Continent, and in fact was going to stay with a friend for a time in Paris. But he'd return to Milan, and suggested we would meet again. I could not have that. By this time, my wife was famous enough that the London theatres were clamoring to have her. I had no wish to return to England, but I reasoned we could go while Turner was in Paris. I thought, you see, if it proved too difficult and too expensive for Turner to pursue me, I'd be rid of the fellow. He'd been so sincere in his declaration he'd live on the Continent for good."

"But Turner came to London."

Bennington grimaced. "Yes, to my misfortune. I'd thought myself safe at last, and then he turns up on my doorstep, smiling and demanding more money. I knew if he told anyone my secret, I was finished."

"So you killed him."

"I had no choice. I feared to call him out, because if I did, he'd likely spread the tale of why we had the appointment, and second . . ." He smiled. "Henry Turner was young and robust, and I am not as steady of hand as I once was. He'd have potted me good."

"You would have died with honor," I said.

He laughed. "Dear me, I have no honor. Honor is for cavalry captains. If I had honor, I'd not have pushed my friend Mr. Worth down the mountain after I learned he'd just come into a large inheritance. His face was completely smashed, and there we were, in a foreign country, no one there knowing which of us was which. The old me was buried, and a new George Worth wrote to the solicitors saying he was moving on to Italy and to send the funds there. I knew it would be a bit risky pretending to be someone else, but then I met Claire." His look turned beatific. "I thought all the gods were smiling on me."

"Because you could marry her and hide in her shadow," I said. "You might not make it a deep secret you'd changed your name to hers, but people would assume it was because you generously wanted her to continue to be known by her stage name. In time, people would forget about the name *Worth*, and no longer associate it with you. Let alone what your real name was."

"Precisely, Captain. It was easy to make Claire marry me. She had hordes of young men dancing attendance on her, but

I had one thing she could not resist. Money. I promised to pay her gambling debts if she'd do me the honor of becoming my wife. I have a sad affliction and cannot bother her in the carnal way, which I assure you she does not mind. And I do not mind much myself. The bodily humors are an inconvenience and interfere with my peace and quiet. Claire never pretended she'd married me for anything but my funds, and I had no intention of being besotted with my own wife. The arrangement suited us admirably. When Turner came along to destroy that . . ." He waved his hand, wiping away Mr. Turner.

"You are correct about one thing," I said. "You have no honor."

"Oh, come now, Captain. Where would that legacy have gone? George Worth told me he had no heir he knew of, unless his man of business could find some fellow living in the wilds of America or some such place. Or the solicitors simply would have discovered a way to divide it amongst themselves. Why should all that money go to waste? I put it to excellent use, and besides, I saved Claire Bennington, the great actress, from debtors' prison. Don't pretend Henry Turner threatened to reveal my secret because he was virtuous. The oily little tick wanted to bleed me dry."

"Of money you obtained by killing another."

He laughed softly. "I suppose you are oozing honor, and in the army threw yourself in front of bullets to save others?"

"Not quite," I said. "But I did pull others out of the way of bullets."

"All for pittance. You are a poor man, Captain. You always have been. What can you understand of a man's need for wealth and comfort?"

"Grenville is the wealthiest man I've ever met," I said. "He loves his comfort, and yet he has much generosity and charity."

"Ah, well. Blame it on my birth. My father was a poor man who blew out his brains when he lost his little all on a horse.

He left a son buried in a school with no one to care for him. Pity me."

"I pity your wife. And even Turner, although, by all accounts, he was not a pleasant person."

"He was not. I did the world a favor, my dear fellow."

I stood up, my patience at an end. "Had you killed him in a duel, I might understand. But you deliberately endangered Colonel Brandon and Mrs. Harper, both of whom were innocent—who were as much victims of Turner's blackmailing as you. You tried to implicate Lady Breckenridge, although that, to her good luck, came to nothing."

"Well, I could hardly continue to enjoy my legacy if I owned up to murder, could I? And besides, Colonel Brandon and Mrs. Harper are not innocent. They were carrying on a frightfully sordid affair, and so let themselves come under Turner's power."

I did not correct him about that. "The fact remains that Colonel Brandon is in prison for a murder he did not commit. You used his knife—where did you get it? Did you pick his pocket, or did you have your wife do that for you too?"

"I had no need of such trickery. The knife was lying there, plain as day, on the writing table. I had my own in my pocket, but how much better to use another man's? I had no idea at the time that it belonged to the good colonel."

"I intend to let the good colonel out of prison one way or another, even if I have to drag you by the neck to Bow Street myself."

At last, uneasiness flickered in his eyes. "You are a man of determination."

"I owe Colonel Brandon much. I will not see him die for your crime. And you, if you have spoken the truth today, are long overdue for paying."

He continued to watch me. "Think of my wife, Captain. Claire cannot be left alone for a moment. She is one of the stupidest women alive, even if she is brilliant behind the foot-lights. What will become of her?"

I thought of Grenville. "She will be cared for. Quite well, in fact. She no longer needs you."

"Oh, dear. Never tell me some gentleman is waiting in the wings to sweep her off—if you will pardon the pun."

"I am fortunate to have friends, Mr. Bennington. One of them is a Bow Street Runner."

As if on cue, Pomeroy entered the room.

At the sight of tall, jovial Pomeroy, anticipating a reward for the conviction of Henry Turner's murderer, Bennington's face drained of color. "Oh, God."

"A most illuminating conversation, Captain," Pomeroy boomed. "Criminals, especially the clever ones, do like to talk. Mr. Bennington, or Mr. Worth—or whatever you would like to be called—I arrest you in the King's name for the murder of Henry Turner. Shall you come with me and speak to the magistrate? Since you like to talk, you'll be able to tell your story all over again. I am looking forward to it, sir."

CHAPTER 19

J wanted the matter to conclude simply, by the magistrates letting Brandon out of his prison room and putting Bennington into it.

But of course, that could not be done. Pomeroy took Bennington to Bow Street, where he would wait until the next morning for Sir Nathaniel to examine him. Pomeroy was gleeful, certain the conversation both he and Grenville had overheard, plus the explanation of how Bennington had managed to kill Turner with no one seeing him, would get Pomeroy his hoped for conviction and the reward offered by Turner's father.

Lady Breckenridge had been delighted to observe us emerging from the hotel with Bennington. Pomeroy and his patrollers took Bennington away with them, and Lady Breckenridge offered to have her coachman drop me and Grenville in Grosvenor Street before she went home. She demanded the full tale on the way, and Grenville gave it to her. I felt strangely reluctant to speak.

Grenville descended first when we reached his house. As I

prepared to follow, Lady Breckenridge stopped me with a hand on my arm.

"I thank you for not shunting me aside, Gabriel. That was most fascinating."

"You ought to curb your fascination for sordid business," I said, but I smiled at her. A fainting flower she was not. Past experience had shown I had not the patience for a fainting flower.

"Nonsense," she said briskly. "It was just the thing. Life in Mayfair is deadly dull, you know. The same people at the same soirees and balls and garden parties, talking of the same things, day after day. You and your investigations are refreshing."

"I am pleased I entertain you."

"Do not tease me. I know you like my interest. When you have finished all you need to finish, Gabriel, pay a call on me. I would be glad to receive you."

Her tone was light, but I sensed caution behind it. She was still not certain where we stood, and somewhere inside her existed the young woman who'd been bruised by her unhappy marriage.

I bowed. "I would be most happy to call on you."

She gave me a nod as though she did not care one way or the other, but her eyes as she turned away told me she was pleased.

I stepped down, and Lady Breckenridge told her coachman to drive on. I followed Grenville into his warm and splendid house.

Grenville invited me to supper, but I declined. "I have many things to do this night," I said. "I must go to Louisa and tell her what has happened."

"You are right. Mrs. Brandon should not suffer another minute."

I hesitated. "Tell Marianne about Mrs. Bennington. She deserves to know."

"Claire does not know yet," Grenville said, his eyes quiet.

"Her mother wrote me a few weeks ago, from Austria. She told me she was very ill, dying, and that Claire was mine. I had not heard from Anna for twenty years, and now she will likely not last twenty days," he finished sadly.

"And you believe her?"

"I do now. I asked Claire when she was born, and the dates correspond exactly with my time with Anna Baumgarten. She was an opera singer I met in Austria, when I was so very young. Our affair did not last long, and I never saw her again. I knew she'd left the stage, but no more than that. Anna never told me of Claire, and in her letter, she admitted she'd not been certain who'd sired Claire at the time. I believe that—Anna was older than me and obviously more experienced. Then, later, she feared I'd take Claire away from her. Not an illogical fear. I probably would have. I also got Claire to tell me her mother had encouraged her to change her surname to Bennington, the better to please English audiences. Always astute, was Anna."

"Not to throw cold water," I said, "but you are very rich, and your Anna could simply claim you are Claire's father, so someone wealthy would look after her."

"I know." Grenville gave me a smile. "When one has a great deal of money, there are those who feel it is natural you should share it with them. But Claire is mine, I am certain of it."

"Are you sure you don't simply wish to be certain?"

"Of course I wish it. I admit I was astonishingly pleased when I learned I had a daughter. Claire is beautiful and gifted, and she drives me to distraction. But I knew she was mine the moment I looked at her." His smile blossomed to a grin. "The poor woman has inherited the Grenville nose."

LOUISA WAS STILL AWAKE WHEN I ARRIVED IN BROOK

Street, but Lady Aline was not with her. Louisa explained, when she received me, that she had sent Lady Aline home.

"She has been very kind to me. But I wanted to be alone." She sighed. "It is difficult to keep up my spirits to please her."

"You will not have to do so much longer," I said.

We sat in her yellow room, a fire on the hearth chasing away the gloom of the night, while I told her about Bennington and his arrest. In the morning, I said, I would ask Sir Nathaniel officially to dismiss the murder charge against Brandon and let him come home.

"You did this for me," Louisa whispered when I finished my tale. "Why? Why are you so impossibly good to me, Gabriel?"

I took her hand, which was too cold, her fingers too thin. "There have been times in my life when you were strong for me. I wanted to be strong for you, this once."

"I have not been strong at all. You say he is truly innocent of this?"

"Your husband did not kill Henry Turner. I knew from the beginning the crime was all wrong for him. Nor is Imogene Harper his lover."

Louisa lifted her head. "But she was. On the Peninsula, she was, however briefly."

"I know. I'm sorry. I am not certain I will forgive him that."

"I will." When I looked surprised, Louisa said, "Aloysius is my husband, Gabriel. We have weathered much together. We will weather this, too."

"You love the idiot."

"Yes. I always have." She touched my cheek. "And I love you too."

"A fact that warms my heart." I kissed her forehead then let her go. "I hope our friendship may weather all this as well."

"It will. I will not be ungrateful and shun you simply because I am embarrassed."

"Good." I paused. The cheerful room had grown more

cheerful still, and in a few moments, I would not be able to bear it. "What did you do with the paper, Louisa?" I asked.

She stilled. "Paper?"

"The one Brandon told you to fetch from the Gillises'."

Her cheeks darkened. "Must you know everything?"

"It is a dangerous document to have."

"I know that. But the greatest danger Aloysius fears is from you."

I held on to my temper. "Does he truly believe I would betray him? After all this? Please give it to me, Louisa. Unless you have already destroyed it."

She rose, agitated, and I rose with her. "I have not. How did you know I had it?"

"Because there is no one else in the world to whom Brandon would have entrusted it. I toyed with the idea that he'd given it to Mrs. Harper, but she did not have it, which was why she went to search Turner's rooms. Brandon probably meant to hide it and fetch it the next day, never dreaming he'd be bound over for trial. *He* knew he did not commit the murder, and he expected everyone else to take him at his word. You read French," I finished. "You must know what the document is."

Louisa wouldn't look at me. "Yes."

"You went to see Brandon after I'd admonished you to, did you not?"

She finally met my gaze. "I did. And he told me an extraordinary tale. He bared his soul to me. He must have been quite desperate to do that. Aloysius hates to appear weak, especially to a woman — most especially to his wife."

"He craves your respect."

"Yes, well, he told me where the paper was, told me to hide it, and begged me, for God's sake, not to give it to you."

"I already know his secrets. Louisa, please, will you trust me and let me have it? No one in the world but you and I and he will know of it."

She looked skeptical. "What about Mrs. Harper?"

"Mrs. Harper should bless her luck Brandon decided to help her at all. I will send word to her it is all over and tell her to return to Scotland."

"Good," Louisa said. She was still pale, but her eyes began to sparkle with their usual fervor. "I will forgive Aloysius, because he can be so easily led into mischief. But Mrs. Harper is another matter. She had no bloody business pinching my husband."

I smiled. "I am pleased to see you will not simply be walked on."

"Indeed no. I expect Aloysius to be quite kind to me for a very long time." Louisa placed her hand on my arm. "Thank you, Gabriel. Drink your coffee, and I will fetch the paper."

AN HOUR LATER FOUND ME AT NEWGATE PRISON WITH THE incriminating letter tucked into my pocket. The turnkey was reluctant to let me in at this late hour, but he was easily bribed.

I found Brandon still dressed, sitting on his bed with his head in his hands. He looked up when I was ushered in and sprang to his feet. "What are you doing here?"

I waited until the turnkey shut the door, waited again until I heard his footsteps retreat.

"I came to tell you that you will soon be free," I said. "I found the man responsible for Henry Turner's death."

Brandon stared at me in shock. "But . . ."

"Had you convinced yourself I never would? Mr. Bennington was arrested this evening. I hoped you could be released at once, but magistrates do things in their own time."

Brandon gaped at me as I told the story for the second time tonight, and when I finished, he began to splutter.

"The blackguard! Using my own knife, sitting by quietly as you please while I waited in here for my trial. Damn the man."

"Would it help to know he is terrified of what is to come?"
I asked.

"What? No, of course not. I long to call the fellow out, but
I suppose that would not be the thing."

He paced the cell, animation flowing into his body.
Brandon dejected was a sad sight, but now his eyes flashed,
and his back was straight and strong.

"If you had told me the truth from the beginning, sir, you
might not have had to come here at all," I said.

Brandon swung to me. "Oh, yes I would have. When I
admitted the knife was mine, Pomeroy blamed me at once,
damn the man."

"Which he would not have if you'd stayed in the ballroom
the entire night with your wife. Why the devil did you not at
least say Stokes saw you wandering the back rooms at the time
of the murder?"

"Because it was none of his business. I didn't want Stokes
standing up in court bellowing every place I'd been."

I thought I understood. "Because if it were mentioned,
someone, Stokes himself perhaps, might recall you slipping
back there after Lord Gillis sent for Pomeroy and his
patrollers. And then Pomeroy, ever thorough, might find what
you'd hidden there." His eyes widened at my guesses, and I
lost my temper. "Damn it, sir, I know all about Naveau, and
the document, and Mrs. Harper. What the hell were you
thinking?"

"You know what the document is?" he asked, watching me.

"I read it. Why the devil didn't you come to me when Mrs.
Harper first approached you? I could have retrieved the paper
without all your machinations at the ball. I know people who
could have made Turner hand it over—Grenville for one, or if
we were more desperate, James Denis. I would have done this
for you. Why did you not trust me?"

Brandon looked at me with infuriating stubbornness.
"Because I know how much you hate me. Why would you not

use the opportunity to bring about my downfall? I could see you doing so, with glee."

"Then you read me entirely wrong. I have been loyal to you since the day I swore allegiance to you, twenty years ago. That has not changed."

Brandon shot a guilty look at my walking stick. "I hurt you."

"I know. And I haven't forgiven you for that, believe me. But you were angry then—you thought I'd taken Louisa from you, the woman you love more than your own life. You feared Louisa would leave you for me, even after you retracted your plan to divorce her. You would have deserved it if she had, but Louisa loves you. The pair of you are so romantic, you make me weep. I never bedded your wife, sir. Never. She never would have done such a thing."

"But you would have," he said sullenly.

"Of course. On an instant. Louisa has always been special to me. If she had wanted to give herself to me in that way, I would have taken what she offered and felt privileged to receive it. But she never offered, it never happened, and it never will."

Brandon glared at me with his old fire. "Such words do not make me disposed to trust you."

"You might be a complete idiot concerning your wife, but it is also true I owe you my life. All of it." I gave him a firm look. "And so I will do my damndest to keep you safe."

I took the document from my pocket and held it up for him to see. I'd read it in Louisa's sitting room and nearly groaned in dismay. In Brandon's handwriting, in French, the letter told Colonel Naveau of Mrs. Harper's husband's death and explained there would be no more information from that source. The letter also included a copy of a dispatch Major Harper had set aside for Naveau.

"This is what everything has been about," I said. "Good God, sir. What possessed you? The chance to convince Mrs.

Harper to marry you and bear your children? Was that truly a reason to betray your own men to the French? Others might have done so, but I never in a thousand years dreamed *you* would."

Brandon ignored my tirade, his gaze on the paper. "Where did you get that?"

"Louisa gave it to me after she'd found where you'd hidden it in the Gillises' house."

"I told Louisa expressly not to show it to you."

"Why not? What did you fear I'd do? Give it back to Naveau? I am, in fact, supposed to do that very thing, on the orders of James Denis."

Brandon whitened. "I will never let you. I will kill you first."

"Your faith in me is overwhelming."

I turned on my heel and stalked to the fireplace. There I knelt and thrust the letter into the flames.

"What are you doing?" Brandon demanded.

"Burning the thing. Or would you like to face charges of treason?"

I took up the poker and pushed the papers into the heart of the fire, then I watched while the whole of the thing burned. When any scrap fell, I lifted it with tongs and shoved it back into the flames.

I waited until the papers had burned completely to ashes, then I rose.

Brandon was staring at me as though he could not believe what I'd just done. "James Denis told you to take that to Naveau?"

"Yes," I said tersely.

"What will you tell him?"

He looked a bit worried. I wondered whether Brandon was anxious on my behalf or feared Denis would retaliate against him for not stopping me.

"I will think of something. Why did you not have Louisa destroy it?"

"I hadn't time to examine the papers at the ball. I wanted to be certain Turner had given me the right document. Turner had closed it and the letter into another paper, and I barely had time to break the seal and see the handwriting was mine before I fled the room. I fancied I'd heard someone coming. Then when I learned Turner had been killed, I panicked."

The last turn of the labyrinth straightened before me. "That is how your knife got into the anteroom. You pulled it from your pocket to break the seal on the paper, and you left the knife on the writing table in your haste."

Brandon looked uninterested. "Yes, I suppose I must have done. At the time I was not concerned about the damned knife."

"Careless of you. You left a murder weapon handy for the ever resourceful Mr. Bennington." I looked at him in anger. "How could you have written such a letter in the first place? How many men did we lose because you sent Naveau that dispatch?"

Brandon gave me a look of contempt. "None at all. The information was false."

I stopped. "I beg your pardon?"

"I changed the dispatch when I copied it. The information Naveau received was false. I imagine that because of it, a French troop uselessly scoured the hills for hours, looking for English artillery. Meanwhile we were far away." Brandon peered at me. "Did you think I would pass information to the French, Gabriel? What do you take me for?"

I let out my breath. "Do you know, sir, sometimes I could cheerfully strangle you."

"We are already in prison. You would not have far to go."

Brandon rarely tried for levity, so I could not know whether he attempted a joke.

"If the information were false, why the devil were you so anxious to get the document back?"

"Well, I could not prove it was false, could I? I would have to have the original dispatch, which I assume has been destroyed by now, or Wellington would have to come forward and claim he remembered every detail of the original battle plans. *I* knew it was false, and Naveau probably realizes it was by this time. A tribunal, on the other hand, especially one influenced by any enemies I made during the war, might not choose to believe me. And even if I could prove I'd passed bad information, Mrs. Harper's husband might still be exposed, and she ruined. I hardly liked to risk it."

I stepped close to him. "If anything of this nature happens again—though I likely *will* strangle you if it does—*tell me.*"

"When I require your help, Gabriel, I will ask for it."

We regarded each other in silence, face to face, eye to eye.

I turned away. "Be happy I am both fond of your wife and bad at obeying orders," I said. "You will be released tomorrow. Good night."

The turnkey let me out. I left Brandon in the middle of the room, staring at me with an unreadable expression.

CHAPTER 20

*T*he next morning, in the Bow Street magistrate's house, I told Sir Nathaniel Conant the story of Bennington's confession to me, verified by Grenville and Pomeroy, who had heard it from the next room.

Mr. Bennington, wearing his usual air of faint scorn, stood before Sir Nathaniel and smoothly agreed that yes, he was a murderer twice over. Love of money, he said, was the root of all evil. That was in the New Testament. In Saint Paul's letters to Timothy, if one wanted to be precise.

Sir Nathaniel, looking neither shocked nor amused, committed Mr. Bennington to trial for the murder of Henry Turner. The murder of Mr. Worth, occurring in another country years ago, with no witnesses, would not be tried here, although Sir Nathaniel would keep Bennington's confession to it in mind.

Bennington, however, never did come to trial. He was found dead the morning before he was to stand in the dock, hanging from his bedsheets in his prison room in Newgate. The turnkeys were supposed to prevent such things, but as I

had observed, the turnkey for the rooms of the wealthy pris-
oners was easily bribed. I assumed the fastidious Mr.
Bennington could not bring himself, in the end, to face the
public hangman.

In any case, Brandon was released the same day
Bennington was taken to Newgate. I do not know what Louisa
did when Brandon arrived home, because I was not there to
witness it. I left the two of them alone to rejoice, to scold, to
decide what they would do from there, together. They did not
need me.

The same afternoon Brandon went home, I received the
inevitable summons to Denis's Curzon Street house.

I met with Denis and Colonel Naveau in Denis's study, the
room in which Denis usually received me. Denis sat behind a
desk that was habitually clean—I did not know if he ever used
it for anything other than intimidating his visitors.

Colonel Naveau, tense and irritated, turned on me as I
entered the room. "Have you got it?"

"No," I answered. "I burned it."

"What?" The colonel trailed off in French, his language
becoming colorful. Denis said nothing.

I laid my walking stick on a small table beside me. "I
burned it because its existence was a threat to Colonel Brandon. I could not risk you would not try to extort money from
him because of it, or from Mrs. Harper."

"Brandon sent it to me," Naveau said. "He took the risk.
He must live with that."

"Not any longer. Why did you keep the paper, by the bye?
To prove you were a good republican and an excellent
exploring officer? Louis Bourbon is not a strong king. Perhaps
the Republic will rise again, and you will need to prove your
loyalty to it."

"Please do not tell my motives to me," Naveau said. "I
kept it for my own reasons." He glanced at Denis, who had
neither moved nor spoken during our exchange. "You

promised he would obtain it for me. I paid you money. Much money."

"I will return your fee," Denis said smoothly. "Like you, Captain Lacey does things for his own reasons."

Naveau gave Denis a hard look. "And you will do nothing?"

Denis cleared his throat, and the two pugilists who stood near the windows came alert. "Please pack your things and return to France, Colonel," Denis said.

Naveau looked at me for a moment longer, stark anger in his eyes. But he was not foolish enough to argue with James Denis. He bowed coolly then strode past me and out of the room.

A lackey in the hall closed the door behind him. Silence fell. The pugilists returned to their stances by the windows. Denis folded his hands on top of his desk and said nothing.

"You must have known I would never give that paper back to him," I said.

Denis inclined his head. "I suspected so, yes."

"Then why did you ask me to find it? Not to placate Naveau, surely."

"It was a test, of sorts."

"A test? And I failed?"

"No," Denis said. "You passed."

I lifted my brows.

"I wished to see where your loyalties lie," he said. "And what you would do for them. You are a man of great loyalty, even when it conflicts with your heart."

I stared at him, not a little annoyed. "I am pleased I could provide you with entertainment."

"No, you are not." He regarded me a moment longer. "Was there something else?"

I hesitated, my fingers brushing my engraved name on my walking stick. "My wife." A familiar lump rose in my throat. "Did she ever marry her French officer?"

"Never officially. I believe they find it easier to let others simply assume them man and wife. Mrs. Lacey has had four other children with this Frenchman, as a matter of fact."

"Good Lord." So, Carlotta had found family and happiness at last. I continued, my lips tight, "If I dissolve the marriage with her, they will no doubt be pleased."

"You will likewise be free," Denis said.

I knew he could help me, that he waited for me to ask him to help. James Denis could no doubt reach out and scoop up my wife, pay the money to get me a divorce or annulment, and land her in France again to marry her Frenchman.

He could, and he would. But I was not yet certain I was ready.

Denis nodded, as though knowing my thoughts. "Good afternoon, Captain. My carriage will return you home."

I left him, still tempted and uncertain. I knew one day soon, I would return to him, hat in hand, and ask for his help. He knew it, too.

I turned away without telling him goodbye, and his butler led me out.

I DID NOT RETURN HOME BUT ASKED DENIS'S COACHMAN TO leave me in South Audley Street. Lady Breckenridge's drawing room this afternoon was filled with highborn ladies, wits and dandies, and a poet and an artist.

They'd heard Mr. Bennington had been arrested for murder, and wasn't that dashed odd? Poor Claire Bennington, they said, but then, her husband had always been a queer chap that no one knew much about. Best she put him behind her as quickly as possible.

Lady Breckenridge smiled at me from across the room. She lounged in a peach silk gown that bared her shoulders, and smoke from her cigarillo wreathed her face. A decadent lady, she liked her sensual pleasures, but she had heart.

When I at last was able to speak to her, she leaned to me and whispered, "Stay behind."

I obeyed. As the callers drifted away, I lingered, shaking hands with the wits and dandies who were trying to become closer to the great Grenville.

Finally, the last guest went away, and Lady Breckenridge and I were alone.

"Let us adjourn upstairs," she said. "This room reeks of perfume. Lady Hartley does like exotic scent, and there's nothing for it that we all must be drenched in it by the time she leaves."

So saying, she ascended to the next floor and to her private boudoir. Barnstable, after his inquiries about the state of my bad leg and rejoicing how quickly my bruises had gone away, brought us coffee and brandy and then left us alone.

I told Lady Breckenridge about Bennington's examination and the fact that Brandon had gone home.

"Thank heavens," she said, pouring a large dollop of brandy into my coffee. "Poor Mrs. Brandon. How awful for her. It will not be easy for her to forgive him."

"No. But she loves him enough to do it."

Lady Breckenridge's brows arched. "Love and loyalty in marriage. What an odd idea."

I smiled over my coffee cup. "Rather old-fashioned."

We drank in companionable silence.

"This summer I will spend time at my father's estate in Oxfordshire," Lady Breckenridge said presently. "It is a beautiful place, and the gardens are quite grand. People pay a shilling on Thursdays to look at them."

"Do they, indeed?"

"I am going to be so bold as to ask you to visit. For a fortnight, perhaps. My mother would approve of you."

"Of a penniless captain who cannot even be a captain any longer?"

"My mother is a true blue blood. She cares nothing for money. Or at least, she does not now her only daughter is provided for. She can retreat into lofty ideals. She does it very well." Lady Breckenridge smiled, the affection in her eyes outweighing her acerbic words.

"I would be honored to accept such an invitation."

"Good," she said.

I set down my cup, and rose. Lady Breckenridge looked surprised. "Goodness, are you going already?"

"No." I reached down, took her cup from her, and put it on the table beside her. Then I closed my hands on hers and raised her to her feet.

"Donata," I said. "I want never to be less than honest with you. You once guessed I had been married, and you assumed me a widower. The truth is I am still married."

Lady Breckenridge's eyes widened. I went on quickly. "Fifteen years ago, Mrs. Lacey deserted me. I have not seen her since. I recently discovered that she lives in a village in France with her lover." I tightened my grip. "I want to find her and dissolve the marriage if I can. And after I have done what I need to set her free, I would like to ask leave to court you."

Lady Breckenridge said nothing. Any other woman might have been overwhelmed by what I'd just told her, or grown furious, or burst into tears. But I knew Lady Breckenridge would forgive honesty far more quickly than she'd accept pleasing lies. She was resilient, this lady.

"I have no idea how to make pretty lover's speeches," I said when the silence had stretched. "Not like your poets."

"Poetry can be tedious. Too many words to say a simple thing." She studied me a moment longer, the pressure of her fingers warm on mine. "Very well, Captain. I give you leave."

Something stirred in my heart. I leaned down and brushed her lips with a soft kiss.

When I made to pull away, to take my leave, she held on to my hands. "Stay," she said.

We looked at each other a moment longer.

"Very well," I replied, and did so.

End

EXCERPT: A COVENT GARDEN MYSTERY

CAPTAIN LACEY REGENCY MYSTERIES
BOOK 6

June 1817

The young woman buying peaches in Covent Garden in the early morning had honey brown hair under a small bonnet, clear white skin, deep brown eyes, and a faint French accent. The stall owner was trying to cheat her.

"Ha'penny for two, miss," the stall owner, a stooped man with a fat red nose and strands of greasy hair under a cap, said. "Best to be had."

He was goading her to take two shriveled specimens. When she pointed to the firm, ripe fruit near the man's hand, he shook his head. "Penny apiece for those, love."

I'd just seen him sell two fine peaches to a housewife for half that price, but he probably thought he could fleece a foreigner, especially an inexperienced girl.

I turned to the peach-seller's stall, walking stick in hand. A lady in distress, even over peaches, spoke to my knight-errant instincts.

"Prices have changed, have they?" I asked the peach seller.

He shot me an irritated look. "They do, Cap'n."

"In a quarter of an hour?" I leaned to him. "Sell her the same as you sold the others."

The peach seller glowered at me, a glint in his eye, but he backed down. I had the reputation for a foul temper, although I believe my acquaintanceship with magistrates and Bow Street Runners decided the matter.

He handed the good peaches to the girl. "Ha'penny," he muttered. To me, he said, "I know why your nose is so long, Cap'n. You use it to poke into business 'tisn't yours."

"True." I touched the offending appendage. "Several men have broken it for me."

"Shouldn't wonder." He took the girl's coin then, with another bellicose look at me, turned to his next customer. "Two for ha'penny."

The girl placed the peaches in the basket on her arm and glanced at me shyly. "I thank you, sir."

I had not seen the young woman in Covent Garden before. Her dress was well made, high-waisted and plain-skirted, the gown of a young, gently born miss. She seemed more suited to strolling formal gardens with smitten young men than roaming Covent Garden shopping for peaches.

Though she spoke English well, her voice held definite French overtones. Perhaps she was an Englishman's paramour, brought home with him from Paris. Or the daughter of émigrés who had fled France long ago and elected to stay in England, even after Louis Bourbon had been restored to his throne.

Whoever she was, she smiled at me, grateful for rescue. Her expression was guileless—too innocent to be a man's paramour, I decided. She possessed an unworldly air that spoke of a simple life. She must be a dutiful daughter, gathering breakfast for her mother or father.

I tipped my hat to her. "Captain Gabriel Lacey, at your service. May I escort you somewhere?"

Her smile was crooked, and her brown eyes sparkled with

good humor. "My father and mother are staying near, sir. I wanted peaches this morning, and so ventured to find them."

That they'd let her come out alone to the markets in Covent Garden did not speak well for them. But perhaps they were provincial people, used to places where everyone knew everyone, where no one would dream of harming the daughters of respectable gentlefolk.

The girl stirred a protective instinct in me. I held out my arm. "Which house? I will walk you there."

She blushed and shook her head. "You are kind, sir, but I must not trouble you."

She thought me forward. At least she was that wise, but anyone in the market could have told her she had nothing to fear from me.

"You can introduce me to your mama and papa," I began, but a shrill voice cut across the market, a startled cry in French.

My young lady turned, and her smile broadened into one of relief. "That is my mama now, sir. I thank you again for your kind assistance."

I barely heard her. Hurrying toward me, through the milling housewives and maids, footmen, carters, and cook's assistants making their morning rounds, came a ghost from my past.

The last time I'd seen her, she'd been thin and frail, a golden-and-white girl looking at me with timid eyes, her dainty mouth shifting between smiles and puckered worry. Her face was still pale and flowerlike, though lines now feathered about her eyes and mouth, and her skin had coarsened a bit. The curls that wreathed her forehead, under her bonnet's brim, were still golden, perhaps a little darker than they'd been fifteen years ago. Time had thickened her figure, but she retained an air of graceful helplessness, one that urged a gentleman to rush to her side and demand to know how he could assist her.

That air had ensnared me as a young man. I had proposed to her within a week of meeting her.

The woman stopped a few feet behind the girl, her lips parting in shock. Though I must have changed a great deal from the unruly and impetuous young man I'd been, she knew me, and I knew her.

Her name was Carlotta Lacey, and she was my wife.

Carlotta's eyes were blue. When I'd proposed in a country meadow near Cambridge, those eyes had glowed with excitement and delight. She'd let me kiss her, and then, full of confidence in our future, we'd consummated our betrothal there on the somewhat damp ground. I remembered the sweet scent of crushed grass, the tiny star flowers that tickled my nose, the warm taste of her skin.

Whether she remembered any of it as we stood closer than we'd stood to each other in fifteen years, I could not tell. I only knew that she looked at me with unblinking eyes, and that she'd deserted me for a French officer a decade and a half ago.

Carlotta recovered first. She closed gloved fingers around the girl's basket, and said in French, "Come away, Gabriella."

The name struck me like a boulder thrown with great force. My gaze shot to the girl, the breath leaving my body.

The young woman looked back at me, her brown eyes innocent and uncomprehending, and the same shade as my own.

Gabriella Lacey. *My daughter.*

"No." The word burst from my tight throat. I stepped around Carlotta, blocking her way.

Gabriella looked startled. Carlotta moved her grip to the girl's arm. "Later," she said to me. "Not now. We will come to it later."

She had not changed in one respect. Anything Carlotta could avoid facing, she would shove away from her with force.

I had recovered from the grief of her leaving me. I had lived through the anger and loneliness and resignation. I could forgive Carlotta for deserting me, because I had made her miserable. But I had never forgiven her, nor would I ever forgive her, for taking away my daughter. I had not seen Gabriella since she was two years old.

I said, "By the laws of England, she belongs to me."

Mothers had no legal guardianship over their children unless they were granted it, which I had not done. Carlotta taking Gabriella away had been a crime in truth.

The worry in Carlotta's eyes told me she knew very well what she had done, and what I could do to retaliate. She looked at me pleadingly. "We must speak of it later. Not here. Not now."

"*Maman,* what is the matter?" Gabriella asked in French. "What is happening?"

Carlotta arranged her face in soothing lines. "Nothing, my dear," she answered, her tone too bright. "We will go home."

I pressed my walking stick against the side of Carlotta's skirt. She could not rush away, her favorite method of solving problems, without pushing past me and making a scene. Gabriella peered at me anxiously. She no doubt thought me a madman, accosting her mother for whatever diabolical reason was in my crazed mind.

I realized then that when I had said to her, *Captain Gabriel Lacey, at your service,* Gabriella had given no beat of recognition. She had no idea who I was.

"You did not tell her," I said to Carlotta.

"Not now," Carlotta repeated. "Please, Gabriel, let us speak of this later. For heaven's sake."

The haze cleared from my mind, and I realized that the denizens of Covent Garden teemed about us, watching with interest. Gabriella looked as though she would shout for help at any moment. The peach seller and the ale seller next to him observed us with blatant curiosity, Londoners always keen for an impromptu drama. A large black carriage with fine gray horses shouldered its way through the crowd, people brushing us as they flowed away from it.

I moved my walking stick. I could not very well seize my daughter and drag her away with me, much as I wanted to. We could not split her in two, Solomon-like, in the middle of Covent Garden.

"Where do you stay?" I asked.

"King Street," Carlotta answered. "I promise you, we will speak of it. We will settle it."

"We shall indeed. I will send a man round to fetch you."

Carlotta shook her head. "No, there will be an appointment. He will see to it."

"Who will?"

Carlotta grasped Gabriella's arm again. "Come," she said to her. "Your father is waiting."

That statement startled me a moment before I realized that Carlotta must mean the Frenchman with whom she'd eloped. The officer who'd thought nothing of living with another man's wife for fifteen years.

Gabriella, with one last bewildered glance at me, let her mother lead her away. Carlotta hurried with her to the north and west side of Covent Garden and out to King Street, and the crowd swallowed them.

I stood in a daze, watching until I could no longer see the two women, the younger one a little taller than the older, walking close, their heads together.

The black carriage still making its way through the market halted nearly on top of me. A woman flung open the window and leaned out, her fashionable hat tilted back to reveal a quantity of golden curls and a childlike, pointed face.

"Devil take it, Lacey," Marianne Simmons cried. "Have your brains addled?"

End of Excerpt

ALSO BY ASHLEY GARDNER

Captain Lacey Regency Mystery Series
The Hanover Square Affair
A Regimental Murder
The Glass House
The Sudbury School Murders
The Necklace Affair
A Body in Berkeley Square
A Covent Garden Mystery
A Death in Norfolk
A Disappearance in Drury Lane
Murder in Grosvenor Square
The Thames River Murders
The Alexandria Affair
A Mystery at Carlton House
Murder in St. Giles
Death at Brighton Pavilion

The Gentleman's Walking Stick
(short stories: in print in
The Necklace Affair and Other Stories)

Kat Holloway "Below Stairs" Victorian Mysteries
(writing as Jennifer Ashley)
A Soupçon of Poison
Death Below Stairs
Scandal Above Stairs
Death in Kew Gardens

Leonidas the Gladiator Mysteries
(writing as Ashley Gardner)
Blood Debts
(More to come)

Mystery Anthologies
Past Crimes

ABOUT THE AUTHOR

Award-winning Ashley Gardner is a pseudonym for *New York Times* bestselling author Jennifer Ashley. Under both names — and a third, Allyson James — Ashley has written more than 85 published novels and novellas in mystery and romance. Her books have won several *RT BookReviews* Reviewers Choice awards (including Best Historical Mystery for *The Sudbury School Murders*), and Romance Writers of America's RITA (given for the best romance novels and novellas of the year). Ashley's books have been translated into more than a dozen different languages and have earned starred reviews in *Booklist* and *Publisher's Weekly*. When she isn't writing, she indulges her love for history by researching and building miniature houses and furniture from many periods.

More about the Captain Lacey series can be found at the website: www.gardnermysteries.com. Stay up to date on new releases by joining her email alerts here:

http://eepurl.com/5n7rz

CPSIA information can be obtained
at www.ICGtesting.com
Printed in the USA
LVHW020029280921
698854LV00006B/590

9 781946 455451